V W Polo Owners Workshop Manual

A K Legg
T Eng (CEI), AMIMI

Models covered
All VW Polo Hatchback, Saloon/Classic and Coupe models, including special and limited edition versions
1043 cc, 1093 cc & 1272 cc

ISBN 1 85010 205 8

© Haynes Publishing Group 1983, 1984, 1986

All rights reserved. No part of this book may be reproduced or transmitted in any form or by any means, electronic or mechanical, including photocopying, recording or by any information storage or retrieval system, without permission in writing from the copyright holder.

Printed in England *(813–1M2)*

ABCDE
FGHIJ
KLMN

THE
BOOK

Haynes Publishing Group
Sparkford Nr Yeovil
Somerset BA22 7JJ England

Haynes Publications, Inc
861 Lawrence Drive
Newbury Park
California 91320 USA

British Library Cataloguing in Publication Data
Legg, A.K.
VW Polo (inc. Classic & Coupe) Owners Workshop Manual.
– 2nd ed. – (Owners workshop manuals/Haynes)
1. Polo automobile
I. Title   II. Legg, A.K. VW Polo owners workshop
manual. III. Series
629.28'722   TL215.P67/
ISBN 1–85010–205–8

Acknowledgements

Special thanks are due to Volkswagenwerk Aktiengesellschaft for the supply of technical information and certain illustrations. Castrol Limited provided lubrication data, and the Champion Sparking Plug Company supplied the illustrations showing the various spark plug conditions.

Sykes-Pickavant provided some of the workshop tools. Thanks are also due to all those people at Sparkford who helped in the production of this manual.

About this manual

Its aim

The aim of this manual is to help you get the best value from your vehicle. It can do so in several ways. It can help you decide what work must be done (even should you choose to get it done by a garage), provide information on routine maintenance and servicing, and give a logical course of action and diagnosis when random faults occur. However, it is hoped that you will use the manual by tackling the work yourself. On simpler jobs it may even be quicker than booking the car into a garage and going there twice, to leave and collect it. Perhaps most important, a lot of money can be saved by avoiding the costs a garage must charge to cover its labour and overheads.

The manual has drawings and descriptions to show the function of the various components so that their layout can be understood. Then the tasks are described and photographed in a step-by-step sequence so that even a novice can do the work.

Its arrangement

The manual is divided into twelve Chapters, each covering a logical sub-division of the vehicle. The Chapters are each divided into Sections, numbered with single figures, eg 5; and the Sections into paragraphs (or sub-sections), with decimal numbers following on from the Section they are in, eg 5.1, 5.2, 5.3 etc.

It is freely illustrated, especially in those parts where there is a detailed sequence of operations to be carried out. There are two forms of illustration: figures and photographs. The figures are numbered in sequence with decimal numbers, according to their position in the Chapter – eg Fig. 6.4 is the fourth drawing/illustration in Chapter 6. Photographs carry the same number (either individually or in related groups) as the Section or sub-section to which they relate.

There is an alphabetical index at the back of the manual as well as a contents list at the front. Each Chapter is also preceded by its own individual contents list.

References to the 'left' or 'right' of the vehicle are in the sense of a person in the driver's seat facing forwards.

Unless otherwise stated, nuts and bolts are removed by turning anti-clockwise, and tightened by turning clockwise.

Vehicle manufacturers continually make changes to specifications and recommendations, and these, when notified, are incorporated into our manuals at the earliest opportunity.

Whilst every care is taken to ensure that the information in this manual is correct, no liability can be accepted by the authors or publishers for loss, damage or injury caused by any errors in, or omissions from, the information given.

Introduction to the VW Polo and Classic

The VW Polo was introduced in December 1981 as a hatchback, although its shape is more like an estate car. In March 1982 the Polo Classic was introduced which is the saloon car version, and then in 1983 the Polo Coupe was introduced. The engine is available in 1043 cc, 1093 cc and 1272 cc sizes and additionally the 1093 cc engine is available as an economy version designated the Formel E.

The overhead camshaft engine is mounted transversely at the front of the car with the four-speed gearbox mounted on the left-hand end of the engine. The final drive is located at the rear of the gearbox and driveshafts transmit the drive to the roadwheels. The VW Polo and Classic are well engineered cars returning excellent fuel consumption figures.

Contents

Volkswagen Polo

Volkswagen Polo Classic

Volkswagen Polo Coupe

Fault diagnosis

Introduction

The vehicle owner who does his or her own maintenance according to the recommended schedules should not have to use this section of the manual very often. Modern component reliability is such that, provided those items subject to wear or deterioration are inspected or renewed at the specified intervals, sudden failure is comparatively rare. Faults do not usually just happen as a result of sudden failure, but develop over a period of time. Major mechanical failures in particular are usually preceded by characteristic symptoms over hundreds or even thousands of miles. Those components which do occasionally fail without warning are often small and easily carried in the vehicle.

With any fault finding, the first step is to decide where to begin investigations. Sometimes this is obvious, but on other occasions a little detective work will be necessary. The owner who makes half a dozen haphazard adjustments or replacements may be successful in curing a fault (or its symptoms), but he will be none the wiser if the fault recurs and he may well have spent more time and money than was necessary. A calm and logical approach will be found to be more satisfactory in the long run. Always take into account any warning signs or abnormalities that may have been noticed in the period preceding the fault – power loss, high or low gauge readings, unusual noises or smells, etc – and remember that failure of components such as fuses or spark plugs may only be pointers to some underlying fault.

The pages which follow here are intended to help in cases of failure to start or breakdown on the road. There is also a Fault Diagnosis Section at the end of each Chapter which should be consulted if the preliminary checks prove unfruitful. Whatever the fault, certain basic principles apply. These are as follows:

Verify the fault. This is simply a matter of being sure that you know what the symptoms are before starting work. This is particularly important if you are investigating a fault for someone else who may not have described it very accurately.

Don't overlook the obvious. For example, if the vehicle won't start, is there petrol in the tank? (Don't take anyone else's word on this particular point, and don't trust the fuel gauge either!) If an electrical fault is indicated, look for loose or broken wires before digging out the test gear.

Cure the disease, not the symptom. Substituting a flat battery with a fully charged one will get you off the hard shoulder, but if the underlying cause is not attended to, the new battery will go the same way. Simi'arly, changing oil-fouled spark plugs for a new set will get you moving again, but remember that the reason for the fouling (if it wasn't simply an incorrect grade of plug) will have to be established and corrected.

Don't take anything for granted. Particularly, don't forget that a 'new' component may itself be defective (especially if it's been rattling round in the boot for months), and don't leave components out of a fault diagnosis sequence just because they are new or recently fitted. When you do finally diagnose a difficult fault, you'll probably realise that all the evidence was there from the start.

Electrical faults

Electrical faults can be more puzzling than straightforward mechanical failures, but they are no less susceptible to logical analysis if the basic principles of operation are understood. Vehicle electrical wiring exists in extremely unfavourable conditions – heat, vibration and chemical attack – and the first things to look for are loose or corroded connections and broken or chafed wires, especially where the wires pass through holes in the bodywork or are subject to vibration.

All metal-bodied vehicles in current production have one pole of the battery 'earthed', ie connected to the vehicle bodywork, and in nearly all modern vehicles it is the negative (–) terminal. The various electrical components – motors, bulb holders etc – are also connected to earth, either by means of a lead or directly by their mountings. Electric current flows through the component and then back to the battery via the bodywork. If the component mounting is loose or corroded, or if a path back to the battery is not available, the circuit will be incomplete and malfunction will result. The engine and/or gearbox are also earthed by means of flexible metal straps to the body or subframe; if these are loose or missing, starter motor, generator and ignition trouble may result.

Assuming the earth return to be satisfactory, electrical faults will be due either to component malfunction or to defects in the current supply. Individual components are dealt with in Chapter 9. If supply wires are broken or cracked internally this results in an open-circuit, and the easiest way to check for this is to bypass the suspect wire temporarily with a length of wire having a crocodile clip of suitable connector at each end. Alternatively, a 12V test lamp can be used to verify the presence of supply voltage at various points along the wire and the break can be thus isolated.

If a bare portion of a live wire touches the bodywork or other earthed metal part, the electricity will take the low-resistance path thus formed back to the battery: this is known as a short-circuit. Hopefully a short circuit will blow a fuse, but otherwise it may cause burning of the insulation (and possibly further short-circuits) or even a fire. This is why it is inadvisable to bypass persistently blowing fuses with silver foil or wire.

Spares and tool kit

Most vehicles are supplied only with sufficient tools for wheel changing; the *Maintenance and minor repair* tool kit detailed in *Tools and working facilities*, with the addition of a hammer, is probably sufficient for those repairs that most motorists would consider attempting at the roadside. In addition a few items which can be fitted without too much trouble in the event of a breakdown should be carried. Experience and available space will modify the list below, but the following may save having to call on professional assistance:

Spark plugs, clean and correctly gapped
HT lead and plug cap – long enough to reach the plug furthest from the distributor
Distributor rotor, condenser and contact breaker points
Drivebelt(s) – emergency type may suffice
Spare fuses
Set of principal light bulbs
Tin of radiator sealer and hose bandage
Exhaust bandage
Roll of insulating tape

Length of soft iron wire
Length of electrical flex
Torch or inspection lamp (can double as test lamp)
Battery jump leads
Tow-rope
Ignition waterproofing aerosol
Litre of engine oil
Sealed can of hydraulic fluid
Emergency windscreen
'Jubilee' clips
Tube of filler paste

If spare fuel is carried, a can designed for the purpose should be used to minimise risks of leakage and collision damage. A first aid kit and a warning triangle, whilst not at present compulsory in the UK, are obviously sensible items to carry in addition to the above.

When touring abroad it may be advisable to carry additional spares which, even if you cannot fit them yourself, could save having to wait while parts are obtained. The items below may be worth considering:

Clutch, throttle and choke cables
Cylinder head gasket
Alternator brushes
Tyre valve core

One of the motoring organisations will be able to advise on availability of fuel etc in foreign countries.

Engine will not start

Engine fails to turn when starter operated
Flat battery (recharge, use jump leads, or push start)
Battery terminals loose or corroded
Battery earth to body defective
Engine earth strap loose or broken
Starter motor (or solenoid) wiring loose or broken
Ignition/starter switch faulty
Major mechanical failure (seizure)
Starter or solenoid internal fault (see Chapter 9)

Starter motor turns engine slowly
Partially discharged battery (recharge, use jump leads, or push start)
Battery terminals loose or corroded
Battery earth to body defective
Engine earth strap loose
Starter motor (or solenoid) wiring loose
Starter motor internal fault (see Chapter 9)

Engine turns normally but fails to start
Damp or dirty HT leads and distributor cap (crank engine and check for spark) (photo))
Dirty or incorrectly gapped distributor points
No fuel in tank (check for delivery at carburettor and fuel pump (photo)
Excessive choke (hot engine) or insufficient choke (cold engine)
Fouled or incorrectly gapped spark plugs (remove, clean and regap)
Other ignition system fault (see Chapter 4)
Other fuel system fault (see Chapter 3)
Poor compression (see Chapter 1)
Major mechanical failure (eg camshaft drive)

Engine fires but will not run
Insufficient choke (cold engine)
Air leaks at carburettor or inlet manifold
Fuel starvation (see Chapter 3)
Ignition fault (see Chapter 4)

Engine cuts out and will not restart

Engine cuts out suddenly – ignition fault
Loose or disconnected LT wires
Wet HT leads or distributor cap (after traversing water splash)
Coil or condenser failure (check for spark)
Other ignition fault (see Chapter 4)

Engine misfires before cutting out – fuel fault
Fuel tank empty
Fuel pump defective or filter blocked (check for delivery)
Fuel tank filler vent blocked (suction will be evident on releasing cap)
Carburettor needle valve sticking
Carburettor jets blocked (fuel contaminated)
Other fuel system fault (see Chapter 3)

Engine cuts out – other causes
Serious overheating
Major mechanical failure (eg camshaft drive)

Engine overheats

Temperature gauge reads high
Coolant loss due to internal or external leakage (see Chapter 2)
Thermostat defective
Low oil level
Brakes binding
Radiator clogged externally or internally
Electric cooling fan not operating correctly
Engine waterways clogged
Ignition timing incorrect or automatic advance malfunctioning
Mixture too weak.

Note: *Do not add cold water to an overheated engine or damage may result*

Low engine oil pressure

Warning light flashes with engine running
Oil level low or incorrect grade
Defective sender unit
Wire to sender unit earthed
Engine overheating
Oil filter clogged or bypass valve defective
Oil pressure relief valve defective
Oil pick-up strainer clogged
Oil pump worn or mountings loose
Worn main or big-end bearings

Note: *Low oil pressure in a high-mileage engine at tickover is not necessarily a cause for concern. Sudden pressure loss at speed is far more significant. In any event, check the gauge or warning light sender before condemning the engine.*

Engine noises

Pre-ignition (pinking) on acceleration
Incorrect grade of fuel
Ignition timing incorrect
Distributor faulty or worn
Worn or maladjusted carburettor
Excessive carbon build-up in engine

Whistling or wheezing noises
Leaking vacuum hose
Leaking carburettor or manifold gasket
Blowing head gasket

Tapping or rattling
Incorrect valve clearances
Worn valve gear
Broken piston ring (ticking noise)

Knocking or thumping
Unintentional mechanical contact
Peripheral component fault (alternator, water pump etc)
Worn big-end bearings (regular heavy knocking, perhaps less under load)
Worn main bearings (rumbling and knocking, perhaps worsening under load)
Piston slap (most noticeable when cold)

Using a spark plug to check for HT spark – do not remove plug from engine otherwise fuel/air mixture may ignite causing fire

Checking for fuel delivery at fuel pump

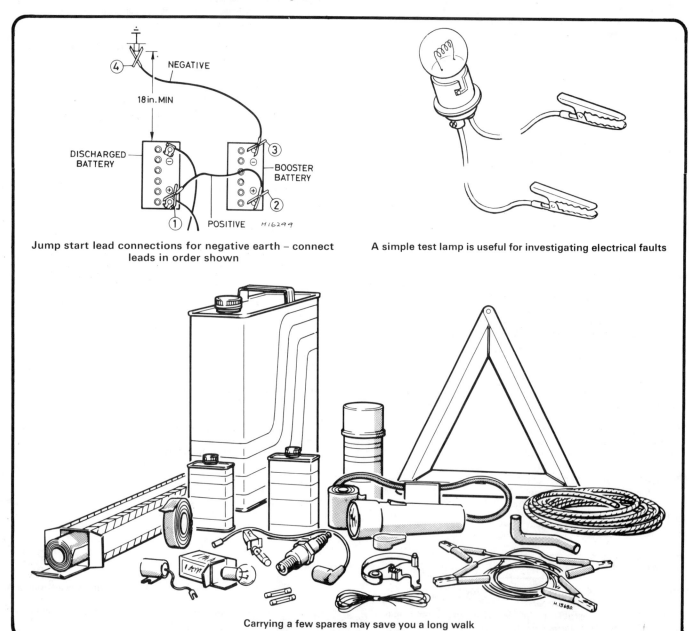

Jump start lead connections for negative earth – connect leads in order shown

A simple test lamp is useful for investigating electrical faults

Carrying a few spares may save you a long walk

Safety first!

Professional motor mechanics are trained in safe working procedures. However enthusiastic you may be about getting on with the job in hand, do take the time to ensure that your safety is not put at risk. A moment's lack of attention can result in an accident, as can failure to observe certain elementary precautions.

There will always be new ways of having accidents, and the following points do not pretend to be a comprehensive list of all dangers; they are intended rather to make you aware of the risks and to encourage a safety-conscious approach to all work you carry out on your vehicle.

Essential DOs and DON'Ts

DON'T rely on a single jack when working underneath the vehicle. Always use reliable additional means of support, such as axle stands, securely placed under a part of the vehicle that you know will not give way.

DON'T attempt to loosen or tighten high-torque nuts (e.g. wheel hub nuts) while the vehicle is on a jack; it may be pulled off.

DON'T start the engine without first ascertaining that the transmission is in neutral (or 'Park' where applicable) and the parking brake applied.

DON'T suddenly remove the filler cap from a hot cooling system – cover it with a cloth and release the pressure gradually first, or you may get scalded by escaping coolant.

DON'T attempt to drain oil until you are sure it has cooled sufficiently to avoid scalding you.

DON'T grasp any part of the engine, exhaust or catalytic converter without first ascertaining that it is sufficiently cool to avoid burning you.

DON'T allow brake fluid or antifreeze to contact vehicle paintwork.

DON'T syphon toxic liquids such as fuel, brake fluid or antifreeze by mouth, or allow them to remain on your skin.

DON'T inhale dust – it may be injurious to health (see *Asbestos* below).

DON'T allow any spilt oil or grease to remain on the floor – wipe it up straight away, before someone slips on it.

DON'T use ill-fitting spanners or other tools which may slip and cause injury.

DON'T attempt to lift a heavy component which may be beyond your capability – get assistance.

DON'T rush to finish a job, or take unverified short cuts.

DON'T allow children or animals in or around an unattended vehicle.

DO wear eye protection when using power tools such as drill, sander, bench grinder etc, and when working under the vehicle.

DO use a barrier cream on your hands prior to undertaking dirty jobs – it will protect your skin from infection as well as making the dirt easier to remove afterwards; but make sure your hands aren't left slippery.

DO keep loose clothing (cuffs, tie etc) and long hair well out of the way of moving mechanical parts.

DO remove rings, wristwatch etc, before working on the vehicle – especially the electrical system.

DO ensure that any lifting tackle used has a safe working load rating adequate for the job.

DO keep your work area tidy – it is only too easy to fall over articles left lying around.

DO get someone to check periodically that all is well, when working alone on the vehicle.

DO carry out work in a logical sequence and check that everything is correctly assembled and tightened afterwards.

DO remember that your vehicle's safety affects that of yourself and others. If in doubt on any point, get specialist advice.

IF, in spite of following these precautions, you are unfortunate enough to injure yourself, seek medical attention as soon as possible.

Asbestos

Certain friction, insulating, sealing, and other products – such as brake linings, brake bands, clutch linings, torque converters, gaskets, etc – contain asbestos. *Extreme care must be taken to avoid inhalation of dust from such products since it is hazardous to health.* If in doubt, assume that they *do* contain asbestos.

Fire

Remember at all times that petrol (gasoline) is highly flammable. Never smoke, or have any kind of naked flame around, when working on the vehicle. But the risk does not end there – a spark caused by an electrical short-circuit, by two metal surfaces contacting each other, by careless use of tools, or even by static electricity built up in your body under certain conditions, can ignite petrol vapour, which in a confined space is highly explosive.

Always disconnect the battery earth (ground) terminal before working on any part of the fuel or electrical system, and never risk spilling fuel on to a hot engine or exhaust.

It is recommended that a fire extinguisher of a type suitable for fuel and electrical fires is kept handy in the garage or workplace at all times. Never try to extinguish a fuel or electrical fire with water.

Fumes

Certain fumes are highly toxic and can quickly cause unconsciousness and even death if inhaled to any extent. Petrol (gasoline) vapour comes into this category, as do the vapours from certain solvents such as trichloroethylene. Any draining or pouring of such volatile fluids should be done in a well ventilated area.

When using cleaning fluids and solvents, read the instructions carefully. Never use materials from unmarked containers – they may give off poisonous vapours.

Never run the engine of a motor vehicle in an enclosed space such as a garage. Exhaust fumes contain carbon monoxide which is extremely poisonous; if you need to run the engine, always do so in the open air or at least have the rear of the vehicle outside the workplace.

If you are fortunate enough to have the use of an inspection pit, never drain or pour petrol, and never run the engine, while the vehicle is standing over it; the fumes, being heavier than air, will concentrate in the pit with possibly lethal results.

The battery

Never cause a spark, or allow a naked light, near the vehicle's battery. It will normally be giving off a certain amount of hydrogen gas, which is highly explosive.

Always disconnect the battery earth (ground) terminal before working on the fuel or electrical systems.

If possible, loosen the filler plugs or cover when charging the battery from an external source. Do not charge at an excessive rate or the battery may burst.

Take care when topping up and when carrying the battery. The acid electrolyte, even when diluted, is very corrosive and should not be allowed to contact the eyes or skin.

If you ever need to prepare electrolyte yourself, always add the acid slowly to the water, and never the other way round. Protect against splashes by wearing rubber gloves and goggles.

When jump starting a car using a booster battery, for negative earth (ground) vehicles, connect the jump leads in the following sequence: First connect one jump lead between the positive (+) terminals of the two batteries. Then connect the other jump lead first to the negative (–) terminal of the booster battery, and then to a good earthing (ground) point on the vehicle to be started, at least 18 in (45 cm) from the battery if possible. Ensure that hands and jump leads are clear of any moving parts, and that the two vehicles do not touch. Disconnect the leads in the reverse order.

Mains electricity

When using an electric power tool, inspection light etc, which works from the mains, always ensure that the appliance is correctly connected to its plug and that, where necessary, it is properly earthed (grounded). Do not use such appliances in damp conditions and, again, beware of creating a spark or applying excessive heat in the vicinity of fuel or fuel vapour.

Ignition HT voltage

A severe electric shock can result from touching certain parts of the ignition system, such as the HT leads, when the engine is running or being cranked, particularly if components are damp or the insulation is defective. Where an electronic ignition system is fitted, the HT voltage is much higher and could prove fatal.

General dimensions, weights and capacities

Dimensions

Overall length:

Without headlight washer	143.9 in (3655 mm)
With headlight washer	144.5 in (3670 mm)
Overall width	62.2 in (1580 mm)
Overall height (unladen)	53.3 in (1355 mm)
Ground clearance	4.2 in (106 mm)
Wheelbase	91.9 in (2335 mm)

Track:

Front	51.4 in (1306 mm)
Rear	52.4 in (1332 mm)
Turning circle..	32.8 ft (10 m)

Weights

Gross vehicle weight..	2492 lb (1130 kg)

Unladen weight:

1.05 litre models...	1543 lb (700 kg)
1.1 litre models...	1566 lb (710 kg)
1.3 litre models...	1588 lb (720 kg)
Maximum roof rack load	110 lb (50 kg)

Maximum trailer weight:

Unbraked (1.05 litre models)...	838 lb (380 kg)
Unbraked (1.1 and 1.3 litre models)...	860 lb (390 kg)
Braked (1.05 litre models)	1323 lb (600 kg)
Braked (1.1 and 1.3 litre models)	1433 lb (650 kg)

Capacities

Engine oil:

With filter	5.3 pt (3.0 litre)
Without filter	4.4 pt (2.5 litre)
Difference between minimum and maximum marks	1.8 pt (1.0 litre)

Cooling system (including heater):

With internal expansion tank	7.9 pt (4.5 litre)
With external expansion tank	11.4 pt (6.5 litre)
Fuel tank	8.0 gal (36.0 litre)
Manual gearbox	3.9 pt (2.2 litre)

Buying spare parts and vehicle identification numbers

Buying spare parts

Spare parts are available from many sources, for example: VW garages, other garages and accessory shops, and motor factors. Our advice regarding spare part sources is as follow:

Officially appointed VW garages – This is the best source of parts which are peculiar to your vehicle and are otherwise not generally available (eg; complete cylinder heads, internal gearbox components, badges, interior trim etc). It is also the only place at which you should buy parts if your car is still under warranty – non-VW components may invalidate the warranty. To be sure of obtaining the correct parts it will always be necessary to give the storeman your car's engine and chassis number and, if possible, to take the 'old' part along for positive identification. Remember that many parts are available on a factory exchange scheme – any parts returned should always be clean! It obviously makes good sense to go straight to the specialists on your car for this type of part for they are best equipped to supply you.

Other garages and accessory shops – These are often very good places to buy materials and components needed for the maintenance of your car (eg; oil filters, spark plugs, bulbs, fanbelts, oils and greases, touch-up paint, filler paste etc). They also sell general accessories, usually have convenient opening hours, may charge lower prices and can often be found not far from home.

Motor factors – Good factors will stock all of the more important components which wear out relatively quickly (eg; clutch components, pistons, valves, exhaust system, brake cylinders/pipes/hoses/seals/shoes and pads, etc). Motor factors will often provide new or reconditioned components on a part exchange basis – this can save a considerable amount of money.

Vehicle identification numbers

Modifications are a continuing and unpublicised process in vehicle manufacture quite apart from major model changes. It is therefore essential to give as much information as possible when ordering spare parts. Quote the car model and year of manufacture, and also if necessary the body and engine numbers.

The vehicle identification plate is located on the front engine compartment panel, next to the bonnet lock.

The chassis number is located on the bulkhead panel behind the air cleaner.

The engine number is located on the front face of the cylinder head at the timing belt end (photo).

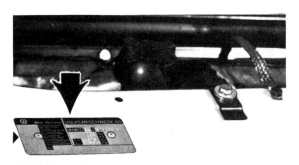

Vehicle identification plate location

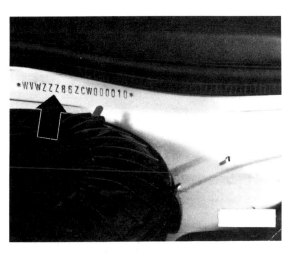

Chassis number location

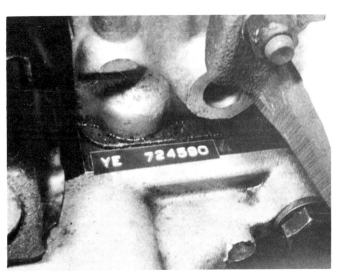

Engine number location

Tools and working facilities

Introduction

A selection of good tools is a fundamental requirement for anyone contemplating the maintenance and repair of a motor vehicle. For the owner who does not possess any, their purchase will prove a considerable expense, offsetting some of the savings made by doing-it-yourself. However, provided that the tools purchased are of good quality, they will last for many years and prove an extremely worthwhile investment.

To help the average owner to decide which tools are needed to carry out the various tasks detailed in this manual, we have compiled three lists of tools under the following headings: *Maintenance and minor repair*, *Repair and overhaul*, and *Special*. The newcomer to practical mechanics should start off with the *Maintenance and minor repair* tool kit and confine himself to the simpler jobs around the vehicle. Then, as his confidence and experience grow, he can undertake more difficult tasks, buying extra tools as, and when, they are needed. In this way, a *Maintenance and minor repair* tool kit can be built-up into a *Repair and overhaul* tool kit over a considerable period of time without any major cash outlays. The experienced do-it-yourselfer will have a tool kit good enough for most repair and overhaul procedures and will add tools from the *Special* category when he feels the expense is justified by the amount of use to which these tools will be put.

It is obviously not possible to cover the subject of tools fully here. For those who wish to learn more about tools and their use there is a book entitled *How to Choose and Use Car tools* available from the publishers of this manual.

Maintenance and minor repair tool kit

The tools given in this list should be considered as a minimum requirement if routine maintenance, servicing and minor repair operations are to be undertaken. We recommend the purchase of combination spanners (ring one end, open-ended the other); although more expensive than open-ended ones, they do give the advantages of both types of spanner.

Combination spanners – 10, 11, 12, 13, 14 & 17 mm
Adjustable spanner – 9 inch
Gearbox drain plug key
Spark plug spanner (with rubber insert)
Spark plug gap adjustment tool
Set of feeler gauges
Brake bleed nipple spanner
Screwdriver – 4 in long × $\frac{1}{4}$ in dia (flat blade)
Screwdriver – 4 in long × $\frac{1}{4}$ in dia (cross blade)
Combination pliers – 6 inch
Hacksaw (junior)
Tyre pump
Tyre pressure gauge
Oil can
Fine emery cloth (1 sheet)

Wire brush (small)
Funnel (medium size)

Repair and overhaul tool kit

These tools are virtually essential for anyone undertaking any major repairs to a motor vehicle, and are additional to those given in the *Maintenance and minor repair* list. Included in this list is a comprehensive set of sockets. Although these are expensive they will be found invaluable as they are so versatile – particularly if various drives are included in the set. We recommend the $\frac{1}{2}$ in square-drive type, as this can be used with most proprietary torque wrenches. If you cannot afford a socket set, even bought piecemeal, then inexpensive tubular box spanners are a useful alternative.

The tools in this list will occasionally need to be supplemented by tools from the *Special* list.

Sockets (or box spanners) to cover range in previous list
Reversible ratchet drive (for use with sockets)
Extension piece, 10 inch (for use with sockets)
Universal joint (for use with sockets)
Torque wrench (for use with sockets)
'Mole' wrench – 8 inch
Ball pein hammer
Soft-faced hammer, plastic or rubber
Screwdriver – 6 in long × $\frac{5}{16}$ in dia (flat blade)
Screwdriver – 2 in long × $\frac{5}{16}$ in dia square (flat blade)
Screwdriver – 1$\frac{1}{2}$ in long × $\frac{1}{4}$ in dia (cross blade)
Screwdriver – 3 in long × $\frac{1}{8}$ in dia (electricians)
Pliers – electricians side cutters
Pliers – needle nosed
Pliers – circlip (internal and external)
Cold chisel – $\frac{1}{2}$ inch
Scriber
Scraper
Centre punch
Pin punch
Hacksaw
Valve grinding tool
Steel rule/straight-edge
Allen keys

Special tools

The tools in this list are those which are not used regularly, are expensive to buy, or which need to be used in accordance with their manufacturers' instructions. Unless relatively difficult mechanical jobs are undertaken frequently, it will not be economic to buy many of these tools. Where this is the case you could consider clubbing together with friends (or joining a motorists' club) to make a joint purchase, or borrowing the tools against a deposit from a local garage or tool hire specialist.

The following list contains only those tools and instruments freely available to the public, and not those special tools produced by the vehicle manufacturer specifically for its dealer network. You will find occasional references to these manufacturers' special tools in the text of this manual. Generally, an alternative method of doing the job without the vehicle manufacturers' special tool is given. However, sometimes, there is no alternative to using them. Where this is the case and the relevant tool cannot be bought or borrowed, you will have to entrust the work to a franchised garage.

> *Valve spring compressor*
> *Piston ring compressor*
> *Balljoint separator*
> *Universal hub/bearing puller*
> *Impact screwdriver*
> *Micrometer and/or vernier gauge*
> *Dial gauge*
> *Stroboscopic timing light*
> *Dwell angle meter/tachometer*
> *Universal electrical multi-meter*
> *Cylinder compression gauge*
> *Lifting tackle*
> *Trolley jack*
> *Light with extension lead*

Buying tools

For practically all tools, a tool factor is the best source since he will have a very comprehensive range compared with the average garage or accessory shop. Having said that, accessory shops often offer excellent quality tools at discount prices, so it pays to shop around.

Remember, you don't have to buy the most expensive items on the shelf, but it is always advisable to steer clear of the very cheap tools. There are plenty of good tools around at reasonable prices, so ask the proprietor or manager of the shop for advice before making a purchase.

Care and maintenance of tools

Having purchased a reasonable tool kit, it is necessary to keep tools in a clean serviceable condition. After use, always wipe off any dirt, grease and metal particles using a clean, dry cloth, before putting the tools away. Never leave them lying around after they have been used. A simple tool rack on the garage or workshop wall, for items such as screwdrivers and pliers is a good idea. Store all normal wrenches and sockets in a metal box. Any measuring instruments, gauges, meters, etc, must be carefully stored where they cannot be damaged or become rusty.

Take a little care when tools are used. Hammer heads inevitably become marked and screwdrivers lose the keen edge on their blades from time to time. A little timely attention with emery cloth or a file will soon restore items like this to a good serviceable finish.

Working facilities

Not to be forgotten when discussing tools, is the workshop itself. If anything more than routine maintenance is to be carried out, some form of suitable working area becomes essential.

It is appreciated that many an owner mechanic is forced by circumstances to remove an engine or similar item, without the benefit of a garage or workshop. Having done this, any repairs should always be done under the cover of a roof.

Wherever possible, any dismantling should be done on a clean, flat workbench or table at a suitable working height.

Any workbench needs a vice: one with a jaw opening of 4 in (100 mm) is suitable for most jobs. As mentioned previously, some clean dry storage space is also required for tools, as well as for lubricants, cleaning fluids, touch-up paints and so on, which become necessary.

Another item which may be required, and which has a much more general usage, is an electric drill with a chuck capacity of at least $\frac{5}{16}$ in (8 mm). This, together with a good range of twist drills, is virtually essential for fitting accessories such as mirrors and reversing lights.

Last, but not least, always keep a supply of old newspapers and clean, lint-free rags available, and try to keep any working area as clean as possible.

Spanner jaw gap comparison table

Jaw gap (in)	Spanner size
0.250	$\frac{1}{4}$ in AF
0.276	7 mm
0.313	$\frac{5}{16}$ in AF
0.315	8 mm
0.344	$\frac{11}{32}$ in AF; $\frac{1}{8}$ in Whitworth
0.354	9 mm
0.375	$\frac{3}{8}$ in AF
0.394	10 mm
0.433	11 mm
0.438	$\frac{7}{16}$ in AF
0.445	$\frac{3}{16}$ in Whitworth; $\frac{1}{4}$ in BSF
0.472	12 mm
0.500	$\frac{1}{2}$ in AF
0.512	13 mm
0.525	$\frac{1}{4}$ in Whitworth; $\frac{5}{16}$ in BSF
0.551	14 mm
0.563	$\frac{9}{16}$ in AF
0.591	15 mm
0.600	$\frac{5}{16}$ in Whitworth; $\frac{3}{8}$ in BSF
0.625	$\frac{5}{8}$ in AF
0.630	16 mm
0.669	17 mm
0.686	$\frac{11}{16}$ in AF
0.709	18 mm
0.710	$\frac{3}{8}$ in Whitworth; $\frac{7}{16}$ in BSF
0.748	19 mm
0.750	$\frac{3}{4}$ in AF
0.813	$\frac{13}{16}$ in AF
0.820	$\frac{7}{16}$ in Whitworth; $\frac{1}{2}$ in BSF
0.866	22 mm
0.875	$\frac{7}{8}$ in AF
0.920	$\frac{1}{2}$ in Whitworth; $\frac{9}{16}$ in BSF
0.938	$\frac{15}{16}$ in AF
0.945	24 mm
1.000	1 in AF
1.010	$\frac{9}{16}$ in Whitworth; $\frac{5}{8}$ in BSF
1.024	26 mm
1.063	$1\frac{1}{16}$ in AF; 27 mm
1.100	$\frac{5}{8}$ in Whitworth; $\frac{11}{16}$ in BSF
1.125	$1\frac{1}{8}$ in AF
1.181	30 mm
1.200	$\frac{11}{16}$ in Whitworth; $\frac{3}{4}$ in BSF
1.250	$1\frac{1}{4}$ in AF
1.260	32 mm
1.300	$\frac{3}{4}$ in Whitworth; $\frac{7}{8}$ in BSF
1.313	$1\frac{5}{16}$ in AF
1.390	$\frac{13}{16}$ in Whitworth; $\frac{15}{16}$ in BSF
1.417	36 mm
1.438	$1\frac{7}{16}$ in AF
1.480	$\frac{7}{8}$ in Whitworth; 1 in BSF
1.500	$1\frac{1}{2}$ in AF
1.575	40 mm; $1\frac{9}{16}$ in Whitworth
1.614	41 mm
1.625	$1\frac{5}{8}$ in AF
1.670	1 in Whitworth; $1\frac{1}{8}$ in BSF
1.688	$1\frac{11}{16}$ in AF
1.811	46 mm
1.813	$1\frac{13}{16}$ in AF
1.860	$1\frac{1}{8}$ in Whitworth; $1\frac{1}{4}$ in BSF
1.875	$1\frac{7}{8}$ in AF
1.969	50 mm
2.000	2 in AF
2.050	$1\frac{1}{4}$ in Whitworth; $1\frac{3}{8}$ in BSF
2.165	55 mm
2.362	60 mm

Jacking and towing

The jack supplied with the car tool kit should only be used for changing roadwheels (photos). When using a trolley jack, position it only beneath the sill panels where indicated by the arrow shape, and preferably use a block of wood between the jack and the body. Always support the car with axle stands before working beneath it.

Towing eyes are provided beneath the front and rear bumpers on the right-hand side (photos). When being towed, the ignition key should be inserted and turned to position 2 so that the direction indicators, the horn, and if required the windscreen wipers can be used. To prevent any overheating of the ignition coil, disconnect the LT lead from the negative terminal on the coil. Note that the brake servo is inoperative with the engine stopped, so more pedal pressure will be required.

Spare wheel location

The tool kit is located under the spare wheel

Jacking point indicated by arrow shape

Front towing eye

Rear towing eye

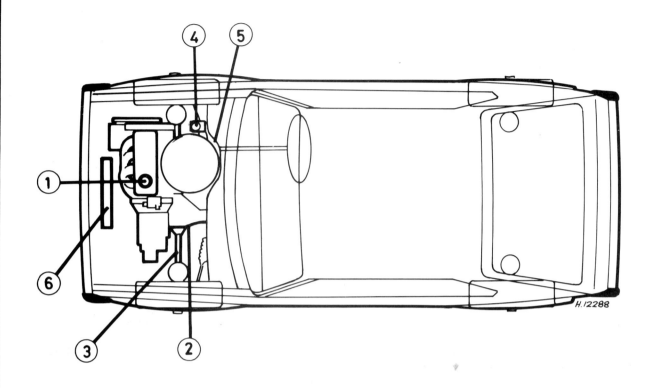

Recommended lubricants and fluids

Component or system	Lubricant type or specification
Engine(1)	SAE 20W/50, SAE 20W/40, SAE 15W/50 or SAE 15W/40
Gearbox (2)	Hypoid SAE 80 or SAE 80W/90
Driveshafts (3)	G 6 2 grease
Brake fluid (4)	FMV SS116 DOT 3
Steering gear (5)	Grease to AOF 063 000 004
Antifreeze (6)	G11

Routine maintenance

Maintenance is essential in the interests of safety, performance and economy. Over the years the need for periodic lubrication – oiling, greasing, and so on – has been greatly reduced if not totally eliminated. This has unfortunately tended to lead some owners to think that because no such action is required, components either no longer exist, or will last for ever. This is certainly not the case; it is essential to carry out regular visual examination as comprehensively as possible in order to spot any possible defects at an early stage before they develop into major expensive repairs.

Note that on pre 1983 models, the lubrication content of the following maintenance was carried out between the main service intervals (ie at 5000 mile/7500 km intervals). However it is recommended that where applicable the lubrication service is now combined with the main service at 10000 mile (15000 km) intervals.

Every 250 miles (400 km) or weekly

Engine
Check the oil level and top up if necessary (photos)
Check the coolant level and top up if necessary

Tyres
Check the tyre pressures and adjust if necessary (photo)

Every 10000 miles (15000 km)

Engine
Check and if necessary adjust the clutch
Check for oil, fuel and coolant leaks
Check antifreeze concentration and adjust if necessary
Check valve clearances and adjust if necessary
Check condition of alternator drivebelt and adjust tension if necessary (photo)
Renew the spark plugs
Renew the contact points and adjust dwell angle
Adjust ignition timing
Change engine oil and renew oil filter
Check exhaust system for leaks and damage
Adjust the slow running

Gearbox
Check oil level and top up if necessary
Check for oil leaks

Driveshafts
Check the CV joint boots for leaks and damage

Braking system
Check the brake lines, hoses and unions for leaks and damage
Check the disc pads and rear brake shoe linings for wear
Check the brake fluid level and top up if necessary (photo)

Electrical system
Check the operation of all electrical components, light bulbs, etc
Check the windscreen/rear window washer fluid level and top up if necessary (photos)
Check the battery electrolyte level and top up with distilled water if necessary
Check headlight beam alignment and adjust if necessary

Steering
Check steering gear bellows for leaks and damage
Check steering tie-rod ends for wear and condition of boots

Tyres
Check tread depth and condition of tyres (photo)

Bodywork
Lubricate all hinges and catches
Check the underbody for corrosion and damage and reseal as necessary

Every 20000 miles (30000 km)

Engine
Renew the air cleaner element
Renew the fuel filter

Every 2 years

Braking system
Renew the brake fluid and check the condition of the visible rubber components of the brake system

Under-bonnet view (air cleaner removed)

1 Battery
2 Brake hydraulic fluid
  reservoir
3 Carburettor

4 Vacuum reservoir
  (1.05 litre models only)
5 Fusebox

6 Windscreen washer
  reservoir
7 Fuel filter
8 Fuel pump

9 Distributor
10 Coil
11 Oil filler cap
12 Radiator filler cap

13 Top hose
14 Radiator

View of front underside of car

1 Lower suspension arm
2 Anti-roll bar
3 Disc brake caliper

4 Driveshaft (RH)
5 Front towing eye

6 Oil filter
7 Sump

8 Exhaust downpipe
9 Gearchange assembly

10 Gearbox
11 Driveshaft (LH)

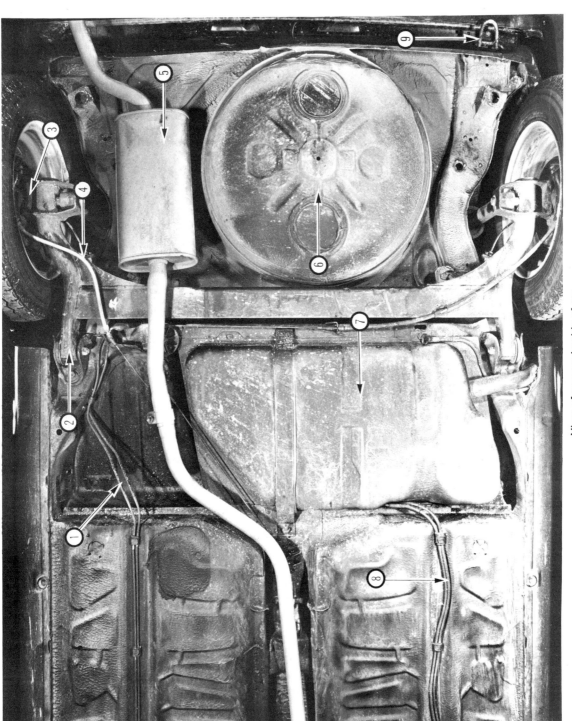

View of rear underside of car

1 Brake hydraulic pipes
2 Rear axle

3 Rear brake drum
4 Handbrake cable

5 Exhaust rear silencer
6 Spare wheel well

7 Fuel tank
8 Fuel feed and return pipes

9 Rear towing eye

Checking engine oil level

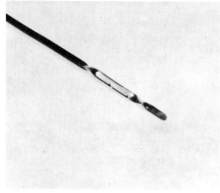
Oil level dipstick markings

Topping up engine oil level

Checking tyre pressures

Checking alternator drivebelt tension

Checking brake fluid level

Topping up windscreen washer fluid

Rear window washer fluid container

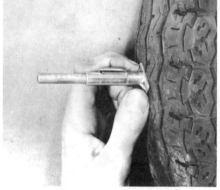
Checking tyre tread depth

Chapter 1 Engine

For modifications, and information applicable to later models, see Supplement at end of manual

Contents

Specifications

Type .... Four cylinder in-line, overhead camshaft, transverse mounting

Engine code letters
GL	1.05 litre
HB	1.1 litre
HH	1.3 litre

General

	GL	HB	HH
Bore	75 mm (2.953 in)	69.5 mm (2.736 in)	75 mm (2.953 in)
Stroke	59 mm (2.323 in)	72 mm (2.835 in)	72 mm (2.835 in)
Capacity	1043 cc	1093 cc	1272 cc
Output	29 kW (40 bhp) at 5300 rpm	37 kW (50 bhp) at 5800 rpm (standard) at 5600 rpm (Formel E)	44 kW (60 bhp) at 5600 rpm
Torque (max)	74 Nm at 2700 rpm	77 Nm at 3500 rpm (standard), 82 Nm at 3300 rpm (Formel E)	95 Nm at 3400 rpm
Compression ratio	9.3 to 1	8.0 to 1 (standard) 9.7 to 1 (Formel E)	8.2 to 1
Compression pressures	8 to 11.5 bar (116 to 166 lbf/in^2)	6 to 10 bar (87 to 145 lbf/in^2) to 799 999 6 to 11 bar (87 to 110 lbf/in^2) from 800 000	6 to 10 bar (87 to 145 lbf/in^2)
Firing order	1-3-4-2 (No 1 at timing belt end)		

Crankshaft
Main journal diameter (standard) .... 53.96 to 53.97 mm (2.124 to 2.125 in)
Undersizes .... −0.25 mm (0.01 in), −0.5 mm (0.02 in), −0.75 mm (0.03 in)
Crankpin journal diameter (standard) .... 41.96 to 41.97 mm (1.651 to 1.652 in)
Undersizes .... −0.25 mm (0.01 in), −0.5 mm (0.02 in), −0.75 mm (0.03 in)
Endfloat .... 0.07 to 0.20 mm (0.003 to 0.008 in)
Main bearing running clearance .... 0.03 to 0.17 mm (0.001 to 0.007 in)
Crankpin running clearance .... 0.02 to 0.095 mm (0.008 to 0.004 in)

Connecting rods
Endfloat on crankpin .... 0.05 to 0.40 mm (0.002 to 0.016 in)

Pistons
Diameter

	GL and HH	HB
Standard	74.98 mm (2.952 in)	69.48 mm (2.735 in)

Oversizes .... +0.25 mm (0.010 in), +0.50 mm (0.020 in), +1.00 mm (0.040 in)
Clearance in cylinder bores (new) .... 0.03 mm (0.001 in)

Piston rings
End gap (15.0 mm/0.6 in from bottom of cylinder):
    Compression rings .... 0.30 to 0.45 mm (0.012 to 0.018 in)
    Oil scraper ring .... 0.25 to 0.40 mm (0.010 to 0.016 in)
Clearance in groove .... 0.02 to 0.15 mm (0.0008 to 0.006 in)

Gudgeon pins
Length:
    GL and HB from 800 000 .... 54 mm (2.126 in)
    HH and HB to 799 999 .... 58 mm (2.284 in)

Cylinder head
Distortion (max) .... 0.1 mm (0.004 in)
Minimum dimension for machining .... 119.3 mm (4.697 in)

Camshaft
Run-out (max) .... 0.02 mm (0.0008 in)
Endfloat .... 0.15 mm (0.006 in)

Valves
Head diameter:
    Inlet .... 34.0 mm (1.339 in)
    Exhaust .... 29.1 mm (1.106 in)
Stem diameter:
    Inlet .... 7.97 mm (0.314 in)
    Exhaust .... 7.95 mm (0.313 in)
Valve length:
    Inlet – GL .... 110.5 mm (4.350 in)
    Inlet – HB, HH .... 104.0 mm (4.094 in)
    Exhaust – GL .... 110.5 mm (4.350 in)
    Exhaust – HB, HH .... 104.0 mm (4.094 in)
Seat angle .... 45°
Seat width .... 2.0 mm (0.079 in)
Valve rock in guide (max):
    Inlet .... 1.0 mm (0.040 in)
    Exhaust .... 1.3 mm (0.051 in)

Valve clearances
Cold engine:
    Inlet .... 0.10 mm (0.004 in)
    Exhaust .... 0.20 mm (0.008 in)
Warm engine:
    Inlet .... 0.15 mm (0.006 in)
    Exhaust .... 0.25 mm (0.010 in)

Valve timing (at 1 mm/0.04 in valve lift with zero valve clearance)

	GL	HB to 799 999	HB from 800 000	HH
Inlet opens	9° ATDC	2° BTDC	3° BTDC	3° BTDC
Inlet closes	13° ABDC	38° ABDC	28° ABDC	3° BTDC
Exhaust opens	15° BBDC	41° BBDC	31° BBDC	46° ABDC
Exhaust closes	11° BTDC	3° BTDC	3° BTDC	47° BBDC
				° TDC

Lubrication system

Oil pressure at 2000 rpm and temperature of 80°C (176° F)	2.0 bar (29.0 lbf/in²)
Oil pressure switch:	
Off pressure (0.3 bar switch)	0.15 to 0.45 bar (2.2 to 6.5 lbf/in²)
On pressure (1.8 bar switch)	1.6 to 2.0 bar (23.2 to 29.0 lbf/in²)
Oil pump:	
Type	Bi-rotor, driven from front of crankshaft

Torque wrench settings

	lbf ft	Nm
Cylinder head bolts (engine cold):		
1st stage	30	40
2nd stage	44	60
3rd stage	55	75
4th stage	Additional $\frac{1}{4}$ turn in one movement	
Valve cover	7	10
Camshaft sprocket	59	80
Sump	15	20
Oil drain plug	22	30
Oil pressure switch	18	25
Crankshaft sprocket	59	80
Drivebelt pulley	15	20
Engine and gearbox mountings:		
M 10 bolts	33	45
M 8 bolts	18	25

1 General description

The engine is of four cylinders, in-line, overhead camshaft type mounted transversely at the front of the car, with the gearbox on the left-hand side. The top of the engine is inclined slightly forwards.

The crankshaft is of five bearing type, and the centre main bearing incorporates thrust washers to control crankshaft endfloat.

The camshaft is driven by a toothed timing belt from a sprocket on the front of the crankshaft, and the timing belt also drives the water pump. The valves are operated by followers which pivot on adjustable ball head studs.

The cylinder block is of cast iron and the cylinder head of light alloy.

The bi-rotor oil pump is located on the front of the cylinder block and driven by the crankshaft.

A positive crankcase ventilation system is incorporated.

2 Major operations possible with the engine in the car

The following operations can be carried out without having to remove the engine from the car:

(a) Removal and servicing of the cylinder head, camshaft, and timing belt.
(b) Removal of the flywheel and clutch after removing the gearbox.
(c) Renewal of the crankshaft front and rear oil seals.
(d) Removal of the sump.
(e) Removal of the oil pump.
(f) Removal of the piston/connecting rod assemblies.
(g) Renewal of the engine mountings.

3 Major operations only possible after removal of the engine from the car

The following operations can only be carried out after removal of the engine from the car:

(a) Renewal of the crankshaft main bearings.
(b) Removal of the crankshaft.

4 Method of engine removal

The engine and gearbox must be lifted from the engine compartment as a complete unit, then separated on the bench.

5 Engine – removal

1 Remove the bonnet as described in Chapter 11.
2 Disconnect the battery negative lead.
3 Remove the air cleaner as described in Chapter 3.
4 Remove the radiator as described in Chapter 2.
5 Loosen the clip and disconnect the top hose from the thermostat housing.
6 Place a suitable container beneath the engine then unscrew the sump drain plug and drain the oil (photo). When completed, clean the drain plug and washer and tighten it into the sump.
7 Identify the fuel supply and return hoses then disconnect them from the fuel pump and carburettor and plug them.
8 Loosen the clip and disconnect the bottom hose from the coolant pipe at the rear of the engine (photo).
9 Disconnect the accelerator and choke cables from the carburettor with reference to Chapter 3.
10 Disconnect the heater hoses from the thermostat housing and rear coolant pipe (photos).

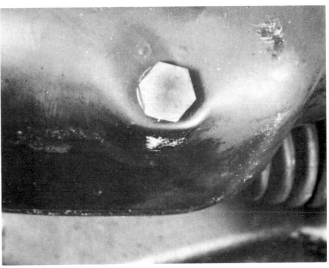

5.6 Sump drain plug

5.8 Removing the bottom hose from the rear engine coolant pipe

5.10A Disconnect the heater hoses from the thermostat housing ...

5.10B ... and coolant pipe

5.11A Oil pressure switch

5.11B Double oil pressure switch fitted to some models

11 Disconnect the following wiring after identifying each lead for location:

(a) Oil pressure switch (rear of the cylinder head) (photo).
(b) Temperature sender unit (thermostat housing).
(c) Cut-off solenoid valve and automatic choke (carburettor).
(d) Inlet manifold pre-heating element and thermo-switch (beneath inlet manifold and in coolant hose) – on 1.05 litre models only.
(e) Distributor HT and LT leads.
(f) Starter.
(g) Reversing light switch (gearbox).
(h) Gearchange and fuel consumption indicator (gearbox and sender in distributor vacuum line) – Formel E models only.
(i) Ignition retard switch (carburettor) – 1.05 litre models only.
(j) Alternator.

12 Disconnect and unclip the vacuum hoses from the distributor and inlet manifold as necessary.

13 Disconnect the clutch cable with reference to Chapter 5.

14 On 1.1 and 1.3 litre engines unbolt the exhaust connecting pipe from the bottom of the inlet manifold and remove the gasket.

15 Disconnect the exhaust downpipe from the exhaust manifold with reference to Chapter 3.

16 Disconnect the speedometer cable from the gearbox and place it on one side.

5.24A Front engine mounting

5.24B Removing the engine earth strap

17 Apply the handbrake then jack up the front of the car and support it on axle stands.

18 Unbolt the front exhaust mounting and lower the exhaust to the floor.

19 If still attached, disconnect the main starter wire from under the car.

20 Unbolt the driveshafts from the drive flanges with reference to Chapter 7 and tie them to one side with wire.

21 Remove the screw from the shift rod coupling and ease the coupling from the rod. The screw threads are coated with a liquid locking agent, and if difficulty is experienced it may be necessary to heat up the coupling with a blowlamp, *however take the necessary fire precautions*.

22 Unscrew the nuts and bolts and remove the rear mounting bracket from the gearbox and mounting.

23 Attach a suitable hoist to the engine lifting hooks and take the weight of the engine and gearbox assembly.

24 Unscrew the mounting bolts from the brackets, also unscrew the bolt securing the earth strap to the right-hand side of the engine compartment (photos).

25 Raise the engine and gearbox assembly from the engine compartment while turning it as necessary to clear the internally mounted components. Make sure that all wires, cables and hoses have been disconnected (photo).

26 Lower the assembly onto a workbench or large piece of wood placed on the floor.

5.25 Removing the engine

6 Engine – separation from gearbox

1 Remove the starter with reference to Chapter 9.

2 Unbolt and remove the cover plate from the clutch housing.

3 Unscrew and remove the engine to gearbox bolts.

4 Withdraw the gearbox from the engine keeping it in a horizontal position until clear of the clutch (photo). If it is seized on the locating dowels use a lever to free it.

7 Engine dismantling – general

1 If possible mount the engine on a proper stand for the dismantling procedure, but failing this support it in an upright position with blocks of wood.

2 Cleanliness is most important, and if the engine is dirty, it should be cleaned with paraffin or a water-soluble degreasant before dismantling.

3 Avoid working with the engine on a concrete floor, as grit presents a real source of trouble.

4 As parts are removed, clean them in a paraffin bath. However, do not immerse parts with internal oilways in paraffin as it is difficult to

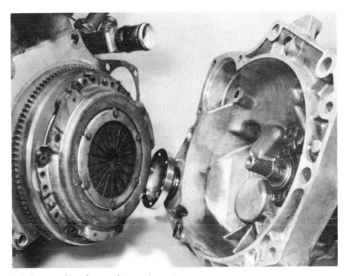

6.4 Separating the engine and gearbox

remove, usually requiring a high pressure hose. Clean oilways with nylon pipe cleaners.

5 It is advisable to have suitable containers to hold small items according to their use, as this will help when reassembling the engine and also prevent possible losses.

6 Always obtain complete sets of gaskets when the engine is being dismantled, but retain the old gaskets with a view to using them as a pattern to make a replacement if a new one is not available.

7 When possible, refit nuts, bolts, and washers in their location after being removed, as this helps to protect the threads and will also be helpful when reassembling the engine.

8 Retain unserviceable components in order to compare them with the new parts supplied.

8 Ancillary components – removal

With the engine removed from the car and separated from the gearbox, the externally mounted ancillary components should now be removed before dismantling begins. The removal sequence need not necessarily follow the order given:

Alternator and drivebelt (Chapter 9)
Inlet manifold and carburettor (Chapter 3)
Exhaust manifold (Chapter 3)

8.1A Crankcase ventilation oil separator and hose

8.1B Removing an engine mounting

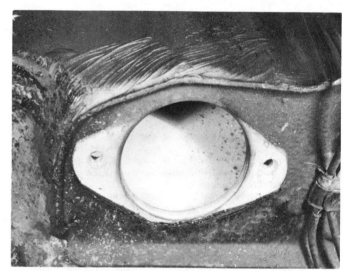

8.1C Rear engine mounting location

8.1D Removing the alternator mounting bracket

8.1E Unscrew the nuts ...

8.1F ... and remove the engine rear coolant pipe

Distributor (Chapter 4)
Fuel pump (Chapter 3)
Thermostat (Chapter 2)
Clutch (Chapter 5)
Crankcase ventilation hose (Section 21 of this Chapter) (photo)
Distributor cap and spark plugs (Chapter 4)
Oil filter (Section 20 of this Chapter)
Engine mountings (photos)
Dipstick
Oil pressure switch
Water temperature switch (Chapter 2)
Alternator mounting bracket and engine earth lead (photo)
Engine rear coolant pipe (photos)

9 Cylinder head – removal

If the engine is still in the car, first carry out the following operations:
(a) Disconnect the battery negative lead.
(b) Remove the air cleaner and fuel pump (Chapter 3).
(c) Drain the cooling system and remove the top hose and thermostat (Chapter 2).
(d) Remove the distributor and spark plugs (Chapter 4).
(e) Remove the inlet and exhaust manifolds (Chapter 3) although if necessary this can be carried out with the cylinder head on the bench.
(f) Disconnect the wiring from the coolant temperature sender and oil pressure switch.

1   Unscrew the nuts and bolts from the valve cover and remove the cover together with the gasket and reinforcement strips (photos).
2   Turn the engine until the indentation in the camshaft sprocket appears in the TDC hole in the timing cover, and the notch in the crankshaft pulley is aligned with the TDC pointer on the front of the oil pump (photos). Now turn the crankshaft one quarter of a turn anti-clockwise so that neither of the pistons is at TDC.
3   Unbolt and remove the timing cover noting that the dipstick tube and earth lead are fitted to the upper bolts. Pull the dipstick tube from the cylinder block (photos).
4   Using a socket through the hole in the camshaft sprocket, unscrew the timing cover plate upper retaining bolt (photo).
5   Loosen the water pump retaining bolts, then turn the pump body clockwise to release the tension from the timing belt (photo). Remove the timing belt from the camshaft sprocket.
6   Remove the bolts and withdraw the timing cover plate followed by the water pump if required.
7   Using a splined socket, unscrew the cylinder head bolts half a turn at a time in the reverse order to that shown in Fig. 1.4. Note the location of the engine lifting hooks (photos).
8   Lift the cylinder head from the block (photo). If it is stuck, tap it free with a wooden mallet. Do not however insert a lever, as damage will occur to the joint faces.
9   Remove the gasket from the cylinder block (photo).

9.1A Unscrew the nuts and bolts ...

9.1B ... and remove the valve cover ...

9.1C ... and gasket

9.2A TDC mark on the camshaft sprocket, and pointer

9.2B Crankshaft pulley notch aligned with the TDC pointer

9.3A Timing cover bolt retaining the dipstick tube

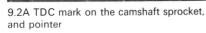

9.3B Timing cover side bolt

9.3C Removing the dipstick tube

9.3D Timing cover side bolt and earth lead

9.3E Removing the timing cover

9.4 Showing timing cover plate upper bolt

9.5 A water pump retaining bolt

9.7A Special splined socket for unscrewing the cylinder head bolts

9.7B Engine lifting hook location

9.8 Removing the cylinder head

9.9 Removing the cylinder head gasket

10 Camshaft – removal

If the engine is still in the car, first carry out the following operations:

(a) *Disconnect the battery negative lead.*
(b) *Remove the air cleaner and fuel pump (Chapter 3).*
(c) *Remove the distributor and spark plugs (Chapter 4).*

If the cylinder head is still fitted to the engine first carry out the procedure described in paragraphs 1 to 4 inclusive.

1 Unscrew the nuts and bolts from the valve cover and remove the cover together with the gasket and reinforcement strips.

2 Turn the engine until the indentation in the camshaft sprocket appears in the TDC hole in the timing cover, and the notch in the crankshaft pulley is aligned with the TDC pointer on the front of the oil pump. Now turn the crankshaft one quarter of a turn anti-clockwise so that neither of the pistons is at TDC.

3 Unbolt and remove the timing cover noting that the dipstick tube and earth lead are fitted to the upper bolts.

4 Loosen the water pump retaining bolts, then turn the pump body clockwise to release the tension from the timing belt. Remove the timing belt from the camshaft sprocket.

5 Prise the oil spray tube from the top of the cylinder head (photo).

6 Note how the cam follower clips are fitted then prise them from the ball studs (photo).

7 Identify each cam follower for location then remove each one by levering with a screwdriver, but make sure that the peak of the relevant cam is pointing away from the follower first by turning the camshaft as necessary (photo).

8 Unscrew the camshaft sprocket bolt and remove the spacer (photo). The sprocket can be held stationary using a metal bar with two bolts, with one bolt inserted in a hole and the other bolt resting on the outer rim of the sprocket.

9 Tap the sprocket from the camshaft with a wooden mallet and prise out the Woodruff key (photo).

10 Using feeler blades check the camshaft endfloat by inserting the blade between the end of the camshaft and the distributor flanges (photo). If it is more than the amount given in the Specifications the components will have to be checked for wear and renewed as necessary.

11 Using an Allen key unscrew the bolts and remove the distributor flange (photo). Remove the gasket.

12 Carefully slide the camshaft from the cylinder head taking care not to damage the three bearing surfaces as the lobes of the cams pass through them (photo).

13 Prise the camshaft oil seal from the cylinder head (photo).

10.5 Removing the oil spray tube

10.6 Removing a cam follower clip

10.7 Removing a cam follower

10.8 Unscrew the bolt ...

10.9 ... and remove the camshaft sprocket

10.10 Checking the camshaft endfloat

10.11 Removing the distributor flange

10.12 Removing the camshaft

10.13 Removing the camshaft oil seal

11 Cylinder head – dismantling

1   Remove the camshaft as described in Section 10.
2   Using a valve spring compressor, compress each valve spring in turn until the split collets can be removed. Release the compressor and remove the retainers and springs (photos). If the retainers are difficult to remove do not continue to tighten the compressor, but gently tap the top of the tool with a hammer. Always make sure that the compressor is held firmly over the retainer.
3   Remove each valve from the cylinder head keeping them identified for location.
4   Prise the valve seals from the valve guides and remove the lower spring seats (photo).
5   Do not remove the cam follower ball studs unless they are unserviceable, as they are likely to be seized in the head.

12 Timing belt and sprockets – removal

If the engine is still in the car, first carry out the following operations:

(a) Disconnect the battery negative lead.
(b) Remove the air cleaner (Chapter 3).
(c) Remove the alternator drivebelt (Chapter 9).

11.2A Compressing the valve spring to remove the split collets

11.2B Removing the valve springs and retainers

11.4 Removing the valve spring lower seats

1   Turn the engine until the indentation in the camshaft sprocket appears in the TDC hole in the timing cover, and the notch in the crankshaft pulley is aligned with the TDC pointer on the front of the oil pump.

2   Unbolt and remove the timing cover noting that the dipstick tube and earth lead are fitted to the upper bolts.

3   Loosen the water pump retaining bolts, then turn the pump body clockwise to release the tension from the timing belt. Remove the timing belt from the camshaft sprocket (photo).

4   Using an Allen key unbolt the pulley from the crankshaft sprocket, then remove the timing belt.

5   To remove the camshaft sprocket unscrew the bolt and remove the spacer. Then tap off the sprocket and remove the Woodruff key. Do not turn the camshaft. The sprocket can be held stationary using a metal bar with two bolts, with one bolt inserted through a sprocket hole and the other bolt resting on the outer rim.

6   To remove the crankshaft sprocket unscrew the bolt and lever the sprocket from the crankshaft. Do not turn the crankshaft otherwise the pistons may touch the valve heads. Hold the crankshaft stationary with a lever inserted in the starter ring gear (remove the starter as applicable). Remove the Woodruff key. Note that if the engine is in the car, the access hole in the right-hand engine compartment panel may be used. Cut a hole if one is not already there (photo).

13 Flywheel – removal

1   Remove the clutch as described in Chapter 5.

2   Hold the flywheel stationary with a lever or angle iron (photo) engaged with the starter ring gear.

3   Unscrew the bolts and lift the flywheel from the crankshaft (photo).

4   Remove the engine plate from the cylinder block (photo).

12.3 Releasing the timing belt from the camshaft sprocket

12.6A Removing the crankshaft sprocket bolt

12.6B Showing access hole for crankshaft sprocket bolt

13.2 One method of holding the flywheel stationary

13.3 Removing the flywheel

13.4 Removing the engine plate

14 Crankshaft front oil seal – renewal

1 Remove the crankshaft sprocket with reference to Section 12.
2 If available use VW tool 2085 to remove the oil seal from the oil pump. Alternatively drill two diagonally opposite holes in the oil seal, insert two self-tapping screws, and pull out the seal with grips.
3 Clean the recess in the oil pump.
4 Smear a little engine oil on the lip and outer edge of the new oil seal, then fit it with tool 10-203 or by tapping it in with a suitable metal tube.
5 Refit the crankshaft sprocket with reference to Section 40.

15 Crankshaft rear oil seal – renewal

1 Remove the flywheel as described in Section 13.

Method 1

2 Drill two diagonally opposite holes in the oil seal, insert two self-tapping screws, and pull out the seal with grips.
3 Clean the recess in the housing.
4 Smear a little engine oil on the lip and outer edge of the new oil seal then tap it into the housing using a suitable metal tube (photo).
5 Refit the flywheel as described in Section 36.

Method 2

6 Remove the sump as described in Section 16.
7 Unscrew the bolts and withdraw the housing from the dowels on the cylinder block. Remove the gasket (photo).
8 Support the housing and drive out the oil seal (photo).
9 Clean the recess in the housing.
10 Smear a little engine oil on the lip and outer edge of the new oil seal then tap it into the housing using a block of wood (photo).
11 Clean the mating faces then refit the housing together with a new gasket and tighten the bolts evenly in diagonal sequence to the specified torque.
12 Refit the sump and flywheel as described in Sections 35 and 36 respectively.

16 Sump – removal

If the engine is still in the car, first carry out the following operations:

(a) *Jack up the front of the car and support it on axle stands. Apply the handbrake.*
(b) *Disconnect the right-hand side driveshaft (Chapter 7) and the exhaust system (Chapter 3).*
(c) *Unclip the alternator wire from the sump (photo).*
(d) *Drain the engine oil into a suitable container. Clean the drain plug and washer and refit it, tightening it to the specified torque.*

1 Unscrew the bolts and withdraw the sump from the cylinder block (photo). If it is stuck, lever it away or cut through the gasket with a knife.
2 Scrape the gasket from the sump and cylinder block.

17 Oil pump – removal

1 Remove the timing belt and crankshaft sprocket as described in Section 12.
2 Remove the sump as described in Section 16.
3 Unbolt and remove the pick-up tube and strainer from the oil pump and cylinder block. Remove the flange gasket (photos).
4 Unscrew the bolts and withdraw the oil pump from the dowels on the front of the cylinder block. Note that the timing pointed bracket is located on the two upper central bolts, and the timing belt guard on the two left-hand side bolts. Remove the gasket (photos).

15.4 The crankshaft rear oil seal and housing

15.7A Removing the crankshaft rear oil seal housing ...

15.7B ... and gasket

15.8 Removing the crankshaft rear oil seal

15.10 Installing the new crankshaft rear oil seal

16.0 Showing the alternator wire clip on the sump

16.1 Removing the sump

17.3A Remove the stay bolts ...

17.3B ... and flange bolts ...

17.3C ... and remove the oil pump pick-up tube and strainer

17.4A Removing the oil pump ...

17.4B ... and gasket

18 Pistons and connecting rods – removal

1 Remove the cylinder head as described in Section 9.
2 Remove the sump as described in Section 16.
3 Unbolt and remove the pick-up tube and strainer from the oil pump and cylinder block. Remove the flange gasket.
4 Using a feeler gauge check that the connecting rod endfloat on each crankpin is within the limits given in the Specifications (photo). If not the components must be checked for wear and renewed as necessary.
5 Check the big-end caps and connecting rods for identification marks, and if necessary use a centre punch to mark them for location and position. Note that the cut-outs in the connecting rods and caps face the timing belt end of the engine. The arrows on the piston crowns also face the timing belt end of the engine (photo).
6 Turn the crankshaft so that No 1 crankpin is at its lowest point.
7 Unscrew the big-end nuts and tap free the cap together with its bearing shell (photo).
8 Using the handle of a hammer tap the piston and connecting rod from the bore and withdraw it from the top of the cylinder block (photo).
9 Loosely refit the cap to the connecting rod (photo).
10 Repeat the procedure given in paragraphs 7 to 9 on No 4 piston and connecting rod, then turn the crankshaft through half a turn and repeat the procedure on No 2 and 3 pistons.

18.4 Checking the connecting rod endfloat

18.5 Piston crown showing arrow which faces the timing belt end of the engine

18.7 Removing a big-end cap

18.8 Removing a piston

18.9 Big-end bearing components

19 Crankshaft and main bearings – removal

1   Disconnect the connecting rods from the crankshaft with reference to Section 18, however it is not essential to remove the pistons or therefore to remove the cylinder head.

2   Remove the oil pump as described in Section 17, and the rear oil seal housing as described in Section 15.

3   Using a feeler gauge check that the crankshaft endfloat is within the limits given in the Specifications (photo). Insert the feeler gauge between the centre crankshaft web and the thrust washers. This will indicate whether new thrust washers are required or not.

4   Check that the main bearing caps are identified for location and position – there should be a cast number in the crankcase ventilation pipe/water coolant pipe side of the caps, numbered from the timing belt end of the engine (photo).

5   Unscrew the bolts and tap the main bearing caps free. Keep the bearing shells and thrust washers identified for position.

6   Lift the crankshaft from the crankcase and remove the remaining bearing shells and thrust washers but keep them identified for position (photo).

19.3 Checking the crankshaft endfloat

19.4 Crankshaft main bearing cap numbering

19.6 Removing the crankshaft

20.2 Removing the oil filter

20 Oil filter – renewal

1   The oil filter should be renewed at the 10000 mile (15000 km) service. First place a suitable container beneath the oil filter. For better access either jack up the front of the car or position it on car ramps.
2   Using a strap wrench unscrew the filter from the cylinder block, and discard it (photo).
3   Wipe clean the sealing face on the block.
4   Smear a little engine oil on the sealing ring of the new filter then fit it to the block and tighten it *by hand only* (photo).
5   Wipe clean the filter and check it for leaks after starting the engine.

21 Crankcase ventilation system – description

The crankcase ventilation system is of the positive type and consists of an oil separator on the rear (water coolant pipe side) of the cylinder block, connected to the air cleaner by a rubber hose. Vacuum from the air cleaner provides a partial vacuum in the crankcase, and the piston blow-by gases are drawn through the oil separator and into the engine combustion chambers.

Periodically the hose should be examined for security and condition. Cleaning will not normally be necessary except when the engine is well worn.

20.4 Tighten the oil filter by hand only

22 Examination and renovation – general

With the engine completely stripped, clean all the components and examine them for wear. Each part should be checked, and where necessary renewed or renovated as described in the following Sections. Renew main and big-end shell bearings as a matter of course, unless you know that they have had little wear and are in perfect condition.

23 Oil pump – examination and renovation

The manufacturers do not supply any clearances for checking the wear of the oil pump gears, so it must be assumed to be in good order provided that the oil pressure is as given in the Specifications. This of course can only be checked with the engine assembled and, as a pressure gauge will not be available to the home mechanic, the work should be entrusted to a VW garage.

However a visual examination of the oil pump can be made if required as follows.

1   Using an Allen key unscrew the relief valve plug and extract the spring and plunger (photos).

23.1A Unscrew the relief valve plug ...

23.1B ... and remove the spring and plunger

23.2A Use an impact screwdriver to remove the screws ...

23.2B ... then remove the oil pump cover ...

23.3A ... and rotors

23.3B The outer rotor indentation should face the cover

2   Using an impact screwdriver remove the cross-head screws and withdraw the cover from the pump (photos).
3   Remove the rotors noting that the indentation on the outer rotor faces the cover (photos).
4   Clean the components in paraffin and wipe dry, then examine them for wear and damage. If evident, renew the oil pump complete, but if in good order reassemble the pump in reverse order and tighten the screws and plug.

24 Crankshaft and bearings – examination and renovation

1   Examine the bearing surfaces of the crankshaft for scratches or scoring and, using a micrometer, check each journal and crankpin for ovality. Where the surfaces are worn or the ovality exceeds 0.03 mm (0.001 in) the crankshaft will have to be reground and undersize bearings fitted. An accurate check of the bearing running clearances can be made using perfect circle plastic such as Plastigage – the plastic strip is placed across the crankpin or journal and the bearing cap tightened to the specified torque. On the removal of the cap the width of the flattened plastic is measured with the gauge supplied (photos).
2   Crankshaft regrinding should be carried out by an engineering works who will supply the matching undersize main and big-end shell bearings.

24.1A Plastigage strip for checking bearing running clearances

24.1B Checking the Plastigage strip with the gauge

25.6 Showing core plugs in the cylinder block

26.6 Checking the piston ring gaps

26.7A Checking the piston ring groove clearance

26.7B The piston ring gaps must be spaced at 120° intervals

3 If the crankshaft endfloat is more than the maximum specified amount, new thrust washers should be fitted to the centre main bearing – these are usually supplied together with the main and big-end bearings on a reground crankshaft.

25 Cylinder block – examination and renovation

1 The cylinder bores must be examined for taper, ovality, scoring, and scratches. Start by examining the top of the bores; if these are worn, a slight ridge will be found which marks the top of the piston ring travel. If the wear is excessive, the engine will have had a high oil consumption rate accompanied by blue smoke from the exhaust.
2 If available, use an inside dial gauge to measure the bore diameter just below the ridge and compare it with the diameter at the bottom of the bore, which is not subject to wear. If the difference is more than 0.006 in (0.152 mm), the cylinders will normally require reboring with new oversize pistons fitted.
3 Provided the cylinder bore wear does not exceed 0.008 in (0.203 mm), however, special oil control rings and pistons can be fitted to restore compression and stop the engine burning oil.
4 If new pistons are being fitted to old bores, it is essential to roughen the bore walls slightly with fine glasspaper to enable the new piston rings to bed properly.
5 Thoroughly examine the crankcase and cylinder block for cracks and damage and use a piece of wire to probe all oilways and waterways to ensure they are unobstructed.
6 Check the core plugs for leaks and security (photo).

26 Pistons and connecting rods – examination and renovation

1 Examine the pistons for ovality, scoring and scratches. Check the connecting rods for wear and damage.
2 To remove the pistons from the connecting rods first mark the two components in relation to each other – the indentation on the bearing

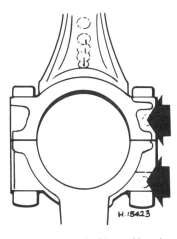

Fig. 1.1 The indentations on the big-end bearings (arrows) must face the same way as the arrow on the piston crown (Sec 26)

end of the connecting rod faces the same way as the arrow on the piston crown.
3 Prise out the circlips then dip the piston in boiling water, press out the gudgeon pin, and separate the piston from the connecting rod.
4 Assemble the pistons in reverse order.
5 If new rings are to be fitted to the original pistons, expand the old rings over the top of the pistons using two or three old feeler blades to prevent the rings dropping into empty grooves.
6 Before fitting the new rings insert each of them into the cylinder bore approximately 15.0 mm (0.6 in) from the bottom and check that the end gaps are as given in the Specifications (photo).
7 When fitting the rings to the pistons make sure that the TOP markings face towards the piston crown, and arrange the end gaps at 120° intervals. Using a feeler gauge check that the clearance of each ring in its groove is within the limits given in Specifications (photo).

27 Flywheel – examination and renovation

1   Examine the clutch driven plate mating surface of the flywheel with reference to Chapter 5.
2   Check the starter ring gear teeth; if they are chipped or worn the ring gear must be renewed. To do this, partially drill the ring gear from the side, then carefully split it with a cold chisel and remove it, taking suitable precautions to prevent injury from flying fragments.
3   Heat the new ring to 392°F (200°C) in an electric oven, then quickly fit it to the flywheel. Allow the ring to cool naturally without quenching.

28 Timing belt and sprockets – examination and renovation

1   The timing belt should be renewed as a matter of course if it has completed more than 20 000 miles (32 000 km) at the time of its removal. Otherwise renew it at 40 000 miles (64 000 km).
2   The camshaft and crankshaft sprockets do not normally require renewal as wear takes place very slowly.

29 Camshaft – examination and renovation

1   Examine the camshaft bearing surfaces, cam lobes, and followers for wear. If excessive renew the shaft and followers.
2   Check the camshaft run-out by turning it between fixed centres with a dial gauge on the centre journal. If the run-out exceeds the amount given in Specifications, renew the shaft.

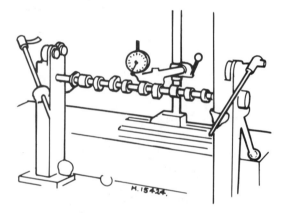

Fig. 1.2 Checking the camshaft run-out (Sec 29)

30 Cylinder head – decarbonising, valve grinding and renovation

1   Decarbonising will normally only be required at comparatively high mileages. However if performance has deteriorated even though engine adjustments are correct decarbonising may be required, although this may be attributable to worn pistons and rings.
2   With the cylinder head removed, use a scraper to remove the carbon. Remove all traces of gasket then wash the cylinder head thoroughly in paraffin and wipe dry.
3   Use a straight edge and feeler blade to check that the cylinder head surface is not distorted. If it is, it must be resurfaced by a suitably equipped engineering works.
4   If the engine is still in the car, clean the piston crowns and cylinder bore upper edges, but make sure that no carbon drops between the pistons and bores. To do this, locate two of the pistons at the top of their bores and seal off the remaining bores with paper and masking tape. Press a little grease between the two pistons and their bores to collect any carbon dust; this can be wiped away when the piston is lowered. To prevent carbon build-up, polish the piston crown with metal polish, but remove all traces of the polish afterwards.
5   Examine the heads of the valves for pitting and burning, especially the exhaust valve heads. Renew any valve which is badly burnt. Examine the valve seats at the same time. If the pitting is very slight, it

can be removed by grinding the valve heads and seats together with coarse, then fine, grinding paste. Note that the exhaust valves should not be recut, therefore they should be renewed if the sealing face is excessively grooved as a result of regrinding.
6   Where excessive pitting has occurred, the valve seats must be recut or renewed by a suitably equipped engineering works.
7   Valve grinding is carried out as follows. Place the cylinder head upside down on a bench with a block of wood at each end.
8   Smear a trace of coarse carborundum paste on the seat face and press a suction grinding tool onto the valve head. With a semi-rotary action, grind the valve head to its seat, lifting the valve occasionally to redistribute the grinding paste. When a dull matt even surface is produced on both the valve seat and the valve, wipe off the paste and repeat the process with fine carborundum paste as before. A light spring placed under the valve head will greatly ease this operation. When a smooth unbroken ring of light grey matt finish is produced on both the valve and seat, the grinding operation is complete.
9   Scrape away all carbon from the valve head and stem, and clean away all traces of grinding compound. Clean the valves and seats with a paraffin soaked rag, then wipe with a clean rag.
10 If the valve guides are worn, indicated by a side-to-side motion of the valve, new guides must be fitted. This work is best carried out by a VW garage as it involves the use of a special reamer.
11 If possible compare the length of the valve springs with new ones, and renew them as a set if any are shorter.

31 Engine reassembly – general

1   To ensure maximum life with minimum trouble from a rebuilt engine, not only must everything be correctly assembled, but it must also be spotlessly clean. All oilways must be clear, and locking washers and spring washers must be fitted where indicated. Oil all bearings and other working surfaces thoroughly with engine oil during assembly.
2   Before assembly begins, renew any bolts or studs with damaged threads.
3   Gather together a torque wrench, oil can, clean rag, and a set of engine gaskets and oil seals, together with a new oil filter.

32 Crankshaft and main bearings – refitting

1   Clean the backs of the bearing shells and the bearing recesses in the cylinder block and main bearing caps.
2   Press the main bearing shells into the cylinder block and caps and oil them liberally (photos).
3   Using a little grease, stick the thrust washers to each robe of the centre main bearings with their oilways facing away from the bearings in the block and cap (photo).
4   Lower the crankshaft into position, then fit the main bearing caps in

32.2A Fitting the centre main bearing shell

32.2B Oiling the main bearing shells

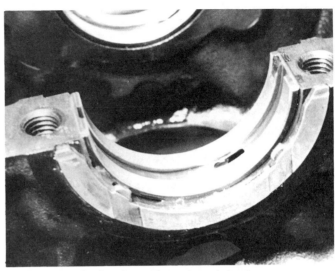
32.3 Thrust washer location on the centre main bearing

32.4 Fitting the centre main bearing cap

32.5 Tightening the main bearing bolts

their previously noted positions (photo). Note that the bearing shell lugs are adjacent to each other.

5   Insert the bolts and tighten them evenly to the specified torque (photo). Check that the crankshaft rotates freely then check that the endfloat is within the limits given in the Specifications by inserting a feeler gauge between the centre crankshaft web and the thrust washers.

6   Refit the rear oil seal bearing (Section 15) and oil pump (Section 34), and reconnect the connecting rods (Section 33).

33 Pistons and connecting rods – refitting

1   Clean the backs of the bearing shells and the recesses in the connecting rods and big-end caps.

2   Press the big-end bearing shells into the connecting rods and caps in their correct positions and oil them liberally (photos).

3   Fit a ring compressor to No 1 piston then insert the piston and

33.2A Fitting a big-end bearing shell

33.2B Showing correct location of tabs on big-end bearings

33.3 Using a ring compressor when installing the pistons

33.4 Tightening the big-end bearing nuts

connecting rod into No 1 cylinder (photo). With No 1 crankpin at its lowest point, drive the piston carefully into the cylinder with the wooden handle of a hammer, and at the same time guide the connecting rod into the crankpin. Make sure that the arrow on the piston crown faces the timing belt end of the engine.

4   Fit the big-end bearing cap in its previously noted position then fit the nuts and tighten them evenly to the specified torque (photo).

5   Check that the crankshaft turns freely and use a feeler gauge to check that the connecting rod endfloat is within the limits given in the Specifications.

6   Repeat the procedure given in paragraphs 3 to 5 for No 4 piston and connecting rod, then turn the crankshaft through half a turn and repeat the procedure for No 2 and 3 pistons.

7   Refit the oil pump pick-up tube and strainer (Section 34), sump (Section 35), and cylinder head (Section 39).

34 Oil pump – refitting

1   Renew the oil seal in the oil pump housing with reference to Section 14 (photos).

2   Locate a new gasket on the dowels on the front of the cylinder block.

3   Locate the oil pump on the block making sure that the inner rotor engages the flats on the crankshaft. Do not damage the oil seal.

4   Insert bolts together with the timing pointer bracket and timing belt guard, and tighten them evenly to the specified torque (photo).

5   Locate a new gasket on the flange face then fit the pick-up tube and strainer, insert the bolts, and tighten them to the specified torque.

6   Refit the sump (Section 35), and timing belt and sprocket (Section 40).

35 Sump – refitting

1   If applicable (ie engine has been dismantled), refit the crankshaft rear oil seal and housing with reference to Section 15.

2   Clean the mating faces of the sump and cylinder block.

3   Locate the new gasket either on the sump or block, then fit the sump, insert the bolts and tighten them evenly in diagonal sequence to the specified torque (photo). If required, the two bolts at the flywheel end of the sump can be replaced by socket head bolts to facilitate their removal with the engine in the car.

4   If the engine is in the car refill the engine with oil, fasten the alternator wire to the sump clip, and lower the car to the ground.

36 Flywheel – refitting

1   Locate the engine plate on the dowels on the cylinder block.

2   Clean the mating faces of the flywheel and crankshaft, then locate

34.1A Prising out the oil pump oil seal

34.1B Fitting the new oil seal to the oil pump

34.4 Fitted location of the oil pump

35.3 Fitting the sump gasket

36.3A Applying liquid locking fluid to the flywheel bolts

36.3B Tightening the flywheel bolts

the flywheel in position. Note that the bolt holes only align in one position as they are offset.

3 Apply liquid locking fluid to the threads of the bolts, then insert them and tighten them in diagonal sequence to the specified torque while holding the flywheel stationary (photos).

4 Refit the clutch as described in Chapter 5.

37 Cylinder head – reassembly

1 Fit the valves in their correct locations in the cylinder head.

2 Working on each valve at a time first locate the valve spring lower seat in position.

3 Before fitting the valve seal, locate the special plastic sleeve provided in the gasket set over the valve stem in order to prevent damage to the seal (photo).

4 Slide the new seal over the valve stem and press it firmly onto the guide using a metal tube (photo). Remove the plastic sleeve.

5 Fit the spring and retainer over the valve stem, then compress the spring with the compressor and insert the split collets. Release the compressor and remove it.

6 Repeat the procedure given in paragraphs 2 to 5 on the remaining valves. Tap the end of each valve stem with a non-metallic mallet to settle the collets.

7 Refit the camshaft as described in Section 38.

38 Camshaft – refitting

1 Smear a little engine oil on the lip and outer edge of the camshaft oil seal, then drive it squarely into the cylinder head with a block of wood.

2 Oil the camshaft bearing surfaces then slide the camshaft into position taking care not to damage the oil seal (photo).

3 Fit the distributor flange together with a new gasket, and tighten the socket head bolts.

4 Using a feeler gauge check that the camshaft endfloat is as specified.

5 Fit the Woodruff key then fit the sprocket to the camshaft followed by the spacer and bolt. Tighten the bolt while holding the sprocket stationary with a metal bar and two bolts (photo).

6 Fit the cam followers by turning the camshaft so that the relevant cam lobe peak is pointing away from the valve, then tap the follower between the valve stem and cam, and onto the ball stud.

7 Slide the cam follower clips into the grooves on the ball studs and locate the upper ends on the cam followers.

37.3 Fit the plastic sleeve on the valve stem ...

37.4 ... then fit the new oil seal

38.2 Oiling the camshaft bearing surfaces

38.5 Method of tightening the camshaft sprocket bolt

38.9 Showing TDC pointer and indentation on camshaft sprocket

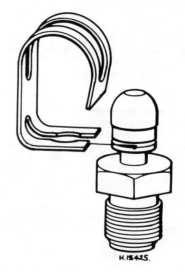

Fig. 1.3 Showing cam follower clip and groove in ball stud
(Sec 38)

8   Adjust the valve clearances as described in Section 41.
9   Turn the camshaft so that the indentation in the sprocket is pointing
downwards and in line with the pointer on the timing cover plate
(photo).
10 Turn the crankshaft a quarter of a turn clockwise so that the notch in
the crankshaft pulley is aligned with the **TDC** pointer on the front of the
oil pump.
11 Fit the timing belt to the camshaft sprocket and water pump.
12 Using a screwdriver in the water pump, turn the pump anti-
clockwise and tension the timing belt until it can just be turned through
90° with the thumb and forefinger midway between the camshaft
sprocket and water pump.
13 Tighten the water pump bolts when the belt tension is correct, and
check the timing marks are still aligned.
14 Fit the dipstick tube to the cylinder block.
15 Fit the timing cover, insert the bolts with the earth lead and dipstick
tube bracket, and tighten the bolts.
16 Press the oil spray tube into the top of the cylinder head.
17 Refit the valve cover with a new gasket, locate the reinforcement
strips, and tighten the nuts and bolts.
18 If the engine is in the car reverse the preliminary procedures given in
Section 10.

39 Cylinder head – refitting

1   Position Nos 1 and 4 pistons at TDC then turn the crankshaft a
quarter of a turn anti-clockwise so that neither of the pistons is at TDC.
2   Make sure that the faces of the cylinder head and block are perfectly
clean then locate the new gasket on the block making sure that all oil
and water holes are visible – the gasket part number should be
uppermost (photo).
3   Lower the cylinder head onto the gasket, then insert the bolts
together with the engine lifting hooks.
4   Using a splined socket tighten the bolts in the four stages given in
the Specifications, using the sequence shown in Fig. 1.4 (photo).
5   Refit the water pump if applicable (Chapter 2).
6   Fit the timing cover plate and insert the water pump bolts loosely.
7   If required refit the camshaft with reference to Section 38.
8   Refit and tighten the timing cover plate upper retaining bolt.
9   If applicable refit the crankshaft sprocket and timing belt to the
crankshaft as described in Section 40 (photo).
10 Turn the camshaft so that the indentation in the sprocket is aligned
with the pointer on the timing cover plate.
11 Turn the crankshaft a quarter of a turn clockwise so that the notch in
the crankshaft pulley (temporarily refit it if necessary) is aligned with the
TDC pointer on the front of the oil pump.
12 Fit the timing belt to the camshaft sprocket and water pump.
13 Using a screwdriver in the water pump, turn the pump anti-

39.2 Correct fitting of the cylinder head gasket

39.4 Tightening the cylinder head bolts

39.9 Fitting the crankshaft sprocket and timing belt

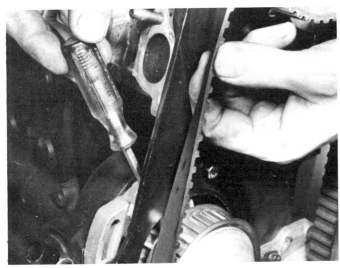

39.13 Tightening the timing belt

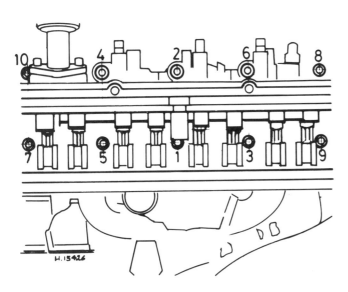

Fig. 1.4 Cylinder head bolt tightening sequence (Sec 39)

clockwise and tension the timing belt until it can just be turned through 90° with the thumb and forefinger midway between the camshaft sprocket and water pump (photo).
14 Tighten the water pump bolts when the tension is correct, and check that the timing marks are still aligned.
15 Fit the dipstick tube to the cylinder block.
16 Fit the timing cover, insert the bolts with the earth lead and dipstick tube bracket, and tighten the bolts.
17 Refit the valve cover with a new gasket, locate the reinforcement strips, and tighten the nuts and bolts.
18 If the engine is in the car reverse the preliminary procedures given in Section 9.

40 Timing belt and sprockets – refitting

1 Fit the Woodruff key in the crankshaft and tap the sprocket into position.
2 Insert the bolt and tighten it to the specified torque while holding the crankshaft stationary with a lever in the starter ring gear.
3 Fit the Woodruff key to the camshaft then fit the sprocket followed by the spacer and bolt. Tighten the bolt while holding the sprocket stationary with a metal bar and two bolts.
4 Locate the timing belt on the crankshaft sprocket then fit the pulley, insert the bolts, and tighten them with an Allen key.
5 Turn the camshaft so that the indentation in the sprocket is aligned with the pointer on the timing cover plate. Check that the notch in the crankshaft pulley is aligned with the TDC pointer on the front of the oil pump.
6 Fit the timing belt to the camshaft sprocket and water pump.
7 Using a screwdriver in the water pump, turn the pump anti-clockwise and tension the timing belt until it can just be turned through 90° with the thumb and forefinger midway between the camshaft sprocket and water pump.
8 Tighten the water pump bolts when the tension is correct, and check that the timing marks are still aligned.
9 Fit the timing cover, insert the bolts with the earth lead and dipstick tube bracket, and tighten the bolts.
10 If the engine is in the car, reverse the preliminary procedures given in Section 12.

41 Valve clearances – adjustments

After overhauling the cylinder head the valve clearances should be adjusted on the bench, then again after the engine has completed 600 miles (1000 km).
1 With the valve cover removed turn the engine or camshaft (ie if head removed) until both cam peaks for No 1 cylinder are pointing away from the valve stems. In this position (TDC) both inlet and exhaust valves can be checked.
2 Insert a feeler blade of the correct thickness (see Specifications) between the cam and cam follower. If the blade is not a firm sliding fit

41.2 Adjusting the valve clearances

turn the adjustable ball stud as necessary using an Allen key (photo). The valves from the timing belt end of the engine are in the following order: Inlet – Exhaust – Inlet – Exhaust – Inlet – Exhaust – Inlet – Exhaust.

3   Repeat the procedure given in paragraphs 1 and 2 for the remaining valves. If the engine is rotated in its normal direction, adjust the valves of No 3 cylinder followed by No 4 cylinder and No 2 cylinder.

4   Refit the valve cover together with a new gasket.

42 Ancillary components – refitting

Refer to Section 8 and refit the listed components with reference to the Chapters or Sections as applicable.

43 Engine – refitting to gearbox

Reverse the procedure given in Section 6.

44 Engine – refitting

Reverse the removal procedure given in Section 5 but note the following additional points:

(a)   *When lowering the assembly into the engine compartment connect the right-hand driveshaft to the drive flange first.*

(b)   *Assemble the engine mountings loosely initially and tighten them only after the assembly is central without straining the mountings.*

(c)   *Adjust the clutch cable as described in Chapter 5.*

(d)   *On 1.05 litre models the white vacuum pipe must be fitted to the bottom (retard) connection on the distributor, and the black pipe to the top (advance) connection.*

(e)   *Adjust the accelerator and choke cables as described in Chapter 3.*

(f)   *Refill the engine with oil and water.*

45 Engine – adjustment after major overhaul

1   With the engine refitted to the car, make a final check to ensure that everything has been reconnected and that no rags or tools have been left in the engine compartment.

2   If new pistons or crankshaft bearings have been fitted, turn the carburettor engine speed screw in about half a turn to compensate for the initial tightness of the new components.

3   Fully pull out the choke and start the engine. This may take a little longer than usual as the fuel pump and carburettor float chamber may be empty.

4   As soon as the engine starts, push in the choke to the detent. Check that the oil pressure light goes out.

5   Check the oil filter, fuel hoses, and water hoses for leaks.

6   Run the engine to normal operating temperature, then adjust the slow running as described in Chapter 3.

7   If new pistons or crankshaft bearings have been fitted, the engine must be run-in for the first 500 miles (800 km). Do not operate the engine at full throttle or allow the engine to labour in any gear.

46 Fault diagnosis – engine

Symptom	Reason(s)
Engine fails to start	Discharged battery Loose battery connection Loose or broken ignition leads Moisture on spark plugs, distributor cap, or HT leads Incorrect spark plug gap or contact points dwell angle Cracked distributor cap or rotor Dirt or water in carburettor Empty fuel tank Faulty fuel pump Faulty starter motor Low cylinder compression
Engine idles erratically	Inlet manifold air leak Cylinder head gasket leaking Worn camshaft lobes Faulty fuel pump Incorrect valve clearances Carburettor slow running adjustment incorrect Uneven cylinder compressions
Engine misfires	Spark plug gap or contact points dwell angle incorrect Faulty coil or condenser Dirt or water in carburettor Burnt out valve Leaking cylinder head gasket Distributor cap cracked Incorrect valve clearances Uneven cylinder compressions
Engine stalls	Carburettor adjustment incorrect Inlet manifold air leak Ignition timing incorrect
Excessive oil consumption	Worn pistons and cylinder bores Valve guides and valve stem seals worn Oil leak from oil seal
Engine backfires	Carburettor adjustment incorrect Ignition timing incorrect Incorrect valve clearances Inlet manifold air leak Sticking valve

Chapter 2 Cooling system

For modifications, and information applicable to later models, see Supplement at end of manual

Contents

Specifications

System type .... Pressurised with pump driven by timing belt, front mounted radiator with internal or external expansion tank, electric cooling fan

Radiator cap pressure .... 17.4 to 21.8lbf/in^2 (1.2 to 1.5 bar)

Thermostat
Opening temperature	92°C (197°F)
Fully open temperature	108°C (226°F)
Minimum stroke	7.0 mm (0.28 in)

Cooling fan thermo-switch
Switch-on temperature	93° to 98°C (199° to 208°F)
Switch-off temperature	88° to 93°C (190° to 199°F)

System capacity (including heater)
With internal expansion tank	7.9 pt (4.5 litre)
With external expansion tank	11.4 pt (6.5 litre)

Antifreeze

Concentration	Protection down to
40%	–25°C (–13°F)
50%	–35°C (–31°F)

Torque wrench settings
	lbf ft	Nm
Temperature sender unit	7	10
Water pump	7	10
Cooling fan thermo-switch	18	25
Cooling fan bracket	7	10
Thermostat cover	15	20

1 General description

The cooling system is of pressurised type and includes a front mounted radiator, water pump driven by the timing belt, and a thermostatically operated electric cooling fan. Circulation through the radiator is controlled by a thermostat located in a housing on the left-hand end of the cylinder head below the distributor. The radiator is of aluminium construction with side tanks, incorporating crossflow circulation, and according to the model the expansion tank may be located internally in the radiator side tank or externally in the engine compartment. No drain plugs are provided.

The system functions as follows. Cold water from the bottom of the radiator circulates through the bottom hose to the water pump via the coolant pipe located at the rear of the engine. The pump impeller forces the water around the cylinder block and head passages. After cooling the cylinder bores, combustion surfaces, and valve seats, the water reaches the cylinder head outlet and is diverted through hoses to the inlet manifold and then to the coolant pipe when the thermostat is closed. A further hose from the cylinder head outlet allows water to circulate through the heater matrix in the passenger compartment and back to the coolant pipe. Initially the circulation is through the engine and heater, but when the coolant reaches the predetermined temperature (see Specifications), the thermostat opens and the water then circulates through the top hose to the top of the radiator. As the water passes through the radiator tubes, it is cooled by the inrush of air when the car is in forward motion, supplemented by the action of the electric cooling fan when necessary. Having reached the bottom of the radiator, the water is cooled and the cycle is repeated.

The electric cooling fan is controlled by a thermo-switch located in the left-hand side of the radiator.

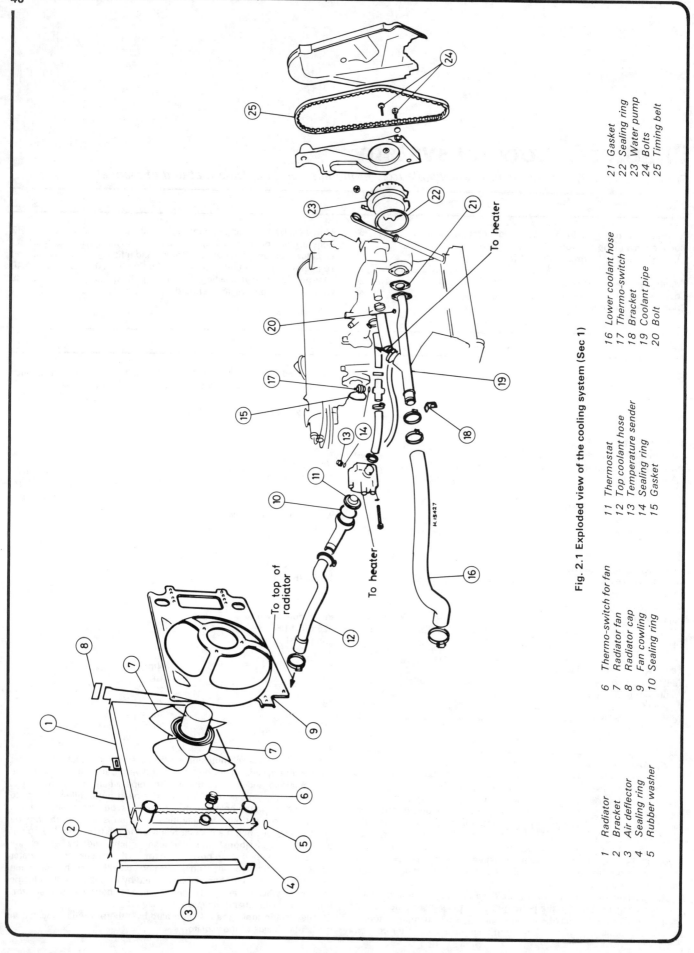

Fig. 2.1 Exploded view of the cooling system (Sec 1)

1 Radiator
2 Bracket
3 Air deflector
4 Sealing ring
5 Rubber washer

6 Thermo-switch for fan
7 Radiator fan
8 Radiator cap
9 Fan cowling
10 Sealing ring

11 Thermostat
12 Top coolant hose
13 Temperature sender
14 Sealing ring
15 Gasket

16 Lower coolant hose
17 Thermo-switch
18 Bracket
19 Coolant pipe
20 Bolt

21 Gasket
22 Sealing ring
23 Water pump
24 Bolts
25 Timing belt

2 Cooling system – draining

1 It is preferable to drain the cooling system when the engine has cooled. If this is not possible, place a cloth over the radiator or expansion tank filler cap and turn it *slowly* in an anti-clockwise direction until the pressure starts to escape.
2 When all the pressure has escaped, remove the filler cap.
3 Set the heater controls to maximum heat, then place a suitable container beneath the left-hand side of the radiator.
4 Loosen the clip and ease the bottom hose away from the radiator outlet. Drain the coolant into the container.

3 Cooling system – flushing

1 After some time the radiator and engine waterways may become restricted or even blocked with scale or sediment which can reduce the efficiency of the cooling system. When this occurs, the coolant will appear rusty and dark in colour and the system should then be flushed. In severe cases, reverse flushing may be required, although if a reputable antifreeze/corrosion inhibitor has been in constant use this is unlikely.
2 With the coolant drained, disconnect the top hose from the radiator. Insert a garden hose and allow the water to circulate through the radiator until it runs clear from the bottom outlet.
3 Disconnect the heater hose from the cylinder head outlet and insert a garden hose in the heater hose. With the heater controls set at maximum heat, allow water to circulate through the heater and out through the bottom hose until it runs clear.
4 In severe cases of contamination the system should be reverse flushed. To do this, remove the radiator, invert it and insert a garden hose in the outlet. Continue flushing until clear water runs from the inlet.
5 The engine should also be reverse flushed. To do this, disconnect the heater hose from the cylinder head outlet and insert a garden hose in the outlet. Continue flushing until clear water runs from the bottom hose.
6 The use of chemical cleaners should only be necessary as a last resort. Regular checking of the antifreeze/corrosion inhibitor concentration at the 10000 mile (15000 km) service should prevent the contamination of the system.

4 Cooling system – filling

1 Reconnect all the hoses and check that the heater controls are set to maximum heat.
2 Remove the rubber strip and plastic cover from the plenum chamber behind the engine compartment, then loosen the bleeder screw on the heater temperature control valve (photo).
3 Pour the recommended coolant into the radiator or expansion tank (as applicable) until it reaches the maximum mark (photo). While doing this watch the heater bleeder, and tighten the screw when bubble-free water comes out.
4 Refit the plastic cover and rubber strip to the plenum chamber.
5 Refit and tighten the filler cap then run the engine at a fast idling speed for approximately 10 seconds.
6 Stop the engine and top-up the coolant level as necessary to the maximum mark. Refit the filler cap.
7 After running the engine to normal operating temperature (ie until the electric cooling fan operates), the coolant level should be rechecked with the engine cold.

5 Antifreeze/corrosion inhibitor mixture – general

1 The manufacturers install G10 antifreeze/corrosion inhibitor mixture in the cooling system when the car is new. Every 10000 miles (15000 km) or 12 months the concentration of the coolant should be checked by a VW garage and if necessary topped up with fresh mixture.
2 The mixture must remain in the cooling system at all times as it prevents the formation of scale and also provides a higher boiling point than plain water – this maintains the efficiency of the coolant particularly when the engine is operating at full load.

4.2 Bleeder screw location for the cooling system

4.3 Filling the cooling system

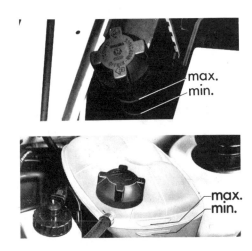

Fig. 2.2 Coolant level marks on radiator with internal expansion tank (top) and external expansion tank (bottom) (Sec 4)

3 The concentration of the mixture can be calculated according to the lowest ambient temperature likely to be encountered as given in the Specifications. However it should never be less than 40%.
4 Before adding new mixture, check all hose connections for tightness.

6 Radiator – removal, inspection, cleaning and refitting

1 Disconnect the battery negative lead.
2 Drain the cooling system as described in Section 2.
3 Disconnect the wiring from the thermo-switch and cooling fan motor (photos).
4 Disconnect the top hose and expansion tank hose (if applicable) from the radiator (photo).
5 Remove the screw and washer, and withdraw the upper retaining

clip from the right-hand side of the radiator (photos).
6 Move the top of the radiator rearwards and remove the air deflectors (2 screws) (photo).
7 Lift the radiator out of the lower mounting rubbers and withdraw it from the engine compartment taking care not to damage the matrix (photos).
8 Remove the screws and withdraw the cowling and fan from the radiator.
9 It is not possible to repair this radiator without special equipment, although minor leaks can be sealed using a proprietary coolant additive.
10 Clean the radiator matrix of flies and small leaves with a soft brush or by hosing, then reverse flush the radiator as described in Section 3. Renew the hoses and clips if they are damaged or deteriorated.
11 Refitting is a reversal of removal, but if necessary renew the radiator lower mounting rubbers. Fill the cooling system as described in Section 4.

6.3A Disconnect the wiring from the thermo-switch ...

6.3B ... and cooling fan motor

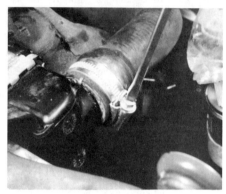
6.4 Disconnecting the top hose

6.5A Remove the screw ...

6.5B ... and lift out the radiator retaining clip

6.6 Removing the radiator air deflectors

6.7A Removing the radiator

6.7B Showing the radiator lower mounting stubs

7.4 Cooling fan and mounting nuts

7 Cooling fan and motor – removal and refitting

1 Disconnect the battery negative lead.
2 Disconnect the wiring from the cooling fan motor.
3 Remove the four screws and lift the cowling together with the cooling fan and motor from the radiator.
4 Remove the nuts and withdraw the cooling fan and motor from the cowling (photo).
5 If necessary the fan can be separated from the motor by prising off the clamp washer. On AEG motors drive out the roll pin, and on Bosch motors remove the shake-proof washer. Assemble the components in reverse order using a new clamp washer.
6 Refitting is a reversal of removal.

8 Cooling fan motor thermo-switch – removal, testing and refitting

1 Disconnect the battery negative lead.
2 Drain the cooling system as described in Section 2.
3 Unscrew the thermo-switch from the left-hand side of the radiator and remove the sealing ring (photo).
4 To test the thermo-switch suspend it with a piece of string so that its element is immersed in a container of water. Connect the thermo-switch in series with a 12 volt test lamp and battery. Gradually heat the

water and note the temperature with a thermometer. The test lamp should light up at the specified switch-on temperature and go out at the specified switch-off temperature. If not, renew the thermo-switch.
5 Refitting is a reversal of removal, but fit a new sealing ring and tighten the thermo-switch to the specified torque. Fill the cooling system as described in Section 4.

9 Thermostat – removal, testing and refitting

1 The thermostat is located in the outlet housing on the left-hand end of the cylinder head. To remove it, first drain the cooling system as described in Section 2.
2 Unscrew the bolts and remove the thermostat cover (photos). Place the cover with top hose still attached to one side.
3 Remove the sealing ring (photo).
4 Extract the thermostat from the outlet housing.
5 To test whether the unit is serviceable, suspend it with a piece of string in a container of water. Gradually heat the water and note the temperature at which the thermostat starts to open. Continue heating the water to the specified fully open temperature then check that the thermostat has opened by at least the minimum amount given in the Specifications. Remove the thermostat from the water and check that it is fully closed when cold.

8.3 Cooling fan motor thermo-switch

9.2A Unscrew the socket head bolts ...

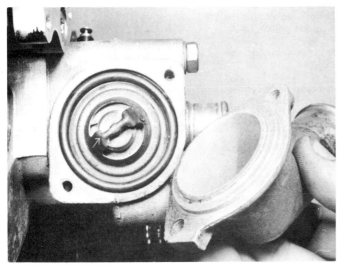

9.2B ... and remove the thermostat cover

9.3 Removing the thermostat cover sealing ring

6   Renew the thermostat if it fails to operate correctly.
7   Clean the thermostat seating and the mating faces of the outlet housing and cover.
8   Refitting is a reversal of removal, but fit a new sealing ring and tighten the cover bolts to the specified torque – the breather hole in the thermostat should face upwards. Fill the cooling system as described in Section 4.

10 Temperature sender unit – removal and refitting

1   It is not necessary to drain the cooling system if some form of plug such as an old sender unit or rubber plug is available. First release any pressure in the system by unscrewing the pressure cap – *if the system is still hot, observe the precaution in Section 2*. With all pressure released, tighten the cap again.
2   Locate the sender unit on the cylinder head outlet housing, then disconnect the wiring lead (photo).
3   Unscrew and remove the temperature sender unit and plug the aperture.
4   Refitting is a reversal of removal, but tighten the sender unit to the

specified torque. Check and if necessary top-up the cooling system with reference to Section 4.

11 Water pump – removal and refitting

1   Drain the cooling system as described in Section 2.
2   Remove the air cleaner and air ducting as described in Chapter 3, and disconnect the battery negative lead.
3   Unbolt and remove the timing belt cover.
4   Turn the engine with a spanner on the crankshaft pulley bolt until the timing cover plate upper retaining bolt is visible through the camshaft sprocket hole. Unscrew and remove the bolt.
5   Align the timing marks and release the timing belt from the water pump and camshaft sprocket with reference to Chapter 1.
6   Remove the bolts and withdraw the timing cover plate followed by the water pump. Remove the sealing ring (photos).
7   It is not possible to repair the water pump, and if faulty it must be renewed. Clean the mating faces of the water pump and cylinder block.
8   Refitting is a reversal of removal, but fit a new sealing ring and refer to Chapter 1 when fitting and tensioning the timing belt. Fill the cooling system as described in Section 4.

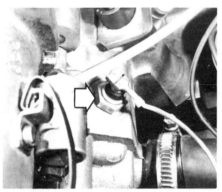

10.2 Temperature sender unit location

11.6A Removing the water pump

11.6B Removing the water pump sealing ring

12 Fault diagnosis – cooling system

Symptom	Reason(s)
Overheating	Low coolant level
	Faulty pressure cap
	Thermostat sticking shut
	Open circuit thermo-switch
	Faulty cooling fan motor
	Clogged radiator matrix
	Retarded ignition timing
Slow warm-up	Thermostat sticking open
	Incorrect thermostat
Coolant loss	Damaged or deteriorated hose, or loose clip
	Leaking water pump
	Leaking cylinder head outlet or coolant pipe gasket
	Leaking cylinder head gasket
	Leaking radiator

Chapter 3 Fuel and exhaust systems

For modifications, and information applicable to later models, see Supplement at end of manual

Contents

Specifications

Air cleaner .... Automatic load and temperature sensitive control, with renewable paper element.

Fuel pump

Type .... Mechanical, diaphragm operated by plunger from the camshaft
Pressure at engine speed of 1000 rpm with return line clamped .... 0.20 to 0.25 bar (2.9 to 3.6 lbf/in^2)

Carburettor

	1.05 litre (29 kW)	1.1 litre (37 kW) up to HB 799 999	1.1 litre Formel E (37 kW) from HB 800 000	1.3 litre (44 kW)
Type	Solex downdraught with manual choke			
Code	31 PIC-7	31 PIC-7	31 PIC-7	34 PIC-6
Venturi	23	25.5	23	24.5
Main jet	X 117.5	X 132.5	X 115	X 120
Air correction jet with emulsion tube	125 Z	105 V	120 Z	85 Z
Idling fuel jet	40	40.5	40	52.5
Idling air jet	100	90	100	130
Auxiliary fuel/air jet (in float chamber) ...	—	—	35/130	35/15° (from 1/82 only)
Auxiliary fuel jet	30	30	—	40 (to 12/81 only)
Auxiliary air jet	130	100	—	100 (to 12/81 only)
Enrichment (primary/secondary)	60/60	100/–	60/60	95/95
Injection capacity (cm^3/stroke)	0.9 ± 0.15	0.9 ± 0.15	0.9 ± 0.15	0.7 ± 0.15
Float needle valve	1.5	1.5	1.5	1.5
Float needle valve washer thickness (mm) ...	2.0	2.0	2.0	0.5
Fast idling speed (rpm)	2400 ± 100	2400 ± 100	2500 ± 100	2600 ± 100
Choke valve gap (mm)	1.8 ± 0.2	2.0 ± 0.2	2.2 ± 0.2	2.0 ± 0.2
Throttle valve gap smooth running detent (mm) ...	2.5 ± 0.3	4.0 ± 0.3	2.5 ± 0.3	4.5 ± 0.5
Idling speed (rpm)	950 ± 50	950 ± 50	950 ± 50	950 ± 50
CO content %	1.0 ± 0.5	1.0 ± 0.5	1.0 ± 0.5	1.0 ± 0.5

Fuel tank capacity .... 8 Imp gal (36 litre)

Fuel octane rating (minimum)

Formel E models .... 98 RON (4 star)
Except Formel E models .... 91 RON (2 star)

Torque wrench settings

	lbf ft	Nm
Fuel pump	15	20
Fuel tank	18	25
Carburettor	18	25
Inlet manifold	18	25
Exhaust heater pipe to inlet manifold	18	25
Intermediate flange nuts	7	10
Inlet manifold cover	7	10
Inlet manifold preheater	7	10
Exhaust manifold	18	25
Hot air shroud	7	10
Downpipe clamp	15	20
Downpipe flange	22	30
Exhaust heater pipe support	15	20
Intermediate exhaust clamps	18	25

1 General description

The fuel system consists of a rear mounted fuel tank, a camshaft operated fuel pump and a Solex PIC downdraught carburettor incorporating a manual choke with automatic override.

The air cleaner is of automatic air temperature control type and incorporates a disposable paper element.

The exhaust system on the 1.05 litre engine is in two sections – the downpipe and front section, and the silencer and tailpipe. On 1.1 and 1.3 litre models the exhaust system is in four sections – the twin downpipe section, intermediate flexible pipe, front silencer and pipe, and the rear silencer and tailpipe. Additionally on 1.1 and 1.3 litre models a flexible and rigid pipe connect the downpipe to the exhaust heated inlet manifold.

On 1.05 litre models the inlet manifold is heated by an electric preheater unit.

2 Air cleaner element and body – removal and refitting

1 The air cleaner element should be renewed every 20 000 miles (30 000 km). To do this prise back the clips and lift off the cover, then lift out the element (photos).

2 Wipe down the inside of the air cleaner with a cloth. Also clean the inside of the cover.

3 Fit the new element and locate the cover on the air cleaner body with the slotted tab over the tab on the intake. Refit the clips.

4 To remove the body first remove the element.

5 Disconnect the hot air hose from the exhaust manifold shroud (photo).

6 Unscrew the retaining nuts then lift the unit from the carburettor and disconnect the vacuum and crankcase ventilation hoses (photos).

7 If necessary unclip and remove the air temperature control vacuum unit and intake pipe.

2.1A Removing the air cleaner cover

2.1B Removing the air cleaner element

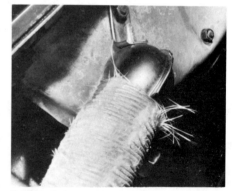
2.5 Hot air hose connected to the exhaust manifold shroud

2.6A Air cleaner retaining nuts

2.6B Air temperature sensor vacuum connections

8   Refitting is a reversal of removal, but make sure that the rubber seal is correctly located on the carburettor.

3   Air cleaner air temperature control – checking

1   Unclip and remove the vacuum unit and intake pipe but leave the vacuum pipe connected (photos).
2   Suspend a thermometer in the flow of air through the inlet duct then start the engine. Between -20°C (-4°F) and +20°C (68°F) the control flap in the unit should be a maximum of ⅔rds open to admit hot air from the exhaust manifold (if a sheet metal type air cleaner is fitted it must not be more than ½ open). Above 20°C (68°F) the control flap must close the hot air supply.
3   The control flap movement can be checked by sucking on the vacuum inlet.
4   With the engine running and inlet air temperature above 20°C (68°F), disconnect the vacuum hose from the vacuum unit. The control flap should fully open within a maximum of 20 seconds.
5   If the control unit does not operate correctly, renew it together with the temperature sensor (photo).
6   Refit the vacuum unit and intake pipe.

4   Fuel pump and filter – testing, removal and refitting

1   The fuel pump is located on the right-hand side of the engine by the air cleaner. To test it accurately, connect a pressure gauge in the outlet pipe and check that the pressure is as given in the Specifications with the engine running at the specified speed.
2   Alternatively a less accurate method is to disconnect the supply pipe from the carburettor (air cleaner removed) and also disconnect the LT lead from the coil positive terminal. Spin the engine on the starter while holding a wad of rag near the fuel pipe. Well defined spurts of fuel should be ejected from the pipe if the fuel pump is operating correctly, provided there is fuel in the fuel tank. If not remove the fuel pump cover (1 screw) and clean out any sediment, and also check the in-line filter for blockage (photo).
3   The in-line filter should be renewed every 20000 miles (30000 km). To do this, remove the clips and extract the filter (photo). If necessary renew the crimped type clips with screw type ones. Fit the new filter in a horizontal position with its arrow facing the flow of fuel towards the fuel pump and make sure that it is firmly held by the plastic support clip.
4   To remove the fuel pump first remove the air cleaner as described in Section 2.

3.1A Air cleaner vacuum unit

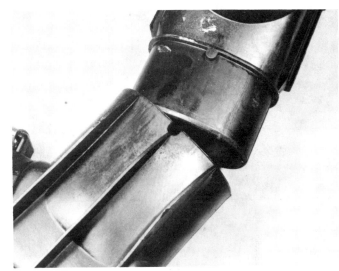

3.1B Removing the air temperature control unit

3.5 Upper view of the air temperature sensor

4.2 Removing the fuel pump cover

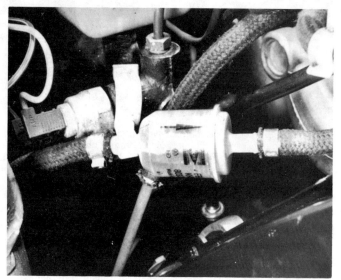

4.3 The in-line fuel filter

4.5 Disconnecting the fuel pump hoses

4.6A Unscrew the bolts ...

4.6B ... and withdraw the fuel pump

4.6C Showing the fuel pump sealing ring

4.8 Alignment indentations on the fuel pump cover

5 Identify the hoses for position, then disconnect them from the pump (photo).
6 Using an Allen key, unscrew the retaining bolts, then withdraw the pump from the cylinder head and remove the sealing ring. Note the earth lead location (photos).
7 Clean the mating faces of the pump and cylinder head.
8 Refitting is a reversal of removal, but renew the sealing ring and tighten both to the specified torque. When refitting the cover make sure that the alignment indentations are correctly engaged (photo). Renew crimped type clips with screw type ones.

5 Fuel tank – removal, servicing and refitting

For safety reasons the fuel tank must always be removed in a well ventilated area, never over a pit.
1 Disconnect the battery negative lead.
2 Siphon or pump all the fuel from the fuel tank (there is no drain plug) (photo).
3 Lift the rear seat cushion, remove the cover plate, and disconnect the wiring from the gauge sender unit.
4 Jack up the rear of the car and support on axle stands. Chock the front wheels and remove the right-hand side rear wheel.

5.2 Fuel tank filler cap

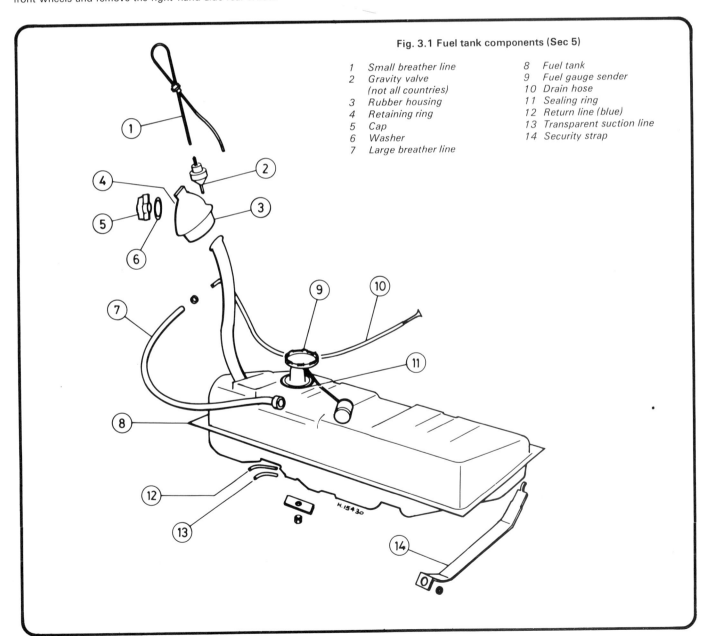

Fig. 3.1 Fuel tank components (Sec 5)

1	Small breather line	8	Fuel tank
2	Gravity valve (not all countries)	9	Fuel gauge sender
		10	Drain hose
3	Rubber housing	11	Sealing ring
4	Retaining ring	12	Return line (blue)
5	Cap	13	Transparent suction line
6	Washer	14	Security strap
7	Large breather line		

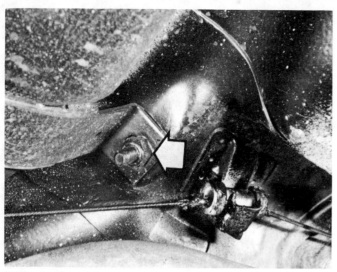

5.8 Fuel tank retaining strap

5.10 Fuel tank vent hose

5   Disconnect the breather hoses from the filler neck.
6   Remove the filler neck rubber tube together with the drain hose.
7   Disconnect the fuel hoses at the front of the fuel tank.
8   Support the fuel tank with a trolley jack and length of wood, then unscrew the retaining nuts and bolts, detach the strips, and lower the tank to the ground (photo).
9   If the tank is contaminated with sediment or water, remove the gauge sender unit as described in Section 6 and swill the tank out with clean fuel. If the tank is damaged or leaks, it should be repaired professionally or alternatively renewed. *Do not under any circumstances solder or weld a fuel tank.*
10 Refitting is a reversal of removal, but the bottom surface of a new tank should first be given a coat of underseal. Make sure that the rubber packing strips are fitted to the retaining straps. Refit the hoses free of any kinks – note that the blue hose goes to the upper connection. Check that the vent (drain) hose is clipped securely to the tank flange (photo).

6 Fuel gauge sender unit – removal and refitting

6.2 Disconnecting the wiring from the fuel tank sender unit

For safety reasons the fuel gauge sender unit must always be removed in a well ventilated area, never over a pit.
1   Disconnect the battery negative lead.
2   Lift the rear seat cushion, remove the cover plate, and disconnect the wiring from the gauge sender unit (photo).
3   Using two crossed screwdrivers turn the sender unit anti-clockwise and withdraw it from the fuel tank. Remove the gasket.
4   Refitting is a reversal of removal, but always fit a new gasket. Note that when correctly fitted the wiring points towards the breather connection. The new gasket should be coated with graphite powder.

7 Accelerator cable – removal, refitting and adjustment

1   Disconnect the battery negative lead.
2   Remove the air cleaner as described in Section 2.
3   Prise the clip from the throttle lever quadrant, then open the throttle by hand and disconnect the inner cable (photos).
4   Release the cable grommet from the support bracket (photos).
5   Working inside the car remove the lower facia panel then unclip the inner cable from the accelerator pedal (photo).
6   Withdraw the complete cable into the engine compartment together with the rubber grommets.
7   Refitting is a reversal of removal, but make sure that it is free of any kinks and correctly aligned. Finally adjust it as follows before refitting the air cleaner.
8   Position a piece of wood 5.0 mm (0.2 in) thick between the accel-

ator pedal arm and the floor, and have an assistant keep the pedal fully depressed.
9   Pull the outer cable so that the throttle is fully open, and insert the spring clip in the groove next to the support bracket grommet washer (photo).
10 Remove the piece of wood and refit the air cleaner.

8 Choke cable – removal, refitting and adjustment

1   Disconnect the battery negative lead.
2   Remove the air cleaner as described in Section 2.
3   Using a screwdriver loosen the inner and outer cable clamps and disconnect the cable from the carburettor (photo).
4   Working inside the car remove the lower facia panel.
5   Pull out the clip and remove the choke knob.
6   Unscrew the ring and withdraw the cable from the facia.
7   Disconnect the wiring and withdraw the complete cable from inside the car.
8   Refitting is a reversal of removal, but make sure that the cable is correctly aligned, and that the grommets are firmly fitted in the bulkhead. Finally adjust it as follows before refitting the air cleaner.
9   Locate the outer cable in the clamp so that its end protrudes

7.3A Accelerator cable and quadrant

7.3B Disconnecting the accelerator inner cable

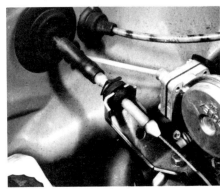

7.4A Showing the accelerator cable support bracket

7.4B Removing the accelerator outer cable

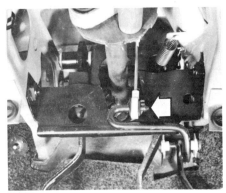

7.5 Inner cable connection to the accelerator pedal

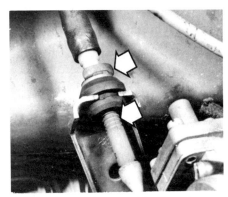

7.9 Showing accelerator cable clip and adjustment grooves

8.3 Removing the choke cable

9.2 Showing accelerator pedal and pivot

approximately 12.0 mm (0.47 in). Tighten the clamp with the outer cable in this position.

10 Push the choke knob fully in then pull it out 3.0 mm (0.12 in) – switch on the ignition and check that the warning lamp is not lit.

11 Insert the inner cable into the choke lever clamp and fully open the choke lever by hand. Tighten the inner cable clamp screw in this position.

12 Refit the air cleaner.

9 Accelerator pedal – removal and refitting

1 Remove the lower facia panel.

2 Disconnect the accelerator cable from the pedal (photo).

3 Prise out the clip and remove the pivot pin.

4 Remove the accelerator pedal. If necessary press out the pivot pin bushes.

5 Refitting is a reversal of removal, but lubricate the bushes with a little grease. Check the cable adjustment with reference to Section 7.

10 Carburettor – general description

The Solex PIC carburettor is of downdraught type incorporating a manual choke with automatic override control. The cut-off solenoid is activated by the ignition switch and cuts the supply of mixture to the idling system when the ignition is switched off, thereby preventing running on (dieselling).

The accelerator pump is of the diaphragm type. When starting from cold, the manual choke valve provides fuel enrichment. A bi-metallic coil is heated by the ignition and gradually opens the choke valve to prevent over-enrichment. Additionally a vacuum operated device opens the choke valve when the engine is accelerated or is running at high speed (photos).

10.1A View of throttle lever end of the carburettor

10.1B View of float chamber end of the carburettor

10.1C View of choke vacuum control end of the carburettor

Certain models are provided with part throttle channel heating in the carburettor for improved cold running, and on some later models the system is controlled by a thermo-switch in contact with the fuel in the float chamber.

11 Carburettor – removal and refitting

1   Disconnect the battery negative lead.
2   Remove the air cleaner as described in Section 2 (photo).
3   Identify the fuel feed and return hoses then disconnect them (photo).
4   Disconnect the accelerator and choke cables with reference to Sections 7 and 8.
5   Disconnect the carburettor earth lead from the fuel pump retaining bolt earth terminal.
6   Disconnect the wiring from the cut-off solenoid, choke control, and throttle valve switch (photo).

7   Disconnect the vacuum hose.
8   Remove the nuts from under the inlet manifold and withdraw the carburettor upwards. Remove the gasket and do not lose the insulator washers (photos).
9   Clean the mating faces of the carburettor and inlet manifold.
10 Refitting in a reversal of removal, but always fit a new gasket and tighten the nuts evenly to the specified torque. Adjust the accelerator and choke cables with reference to Section 7 and 8. Adjust the slow running as described in Section 13.

12 Carburettor – dismantling, reassembly and adjustment

1   With the carburettor removed from the engine clean the external surfaces with paraffin and wipe dry.
2   Remove the screws from the cover noting the location of the earth lead (photo).

11.2 View of carburettor with air cleaner removed

11.3 Disconnecting the fuel hoses

11.6 Cut-off solenoid and wiring

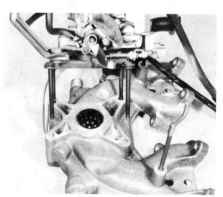

11.8A Removing the carburettor

11.8B Lower view of the carburettor and gasket

12.2 Showing carburettor cover and screws

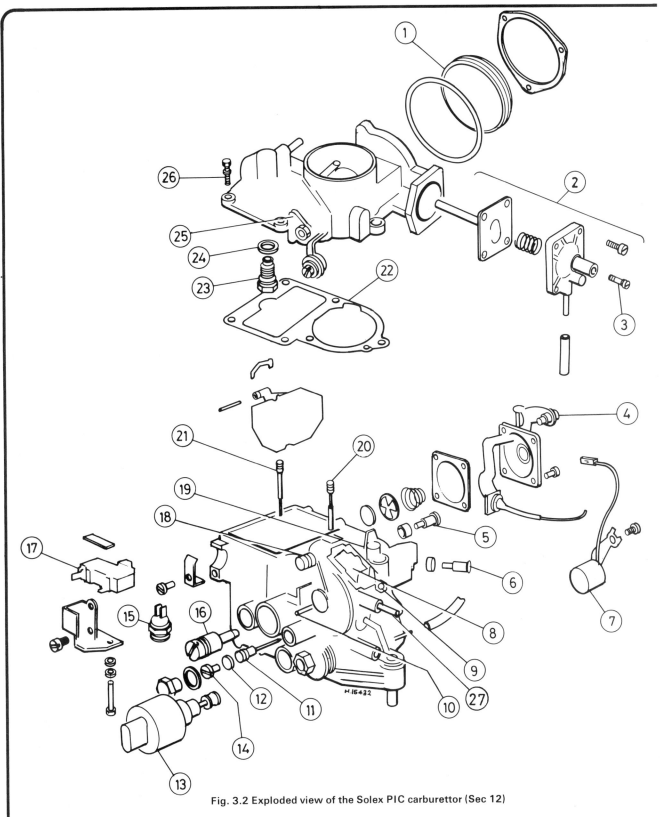

Fig. 3.2 Exploded view of the Solex PIC carburettor (Sec 12)

1 Choke cover
2 Pulldown device
3 Adjustment screw
   (choke valve gap)
4 Adjustment screw
   (injection capacity)
5 Auxiliary fuel jet
   (except 052 129 017 B/D)
6 Pilot jet

7 Bypass passage heater
8 Limiting screw
9 Tamper-proof cap
10 Connector for distributor
   advance unit
11 CO adjusting screw
12 Tamper-proof cap
13 Bypass air cut-off valve

14 Main jet
15 Thermo-switch
16 Idle adjustment screw
17 Throttle valve switch
18 Detent roller
19 Injection pipe
20 Air correction jet with
   emulsion tube

21 Auxiliary fuel/air jet
22 Gasket
23 Float needle valve
24 Washer
25 Eccentric pin
26 Screws
27 Temperature regulator
   connection (air cleaner)

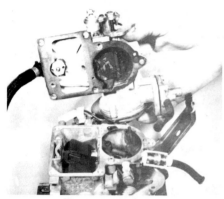

12.3 Removing the carburettor cover

12.4A Prise out the retainer ...

12.4B ... and remove the float

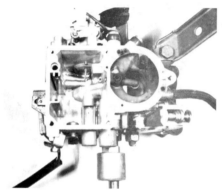

12.5 View of carburettor with cover removed

12.9A Checking the choke valve gap with a twist drill

12.9B Adjusting screw location for choke valve gap

3 Lift off the cover and remove the gasket (photo).

4 Prise out the retainer and remove the float from the carburettor (photos).

5 Clean out the float chamber with clean fuel (photo).

6 If necessary further dismantle the carburettor with reference to Fig. 3.2.

7 To check the cut-off solenoid when removed, depress the pin approximately 3 to 4 mm (0.12 to 0.16 in) then energise it with battery voltage. A click should be heard and the pin should move out.

8 Reassembly is a reversal of dismantling, but renew all gaskets and rubber rings. Finally make the following adjustments.

9 To adjust the choke valve gap operate the choke lever fully then return it to the smooth running detent and hold it there. With the choke spindle lever against the cam check that the clearance between the choke valve and barrel is as given in the Specification. Use a twist drill to make the check and if necessary adjust the screw at the end of the pulldown unit (photos).

10 The accelerator pump injection capacity may be checked with the carburettor fitted or removed, however the air cleaner must be removed and the float chamber must be full. Open the choke valve and retain in the open position with a piece of wire, then push a length of close fitting plastic tube over the injection pipe. Operate the throttle until fuel emerges then place the tube in a measuring glass. Operate the throttle fully five times allowing at least three seconds per stroke. Divide the final quantity by five to determine the amount per stroke and compare with the amount given in the Specifications. If necessary reposition the adjusting screw on the accelerator pump lever. Note that the fuel must be injected into the throttle valve gap – if necessary bend the injection pipe.

---

13 Carburettor – slow running adjustment

Accurate adjustment of the carburettor is only possible after adjustment of the ignition timing, dwell angle, and spark plug gaps. Incorrect valve clearances can also effect carburettor adjustment. Note that

tamperproof caps may be fitted to the slow running adjustment screws and the removal of the caps may be prohibited by legislation in certain countries.

1 Run the engine to normal operating temperature then stop it. Connect a tachometer and if available an exhaust gas analyser.

2 Check that all electrical accessories are switched off and note that slow running adjustments should not be made while the radiator cooling fan is running.

3 Disconnect the crankcase ventilation hose from the air cleaner body and plug the air cleaner outlet.

13.4 Idle speed (A) and mixture (B) adjusting screw locations

4 Start the engine and let it idle. Check that the engine speed and CO content are as given in the Specification. If not, turn the two screws located above the cut-off solenoid alternately as necessary (photos).

5 If an exhaust gas analyser is not immediately available, an approximate mixture setting can be made by turning the mixture screw to give the highest engine speed.

6 Reconnect the crankcase ventilation hose. If this results in an increase in the CO content, the engine oil is diluted with fuel and should be renewed. Alternatively, if an oil change is not due, a long fast drive will reduce the amount of fuel in the oil.

7 Stop the engine and remove the tachometer and exhaust gas analyser.

8 To adjust the fast idle speed first check that the engine is still at normal operating temperature. Remove the air cleaner.

9 With the engine stopped, pull the choke control knob fully out then push it in to the smooth running detent.

10 Retain the choke valve in its open position using an elastic band.

11 Connect a tachometer then start the engine and check that the fast idling speed is as given in the Specification. If not turn the adjustment screw on the side of the choke lever cam. Note that this screw may also have a tamperproof cap.

12 Stop the engine, disconnect the tachometer and elastic band, and refit the air cleaner. Push the choke control knob fully in.

14 Inlet manifold preheating – description and testing

1 On 1.05 litre engines the inlet manifold is heated by water from the cooling system and by a heater element located in the bottom of the manifold beneath the carburettor.

2 On 1.1 and 1.3 litre engines the inlet manifold is heated by exhaust gas channelled from the exhaust downpipe by a connecting pipe (photo).

3 The heater element fitted to 1.05 litre engines can be checked by disconnecting the supply wire and connecting on ohmmeter between the wire and earth – 0.25 to 0.50 ohms should be recorded.

4 To remove the element disconnect the wire, then unscrew the bolt and withdraw the unit. Remove the sealing ring and gasket (photos). When refitting always renew the sealing ring and gasket.

5 The heater element is controlled by a thermo-switch located in the coolant supply hose to the inlet manifold. To test the thermo-switch unscrew it from the housing and plug the hole. With an ohmmeter connected to the terminals gradually heat the base of the unit in hot water. Below approximately 65°C (149°F) there should be zero resistance (ie internal contacts closed), and above approximately 75°C (167°F) there should be maximum resistance (ie internal contacts open). If not, renew the thermo-switch (photos).

14.2 Exhaust connecting pipe for heating the inlet manifold on 1.1 and 1.3 litre engines

14.4A Unscrew the bolts ...

14.4B ... and remove the heater element from the inlet manifold

14.4C Removing the sealing ring from the heater element

14.5A Location of thermo-switch for controlling the inlet manifold heater element

14.5B Inlet manifold preheater thermo-switch and housing

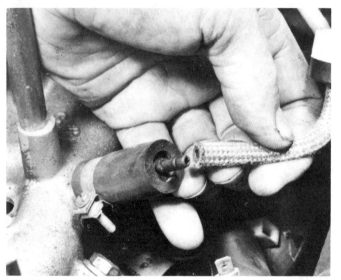

15.4 Disconnecting the vacuum reservoir hose from the inlet manifold

15.5A Unscrew the nuts and bolts ...

15.5B ... and withdraw the inlet manifold

15.5C Removing the inlet manifold gasket

15 Inlet manifold – removal and refitting

1 Remove the carburettor as described in Section 11.

2 On 1.05 litre models disconnect the preheater element wire, drain the cooling system (Chapter 2) and disconnect the coolant hoses from the manifold.

3 On 1.1 and 1.3 litre models unscrew the nuts and disconnect the exhaust connecting pipe. Remove the gasket.

4 Where applicable disconnect the vacuum hose(s) (photo).

5 Unscrew the nuts and bolts and withdraw the inlet manifold from the cylinder head (photos). Remove the gasket.

6 Clean the mating faces of the manifold and cylinder head. If necessary the endplate and gasket, heat deflector and insulator may be removed from the inlet manifold on 1.1 and 1.3 litre models.

7 Refitting is a reversal of removal, but always fit new gaskets and tighten nuts and bolts evenly to the specified torque.

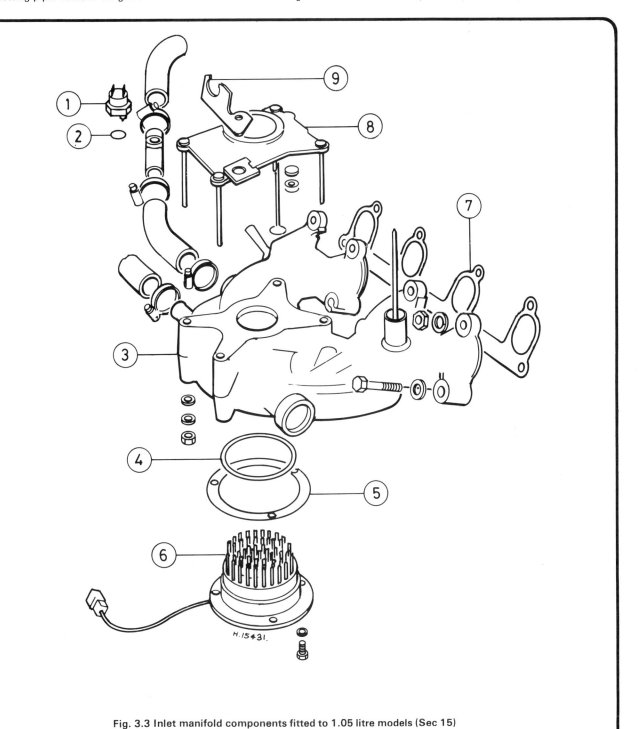

H.15431.

Fig. 3.3 Inlet manifold components fitted to 1.05 litre models (Sec 15)

1 Thermo-switch for inlet manifold preheating	3 Intake manifold	6 Intake manifold preheater	8 Intermediate flange
2 Sealing ring	4 Sealing ring	7 Gasket	9 Bracket
	5 Gasket		

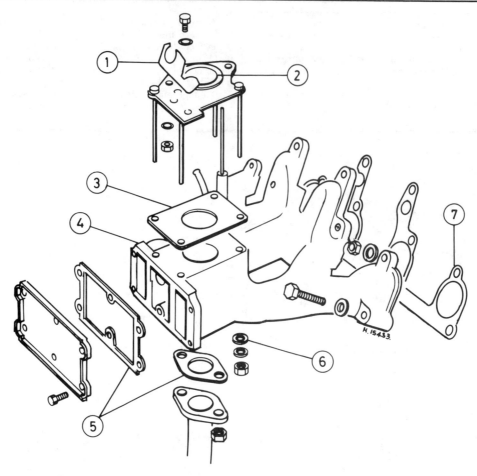

Fig. 3.4 Inlet manifold components fitted to 1.1 and 1.3 litre models (Sec 15)

1 Bracket	3 Heat insulator	5 Gasket	7 Gasket
2 Intermediate flange	4 Intake manifold	6 Insulating washer	

16 Exhaust manifold – removal and refitting

1   Disconnect the flexible hose from the hot air shroud on the exhaust manifold.

2   Unscrew the three nuts and remove the hot air shroud and outlet tube (photos).

3   On 1.05 litre models unscrew the bolts and remove the clamp securing the downpipe to the manifold (photo).

4   On 1.1 and 1.3 litre models unscrew the nuts and detach the twin downpipe from the manifold (photo). Remove the gasket.

5   Unscrew the nuts and withdraw the exhaust manifold from the cylinder head. Remove the gaskets (photos).

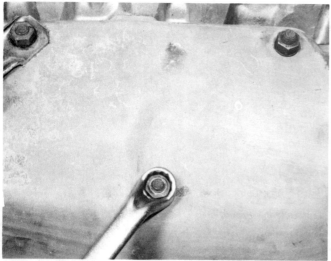

16.2A Unscrew the nuts ...

16.2B ... and remove the hot air shroud and outlet tube

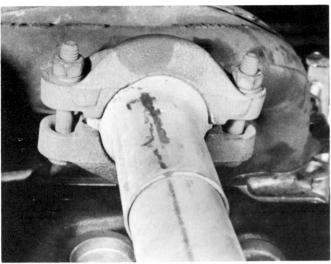

16.3 Exhaust downpipe clamp on 1.05 litre models

16.4 Exhaust downpipes on 1.1 and 1.3 litre models

16.5A Removing the exhaust manifold

16.5B Showing the exhaust manifold gaskets

6   Clean the mating faces of the manifold and cylinder head, also the downpipe faces.

7   Refitting is a reversal of removal, but always fit new gaskets and tighten nuts and bolts evenly to the specified torque. On 1.05 litre models smear a little exhaust jointing paste on the downpipe flange before fitting it to the manifold.

17 Exhaust system – checking, removal and refitting

1   The exhaust system should be examined for leaks, damage, and security every 10000 miles (15000 km). To do this, apply the handbrake and allow the engine to idle. Check the full length of the exhaust system for leaks from each side of the car in turn while an assistant temporarily places a wad of cloth over the tailpipe. If a leak is evident, stop the engine and use a proprietary repair kit to seal it. If the leak is excessive or damage is evident, renew the section. Check the rubber mountings for deterioration, and renew them if necessary.

2   To remove the exhaust system jack up the front and rear of the car and support it on axle stands. Alternatively locate the front wheels on car ramps and jack up the rear, supporting it on axle stands.

3   Unscrew the clamp bolts or flange nuts securing the downpipe(s) to the manifold.

4   On 1.1 and 1.3 litre models loosen the clip and disconnect the flexible hose from the downpipe (photo).

17.4 Flexible pipe fitted to the front of the exhaust pipe on 1.1 and 1.3 litre models

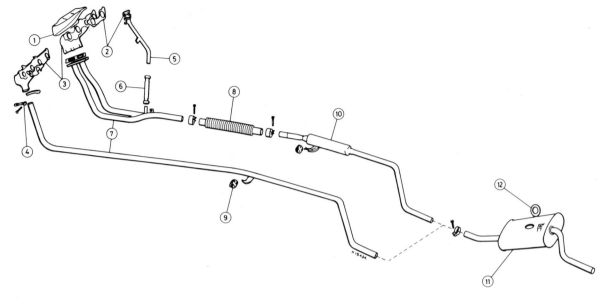

Fig. 3.5 Exhaust system components (Sec 17)

1	Warm air shroud	4	Clamp	7	Front exhaust pipe	10	Front silencer
2	Gasket	5	Connecting pipe	8	Flexible pipe	11	Main silencer
3	Exhaust manifold	6	Flexible pipe	9	Support loop	12	Rubber mounting

5 Unbolt the front of the system from the mounting strap (photo).

6 Release the mounting rubbers from the hooks and lower the exhaust system to the ground (photos).

7 If necessary remove the relevant section by releasing the clamps. Tap around the joint with a hammer and twist the two sections from each other. If difficulty is experienced, heat the joint with a blow lamp to assist removal.

8 Refitting is a reversal of removal, but fit new gaskets as applicable and assemble the complete system loosely in position before finally tightening the clamps and mounting bolt. On 1.05 litre models smear a little exhaust jointing paste on the downpipe flange before fitting it to the manifold. Finally run the engine and check for leaks as described in paragraph 1.

17.5 Detaching the exhaust from the front mounting strap

17.6A An exhaust mounting rubber

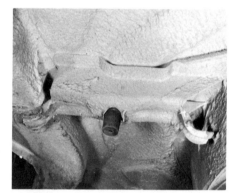

17.6B Exhaust rear mounting bracket

18 Fault diagnosis – fuel and exhaust systems

Sympton	Reason(s)
Excessive fuel consumption	Air cleaner element choked
	Leak in fuel tank, carburettor or fuel lines
	Mixture adjustment incorrect
	Valve clearances incorrect
	Worn carburettor
	Needle valve sticking open
Insufficient fuel supply or weak mixture	Faulty fuel pump
	Leak in fuel lines
	Leaking inlet manifold gasket
	Leaking carburettor gasket
	Mixture adjustment incorrect

Chapter 4 Ignition system

For modifications, and information applicable to later models, see Supplement at end of manual

Contents

Specifications

System type .... 12 volt battery, coil, and distributor with contact breaker points

Coil
Primary winding resistance .... 1.7 to 2.1 ohm
Secondary winding resistance .... 7000 to 12000 ohm

Distributor
Rotor rotation .... Anti-clockwise (viewed from flywheel end)
Rotor cut-out speed (if applicable) .... 6300 to 6700 rpm
Dwell angle:
    Setting .... 47° ± 3° (53% ± 3%)
    Wear limit .... 42° to 58° (47% to 64%)
Contact breaker gap (for initial setting) .... 0.4 mm (0.016 in)
Centrifugal advance:
    1.05 litre .... Begins 1500 to 1700 rpm, 27° to 31° at 4000 rpm
    1.1 litre (standard) .... Begins 1050 to 1450 rpm, 26° to 30° at 4400 rpm
    1.1 litre (economy) .... Begins 1200 to 1450 rpm, 20° to 24° at 5300 rpm
    1.3 litre .... Begins 1050 to 1450 rpm, 26° to 30° at 4400 rpm
Firing order .... 1–3–4–2 (No 1 at timing belt end)

Ignition timing (at idling speed)
1.05 litre (vacuum hoses connected) .... 5° ± 1° BTDC
1.1 litre (vacuum hose disconnected) .... 10° ± 1° BTDC
1.3 litre (vacuum hose disconnected) .... 5° ± 1° BTDC

Spark plugs
Type:
    1.05 litre .... Bosch W7D
               Beru 14-7D
               Champion N8Y
    1.1 litre (standard) .... Bosch W7D or W7DC
               Beru 14-7D or 14-7DU
               Champion N8Y
    1.1 litre (economy) .... Bosch W7D
    1.3 litre .... Bosch W7D or W7DC
               Beru 14-7D or 14-7DU
               Champion N8Y
Gap .... 0.6 to 0.7 mm (0.024 to 0.028 in)

Torque wrench settings

	lbf ft	NM
Spark plugs	22	30
Distributor clamp bolt	7	10

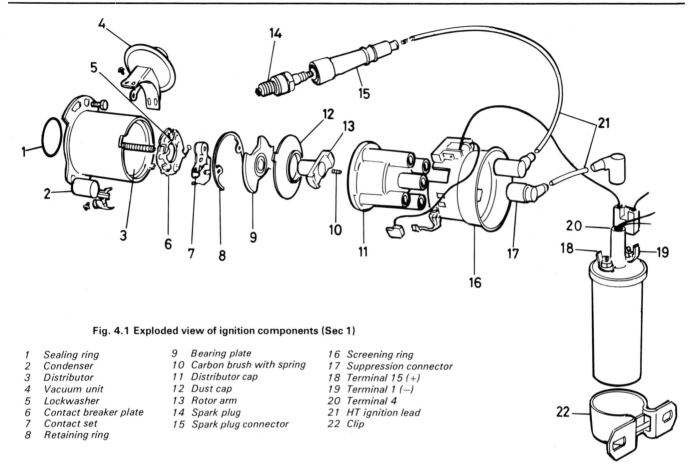

Fig. 4.1 Exploded view of ignition components (Sec 1)

1 Sealing ring	9 Bearing plate	16 Screening ring
2 Condenser	10 Carbon brush with spring	17 Suppression connector
3 Distributor	11 Distributor cap	18 Terminal 15 (+)
4 Vacuum unit	12 Dust cap	19 Terminal 1 (−)
5 Lockwasher	13 Rotor arm	20 Terminal 4
6 Contact breaker plate	14 Spark plug	21 HT ignition lead
7 Contact set	15 Spark plug connector	22 Clip
8 Retaining ring		

1 General description

A conventional ignition system is fitted consisting of the battery, coil, distributor, and spark plugs. The distributor is mounted on the left-hand end of the cylinder head and is driven directly from the camshaft.

In order that the engine can run correctly, it is necessary for an electrical spark to ignite the fuel/air mixture in the combustion chamber at exactly the right moment in relation to engine speed and load. The ignition system is based on feeding low tension voltage from the battery to the coil, where it is converted to high tension voltage. The high tension voltage is powerful enough to jump the spark plug gap in the cylinders many times a second under high compression, providing that the system is in good condition and that all adjustments are correct.

The ignition system is divided into two circuits, the low tension circuit and the high tension circuit. The low tension (sometimes known as the primary) circuit consists of the battery, lead to the ignition switch, lead from the ignition switch to the low tension or primary coil windings (terminal +), and the lead from the low tension coil windings (coil terminal −) to the contact breaker points and condenser in the distributor. The high tension circuit consists of the high tension or secondary coil windings, the heavy ignition lead from the coil to the distributor cap, the rotor arm, and the spark plug leads and spark plugs.

The system functions in the following manner. Low tension voltage is changed in the coil into high tension voltage by the opening and closing of the contact breaker points in the low tension circuit. High tension voltage is then fed via the carbon brush in the centre of the distributor cap to the rotor arm of the distributor, and each time it comes in line with one of the four metal segments in the cap, which are connected to the spark plug leads, the opening and closing of the contact breaker points causes the high tension voltage to build up, jump the gap from the rotor arm to the appropriate metal segment, and so via the spark plug lead to the spark plug, where it finally jumps the spark plug gap before going to earth. The ignition is advanced and retarded automatically, to ensure that the spark occurs at just the right instant for the particular load at the prevailing engine speed.

The ignition advance is controlled both mechanically and by a vacuum operated system. The mechanical governor mechanism com-

prises two weights, which move out from the distributor shaft as the engine speed rises due to centrifugal force. As they move outwards they rotate the cam relative to the distributor shaft, and so advance the spark. The weights are held in position by two light springs and it is the tension of the springs which is largely responsible for correct spark advancement.

The vacuum control consists of a diaphragm, one side of which is connected via a small bore tube to the carburettor, and the other side to the contact breaker plate. Depression in the inlet manifold and carburettor, which varies with engine speed and throttle opening, causes the diaphragm to move, so moving the contact breaker plate, and advancing or retarding the spark. 1.05 litre engines are also equipped with a lead and speed sensitive vacuum retard system.

The ignition system incorporates a sensitive wire which is in circuit all the time that the engine is running. When the starter is operated, the resistance is bypassed to provide increased voltage at the spark plugs.

2 Contact breaker points – checking and adjustment

If the contact breaker points are renewed regularly as described in Section 3, it will not normally be necessary to check them, however the following information is given for in the event of breakdown, starting difficulties or power loss.

1 Remove the polythene cover then prise the two clips from the distributor cap (photo). Where an interference screen is fitted, disconnect the earth cable and low tension lead if applicable. Remove the cap from the distributor.

2 Pull off the rotor arm and remove the dust cover (photo).

3 Using a screwdriver open the points and check the condition of the faces. If they are pitted and discoloured, remove them as described in Section 3 and dress them using emery tape or a grindstone making sure that the surfaces are flat and parallel with each other. If the points are worn excessively, renew them. If the points are in good condition check their adjustment as follows.

Adjustment

4 Turn the engine with a spanner on the crankshaft pulley bolt until the

2.1 The distributor, showing cap retaining clips

2.2 Removing the dust cover

2.5A Checking the contact points gap with a feeler gauge

2.5B Adjusting the contact points gap

2.5C Showing the two pips and notch for inserting a screwdriver when adjusting the contact points gap

moving contact point is fully open with the contact heel on the peak of one of the cam lobes.

5 Using a feeler blade check that the gap between the two points is as given in the Specifications. If not, loosen the fixed contact screw and reposition the fixed contact until the feeler blade is a firm sliding fit between the two points. In order to make a fine adjustment slightly loosen the screw then position the screwdriver in the fixed contact notch and the two pips on the contact plate. With the gap adjusted tighten the screw (photos).

6 Using a dwell meter check that the dwell angle of the contact points is as given in the Specifications while spinning the engine on the starter. If not, re-adjust the points gap as necessary – reduce the gap in order to increase the dwell angle, or increase the gap in order to reduce the dwell angle.

7 Clean the dust cover and rotor arm then refit them. Do not remove any metal from the rotor arm segment.

8 Wipe clean the distributor cap and make sure that the carbon brush moves freely against the tension of the spring. Clean the metal segments in the distributor cap, but do not scrape away any metal otherwise the HT spark at the spark plugs will be reduced. Also clean the HT leads and coil tower.

9 Refit the distributor cap and interference screen where applicable. Refit the polythene cover.

10 Start the engine and check that the dwell angle is as given in the

Specifications both at idling and higher engine speeds. A decrease in dwell angle at high engine speeds indicates a weak spring on the moving contact point.

11 After making an adjustment to the contact points the ignition timing should be checked and adjusted as described in Section 6.

3 Contact breaker points – renewal

1   The contact breaker points should be renewed at the 10 000 mile (15 000 km) service.

2   Remove the polythene cover then prise the two clips from the distributor cap. Where an interference screen is fitted, disconnect the earth cable and low tension lead if applicable. Remove the cap from the distributor.

3   Pull off the rotor arm and remove the dust cover.

4   Remove the screws and withdraw the bearing plate (photos).

5   Disconnect the moving contact low tension lead from the terminal then remove the retaining screw and withdraw the contact breaker set from the distributor (photos).

6   Wipe clean the contact breaker plate in the distributor and make sure that the contact surfaces of the new contact breaker set are clean. Lubricate the arm surface and moving contact pivot with a little multi-purpose grease. Use only a small amount otherwise the contact points may become contaminated.

7   Fit the contact set on the baseplate and refit the retaining screw. Connect the low tension lead to the terminal.

8   Refit the bearing plate and tighten the screws.

9   Adjust the contact breaker points as described in Section 2, paragraphs 4 to 11 inclusive.

4 Condenser – testing, removal and refitting

1   The condenser is fitted in parallel with the contact points and its purpose is to reduce arcing between the points and also to accelerate the collapse of the coil low tension magnetic field. A faulty condenser can cause the complete failure of the ignition system, as the points will be prevented from interrupting the low tension circuit.

2   To test the condenser, remove the distributor cap, rotor arm and dust cover and rotate the engine until the contact points are closed. Switch on the ignition and separate the points – if this is accompanied by a *strong* blue flash the condenser is faulty (a *weak* white spark is normal).

3   A further test can be made for short circuiting by removing the condenser and connect a test lamp and leads to the supply lead and body (ie connect the condenser in series with a 12 volt supply). If the test lamp lights, the condenser is faulty.

4   If the correct operation of the condenser is in doubt, substitute a new unit and check whether the fault persists.

5   To remove the condenser remove the polythene cover from the distributor then unscrew the condenser retaining screw and disconnect the low tension supply lead (at the coil on some models) (photo).

6   Withdraw the condenser sufficient to disconnect the moving contact supply lead then withdraw the condenser. If the moving contact supply lead has insufficient length it will be necessary to remove the distributor cap, rotor arm, dust cover and bearing plate first.

7   Refitting is a reversal of removal.

5 Distributor – removal, overhaul and refitting

1   Disconnect the battery negative lead.

2   Remove the polythene cover then prise the two clips from the distributor cap. Where an interference screen is fitted disconnect the earth cable.

3   Remove the distributor cap and disconnect the low tension lead (at the coil on some models).

4   Disconnect the vacuum hose(s) – where two are fitted, identify them for position (photo).

5   The distributor driveshaft is located in the end of the camshaft by an off centre key, and therefore the procedure in this paragraph is only strictly necessary for checking purposes such as when fitting a new distributor. Turn the engine so that the rotor arm points to the No 1 cylinder TDC groove on the distributor arm (lift the dust cover first) (photo). The mark on the crankshaft pulley should be aligned with the TDC pointer with No 1 piston (timing belt end) at TDC compression.

3.4 Removing the bearing plate (late models)

3.5 Showing the contact points fitted to the distributor

4.5 Condenser location

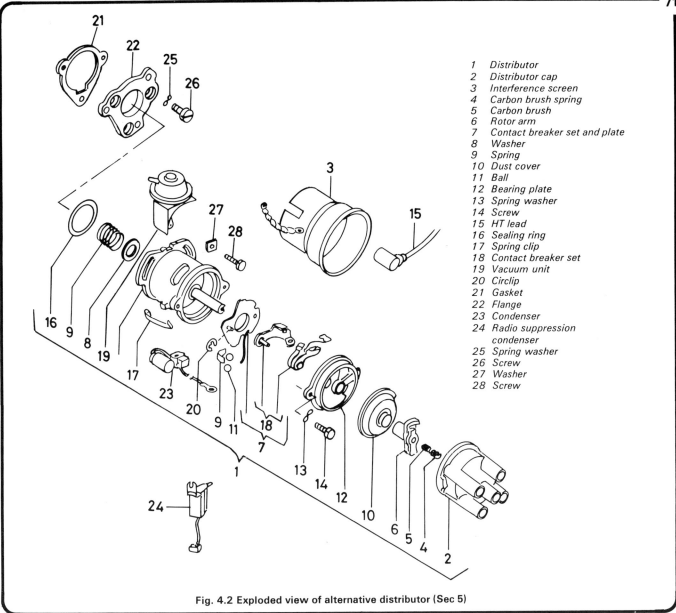

1 Distributor
2 Distributor cap
3 Interference screen
4 Carbon brush spring
5 Carbon brush
6 Rotor arm
7 Contact breaker set and plate
8 Washer
9 Spring
10 Dust cover
11 Ball
12 Bearing plate
13 Spring washer
14 Screw
15 HT lead
16 Sealing ring
17 Spring clip
18 Contact breaker set
19 Vacuum unit
20 Circlip
21 Gasket
22 Flange
23 Condenser
24 Radio suppression
   condenser
25 Spring washer
26 Screw
27 Washer
28 Screw

Fig. 4.2 Exploded view of alternative distributor (Sec 5)

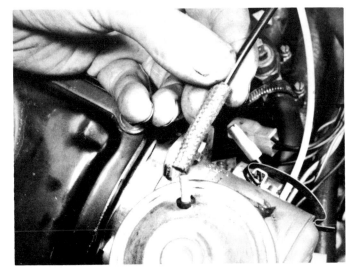

5.4 Disconnecting the vacuum hose

5.5 Showing the rotor arm aligned with the No 1 cylinder TDC groove on the distributor rim

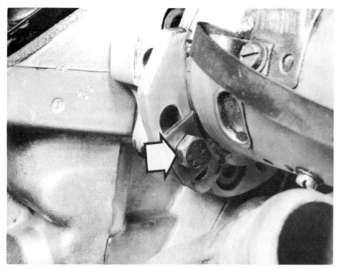

5.7A Unscrew the retainings bolts ...

5.7B ... and remove the distributor

5.9A Correct fitted position of the bearing plate retaining ring

5.9B Removing the bearing plate retaining ring

5.15 Align the rotor arm with the No 1 cylinder TDC groove on the rim before refitting the distributor

6   Mark the distributor flange and cylinder head in relation to each other.

7   Unscrew the bolts and withdraw the distributor (photos). Remove the sealing ring and gasket as applicable.

8   Remove the contact points and condenser with reference to Sections 3 and 4.

9   If applicable mark the position of the bearing plate retaining ring then remove it (photos).

10 Extract the circlip securing the vacuum unit arm to the contact breaker plate.

11 Remove the retaining screws then unhook the arm and withdraw the vacuum unit.

12 Remove the side screws noting the location of the earth lead terminal, then remove the contact breaker plate by turning it anti-clockwise to align the lugs with the cut-outs if applicable.

13 Wipe clean all the electrical components and clean the distributor body assembly with paraffin then wipe dry.

14 Check all components for wear and damage referring to Sections 2 and 4 for the contact breaker points, distributor cap, rotor and condenser.

15 Reassembly and refitting is a reversal of removal and dismantling, but lubricate the centrifugal mechanism and contact breaker plate with a little multi-purpose grease (photo). Adjust the contact breaker points as described in Section 2 and the ignition timing as described in Section 6. Always renew the sealing ring and gasket.

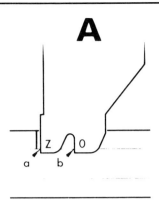
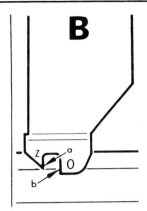

Fig. 4.3 Ignition timing pointers (Sec 6)

a = Z reference edge for timing
    degrees BTDC
b = O reference edge for No 1
    cylinder TDC

A 1.1 litre engines
B 1.05 and 1.3 litre engines

6 Ignition timing – adjustment

Accurate ignition timing is only possible using a stroboscopic timing light or by using a special instrument connected to the flywheel TDC sender unit through the aperture in the top of the gearbox bellhousing. The latter will not normally be available to the home mechanic. For initial setting-up purposes, the test bulb method can be used, but this must always be followed by the stroboscopic timing light method.

Test bulb method (initial setting-up)

1 Remove No 1 spark plug (timing belt end) with reference to Section 8 and place a finger or thumb over the aperture.
2 Turn the engine in the normal running direction (clockwise viewed from the crankshaft pulley end) until pressure is felt in No 1 cylinder indicating that the piston is commencing its compression stroke. Use a spanner on the crankshaft pulley bolt, or engage top gear and pull the car forwards.
3 Continue turning the engine until the line on the crankshaft pulley is aligned with the first pointer projecting out of the timing cover. *Do not align the mark with the second pointer which is at top dead centre (TDC).*
4 Remove the distributor cap and check that the rotor arm is pointing towards the No 1 HT lead location in the cap.
5 Connect a 12 volt test bulb between the distributor (or coil-) LT terminal and a suitable earthing point.
6 Loosen the distributor retaining bolts sufficient to turn the distributor.
7 Switch on the ignition. If the bulb is already lit turn the distributor slightly anti-clockwise until the bulb goes out.
8 Turn the distributor clockwise until the bulb just lights up, indicating that the points have just opened. Tighten the bolts.
9 Switch off the ignition and remove the test bulb.
10 Refit the distributor cap and No 1 spark plug. Once the engine has been started, check the timing stroboscopically as follows.

Stroboscopic timing light method

11 On 1.1 and 1.3 litre engines disconnect and plug the distributor vacuum advance hose.
12 Wipe clean the timing mark on the crankshaft pulley and if necessary highlight it with chalk or white paint.
13 Connect the timing light to the engine in accordance with the manufacturers instructions.
14 Start the engine and run it at idling speed. To ensure that the engine speed variation is minimal, it should be at normal operating temperature.
15 Point the timing light at the timing mark and the left-hand pointer – they should appear to be stationary and aligned. If they are not aligned loosen the retaining bolts and turn the distributor clockwise to advance and anti-clockwise to retard the ignition timing. Tighten the bolts when the setting is correct.

16 Gradually increase the engine speed while still pointing the timing light at the timing marks. The mark on the crankshaft pulley should appear to move anti-clockwise proving that the centrifugal weights are operating correctly. If not, the centrifugal mechanism is faulty and the distributor should be renewed.
17 Accurate checking of the vacuum advance (and retard where fitted) requires the use of a vacuum pump and gauge. However, providing that the diaphragm unit is serviceable, the vacuum hose(s) firmly fitted, and the internal mechanism not seized, the system should work correctly.
18 Switch off the engine, remove the timing light and refit the vacuum hose where applicable.

7 Coil – description and testing

1 The coil is located on the left-hand side of the engine compartment, and it should be periodically wiped clean to prevent high tension voltage loss through possible arcing (photo).
2 To ensure the correct HT polarity at the spark plugs, the coil LT leads must always be connected correctly. The ignition lead from the fusebox must be connected to the positive (+) terminal 15, and the distributor lead (usually green) must be connected to the negative (–) terminal 1. Incorrect connections can cause bad starting, misfiring, and short spark plug life.
3 Complete testing of the coil requires special equipment, however if

7.1 The coil

an ohmmeter is available the primary and secondary winding resistances can be checked and compared with those given in the Specifications. During testing the LT and HT wires must be disconnected from the coil. To test the primary winding, connect the ohmmeter between the two LT terminals. To test the secondary winding, connect the ohmmeter between the negative (–) terminal 1 and the HT terminal.

8 Spark plugs and HT leads – general

1   The correct functioning of the spark plugs is vital for the correct running and efficiency of the engine. The spark plugs should be renewed every 10000 miles (15000 km), however if misfiring or bad starting is experienced before renewal is due, they must be removed, cleaned and regapped.

2   To remove the spark plugs first remove the air cleaner as described in Chapter 3, then disconnect the HT leads after noting their positions. Always pull on the end fittings otherwise the leads may be damaged internally. Unscrew and remove the spark plugs using a proper plug spanner (photo).

3   The condition of the spark plugs will also tell much about the overall condition of the engine. If the insulator nose of the spark plug is clean and white, with no deposits, this is indicative of a weak mixture, or too hot a plug. (A hot plug transfers heat away from the electrode slowly – a cold plug transfers it away quickly.)

4   If the tip and insulator nose is covered with hard black-looking deposits, then this is indicative that the mixture is too rich. Should the plug be black and oily, then it is likely that the engine is fairly worn, as well as the mixture being too rich.

5   If the insulator nose is covered with light tan to greyish brown deposits, then the mixture is correct and it is likely that the engine is in good condition.

6   If there are any traces of long brown tapering stains on the outside of the white portion of the plug, then the plug will have to be renewed, as this shows that there is a faulty joint between the plug body and the insulator, and compression is being lost.

7   Plugs should be cleaned by a sand blasting machine, which will free them from carbon more thoroughly than cleaning by hand. The machine will also test the condition of the plugs under compression. Any plug that fails to spark at the recommended pressure should be renewed.

8   The spark plug gap is of considerable importance, as, if it is too large or too small, the size of the spark and its efficiency will be seriously impaired. The spark plug gap should be set to the figure given in the Specifications at the beginning of this Chapter.

9   To set it, measure the gap with a feeler gauge, and then bend open,

8.2 Removing a spark plug

or close, the *outer* plug electrode until the correct gap is achieved. The centre electrode should *never* be bent as this may crack the insulation and cause plug failure, if nothing worse.

10 Always tighten the spark plugs to the specified torque.

11 Periodically the spark plug leads should be wiped clean and checked for security to the spark plugs.

9 Load and speed sensitive vacuum retard – description and checking

1   1.05 litre engines are equipped with a load and speed sensitive vacuum retard system which prevents engine pinking (spontaneous combustion as opposed to controlled combustion). The system operates at engine speeds below 3600 rpm with the carburettor throttle valve opened more than 30°, and under these conditions the ignition timing is retarded by 6°.

2   The speed sensitive switch is located behind the facia panel and the throttle valve switch is located on the carburettor. With both switches closed, vacuum passes from the spherical reservoir on the bulkhead, through the solenoid valve to the retard side of the vacuum unit. With

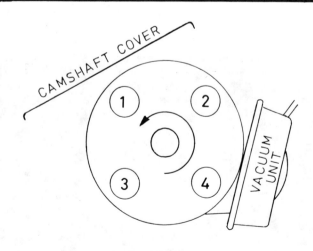

Fig. 4.4 Showing HT lead positions in distributor cap (Sec 8)
Vacuum unit position may vary

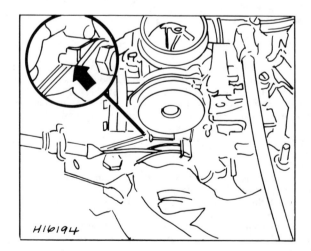

Fig. 4.5 Using a drill to check the throttle valve switch operation (Sec 9)

Measuring plug gap. A feeler gauge of the correct size (see ignition system specifications) should have a slight 'drag' when slid between the electrodes. Adjust gap if necessary

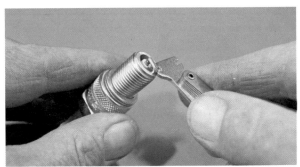

Adjusting plug gap. The plug gap is adjusted by bending the earth electrode inwards, or outwards, as necessary until the correct clearance is obtained. Note the use of the correct tool

Normal. Grey-brown deposits, lightly coated core nose. Gap increasing by around 0.001 in (0.025 mm) per 1000 miles (1600 km). Plugs ideally suited to engine, and engine in good condition

Carbon fouling. Dry, black, sooty deposits. Will cause weak spark and eventually misfire. Fault: over-rich fuel mixture. Check: carburettor mixture settings, float level and jet sizes; choke operation and cleanliness of air filter. Plugs can be re-used after cleaning

Oil fouling. Wet, oily deposits. Will cause weak spark and eventually misfire. Fault: worn bores/piston rings or valve guides; sometimes occurs (temporarily) during running-in period. Plugs can be re-used after thorough cleaning

Overheating. Electrodes have glazed appearance, core nose very white – few deposits. Fault: plug overheating. Check: plug value, ignition timing, fuel octane rating (too low) and fuel mixture (too weak). Discard plugs and cure fault immediately

Electrode damage. Electrodes burned away; core nose has burned, glazed appearance. Fault: pre-ignition. Check: as for 'Overheating' but may be more severe. Discard plugs and remedy fault before piston or valve damage occurs

Split core nose (may appear initially as a crack). Damage is self-evident, but cracks will only show after cleaning. Fault: pre-ignition or wrong gap-setting technique. Check: ignition timing, cooling system, fuel octane rating (too low) and fuel mixture (too weak). Discard plugs, rectify fault immediately

9.2A The vacuum retard system throttle valve switch fitted to the carburettor on 1.05 litre engines

9.2B The vacuum retard system vacuum reservoir located on the bulkhead on 1.05 litre engines

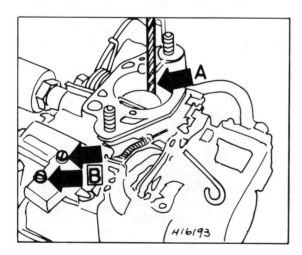

Fig. 4.6 Adjusting the throttle valve switch (Sec 9)

A   Drill   B   Adjusting screws

both switches open, the retard side of the vacuum unit is ventilated to atmosphere and no ignition retard occurs (photos).

3   A check valve is fitted into the vacuum line to the reservoir. Note that the white side of the valve must be towards the reservoir.

4   To check the system first remove the air cleaner and plug the intake temperature control vacuum hose.

5   Connect a stroboscopic timing light to the engine. Start the engine and note the ignition timing at idling speed.

6   Manually close the throttle valve switch (ie with the engine still at idling speed), and check that the ignition is retarded by 6°.

7   To check the engine speed switch, connect a 12 volt test lamp between the battery positive terminal and each of the terminals on the throttle valve switch in turn. With the ignition on (engine stopped) disconnect the lead from the terminal on which the test lamp lights up – this is the lead to the speed switch. With the test lamp lead connected to the lead, start the engine and slowly increase its speed – at 3600 ± 100 rpm the test lamp should go out. If not, the speed switch is defective and should be renewed.

8   To check the throttle valve switch connect the test lamp between the free terminal and a suitable earth point with the engine stopped. Insert a 10.5 mm drill between the throttle valve lever and the full throttle stop in order to open the throttle valve by approximately 25°. Switch on the ignition and check that the test lamp remains off. Repeat the test using a 9.0 mm drill and the test lamp should now light up as the throttle valve is approximately 35° open.

9   Adjustment of the throttle valve switch is only possible with the carburettor removed. With the carburettor inverted, insert a 4.0 mm drill between the throttle valve and the carburettor barrel wall. Loosen the screws and adjust the switch so that the points just close. Tighten the screws and check that the switch operates at the correct throttle valve opening, then refit the carburettor.

10 Fault diagnosis – ignition system

By far the majority of breakdown and running troubles are caused by faults in the ignition system, either in the low tension or high tension circuit. There are two main symptoms indicating ignition faults. Either the engine will not start or fire, or the engine is difficult to start and misfires. If it is a regular misfire, ie the engine is only running on two or three cylinders, the fault is almost sure to be in the secondary, or high tension, circuit. If the misfiring is intermittent, the fault could be in either the high or low tension circuits. If the car stops suddenly, or will not start at all, it is likely that the fault is in the low tension circuit. Loss of power and overheating, apart from faulty carburation settings, are normally due to faults in the distributor or incorrect ignition timing.

Engine fails to start

1   If the engine fails to start and the car was running normally when it was last used, first check there is fuel in the petrol tank. If the engine turns over normally on the starter motor and the battery is evidently well charged, then the fault may be in either the high or low tension circuits. First check the HT circuit. If the battery is known to be fully charged, the ignition light comes on, and the starter motor fails to turn the engine, check the tightness of the leads on the battery terminals and the security of the earth lead to its connection to the body. It is quite common for the leads to have worked loose, even if they look and feel secure. If one of the battery terminal posts gets very hot when trying to work the starter motor, this is a sure indication of a faulty connection to that terminal.

2   One of the most common reasons for bad starting is wet or damp spark plug leads and distributor. Remove the distributor cap. If condensation is visible internally dry the cap with a rag and wipe over the leads. Refit the cap.

3   If the engine still fails to start, check that current is reaching the plugs, by disconnecting each plug lead in turn at the spark plug end, and holding the end of the cable about $\frac{3}{16}$ inch (5 mm) away from the cylinder head. Spin the engine on the starter motor.

4   Sparking between the end of the cable and the head should be fairly strong with a regular blue spark. (Hold the lead with rubber to avoid electric shocks.) If current is reaching the plugs, then remove them and clean and regap them. The engine should now start.

5   If there is no spark at the plug leads, take off the HT lead from the centre of the distributor cap and hold it to the block as before. Spin the engine on the starter once more. A rapid succession of blue sparks

between the end of the lead and the block indicate that the coil is in order and that the distributor cap is cracked, the rotor arm faulty or the carbon brush in the top of the distributor cap is not making good contact with the rotor arm. Or possibly the points are in bad condition; clean and reset them.

6 If there are no sparks from the end of the lead from the coil, check the connections at the coil end of the lead. If it is in order start checking the low tension circuit.

7 Use a 12 volt voltmeter, or a 12 volt bulb and two lengths of wire. With the ignition switch on and the points open test between the low tension wire to the coil (it is marked +) and earth. No reading indicates a break in the supply from the ignition switch. Check the connections at the switch to see if any are loose. Refit them and the engine should run. A reading shows a faulty coil or condenser or broken lead between the coil and the distributor.

8 Remove the condenser from the distributor and remove the distributor cap, rotor and dust cover. With the points open, test between the moving point and earth. If there now is a reading then the fault is in the condenser. Fit a new one and the fault is cleared.

9 With no reading from the moving point to earth, take a reading between earth and the negative (–) terminal of the coil. A reading here indicates a broken wire which must be renewed between the coil and distributor. No reading confirms that the coil has failed and must be renewed. For these tests it is sufficient to separate the contact breaker points with a piece of paper.

10 If the engine starts when the starter motor is operated, but stops as soon as the ignition key is returned to the normal running position, the resistive wire may have an open circuit. Connect a temporary lead between the coil positive (+) terminal and the battery positive (+) terminal. If the engine now runs correctly, renew the resistive wire. Note that the resistive wire must not be permanently bypassed, otherwise the coil will overheat and be irreparably damaged.

Engine misfires

11 If the engine misfires regularly, run it at a fast idling speed. Pull off each of the plug caps in turn and listen to the note of the engine. Hold the plug cap in a dry cloth or with a rubber glove as additional protection against a shock from the HT supply.

12 No difference in engine running will be noticed when the lead from the defective circuit is removed. Removing the lead from one of the good cylinders will accentuate the misfire.

13 Remove the plug lead from the end of the defective plug and hold it about $\frac{3}{16}$ inch (5 mm) away from the block. Restart the engine. If the sparking is fairly strong and regular, the fault must lie in the spark plug.

14 The plug may be loose, the insulation may be cracked, or the points may have burnt away, giving too wide a gap for the spark to jump. Worse still, one of the points may have broken off. Either renew the plug, or clean it, reset the gap, and then test it.

15 If there is no spark at the end of the plug lead, or if it is weak and intermittent, check the ignition lead from the distributor to the plug. If the insulation is cracked or perished, renew the lead. Check the connections at the distributor cap.

16 If there is still no spark, examine the distributor cap carefully for tracking. This can be recognised by a very thin black line running between two or more electrodes, or between an electrode and some other part of the distributor. These lines are paths which now conduct electricity across the cap, thus letting it run to earth. The only answer in this case is a new distributor cap.

17 Apart from the ignition timing being incorrect, other causes of misfiring have already been dealt with under the section dealing with the failure of the engine to start. To recap, these are that:

(a) The coil may be faulty giving an intermittent misfire
(b) There may be a damaged wire or loose connection in the low tension circuit
(c) The condenser may be short circuiting

18 If the ignition timing is too far retarded it should be noted that the engine will tend to overheat, and there will be a quite noticeable drop in power. If the engine is overheating and the power is down, and the ignition timing is correct, then the carburettor should be checked, as it is likely that this is where the fault lies.

Chapter 5 Clutch

For modifications, and information applicable to later models, see Supplement at end of manual

Contents

Specifications

Clutch type .... Single dry plate, diaphragm spring pressure plate, cable actuation

Free play at clutch pedal .... 15 to 20 mm (0.6 to 0.8 in)

Clutch drive
Diameter .... 180 mm (7.09 in)
Maximum run-out (2.5 mm/0.1 in from outer edge) .... 0.4 mm (0.016 in)

Pressure plate
Maximum inward taper .... 0.3 mm (0.012 in)
Diaphragm spring finger scoring depth (maximum) .... 0.3 mm (0.012 in)

Torque wrench settings

	lbf ft	Nm
Pressure plate	18	25
Flywheel	55	75
Guide sleeve	11	15

1 General description

The clutch is of single dry plate type with a diaphragm spring pressure plate, and actuation is by cable. The pressure plate assembly is bolted to the flywheel and transmits drive to the friction disc which is splined to the gearbox input shaft. Friction linings are rivetted to each side of the disc and radial damper springs are incorporated in the hub in order to cushion rotational shocks.

When the clutch pedal is depressed, the cable pulls the arm on the release shaft, and the release bearing is pushed along the guide sleeve against the diaphragm spring fingers. Further movement causes the diaphragm spring to withdraw the pressure plate from the friction disc which also moves along the splined input shaft away from the flywheel. Drive then ceases to be transmitted to the gearbox.

Then the clutch pedal is released, the diaphragm spring forces the pressure plate back into contact with the friction disc which then moves along the input shaft into engagement with the flywheel. Drive is then transmitted directly through the clutch to the gearbox.

Wear of the friction disc linings causes the pressure plate to move closer to the flywheel and the cable free play to decrease. Cable adjustment must therefore be carried out as described in Section 2.

2 Clutch cable – adjustment

1 The clutch cable adjustment must be checked every 10 000 miles (15 000 km). To do this, check the free play at the clutch pedal by measuring the distance it has to be moved in order to take up the slack in the cable. If the distance is not as given in the Specification adjust the cable as follows.

2 Locate the release arm on the gearbox clutch housing then turn the adjusting nut and half-round seating until the adjustment is correct (photo). Depress the arm if necessary to enable the nut to be turned more easily, and if the nut is tight on its thread, hold the inner cable with a spanner.

3 Make sure that the adjusting nut is correctly seated in the release arm before finally checking the adjustment.

2.2 Clutch cable and release arm showing adjustment nut

3.2 Clutch cable support clip location

3.4 Pulling the clutch cable through the steering gear

3 Clutch cable – renewal

1   Unscrew the clutch cable adjusting nut and slide the end fitting from the release arm on the gearbox clutch housing. Alternatively push the release arm inwards and remove the end fitting.
2   Release the outer cable from the gearbox and support clip (photo).
3   Working inside the car reach up behind the facia and unhook the inner cable from the clutch pedal.
4   Pull the cable assembly through the bulkhead and withdraw it from the engine compartment. On left-hand drive models release the cable

from the retaining clip. On right-hand drive models press the retaining sleeve downwards from the steering gear (photo).
5   Fit the new cable using a reversal of the removal procedure, but first lightly grease the inner cable by pulling it from the outer cable at each end. Finally adjust the cable as described in Section 2.

4 Clutch pedal – removal and refitting

1   Disconnect the clutch cable from the release arm on the gearbox

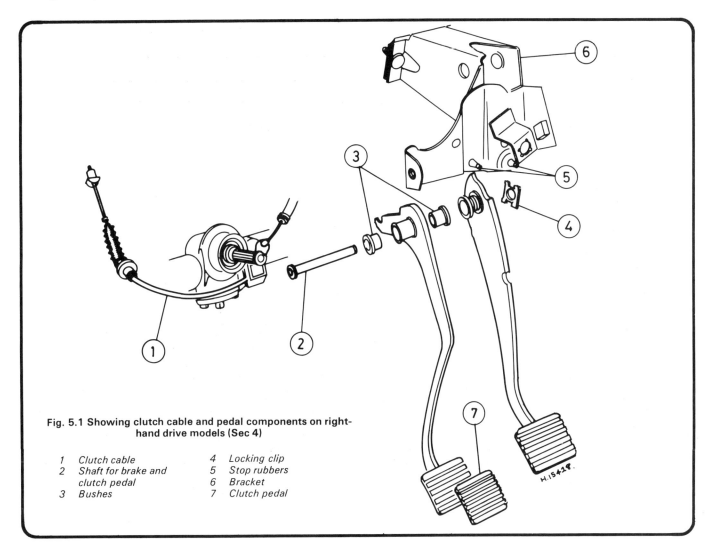

Fig. 5.1 Showing clutch cable and pedal components on right-hand drive models (Sec 4)

1   Clutch cable
2   Shaft for brake and
    clutch pedal
3   Bushes

4   Locking clip
5   Stop rubbers
6   Bracket
7   Clutch pedal

clutch housing and from the top of the clutch pedal with reference to Section 3.

2 Prise the clip from the end of the pedal pivot shaft.

3 On left-hand drive models withdraw the pivot shaft sufficient to remove the clutch pedal from the bracket. On right-hand drive models the pivot shaft must first be withdrawn through the brake pedal.

4 Clean the pedal and pivot shaft and examine them for wear. If the bushes are worn they can be removed using a soft metal drift, and the new bushes installed using a vice to press then into position. Check the rubber foot pad and the stop rubber on the bracket, and renew them if necessary.

5 Refitting is a reversal of removal, but apply a little multi-purpose grease to the pivot shaft and bushes. Finally adjust the cable as described in Section 2.

5 Clutch – removal and refitting

1 Remove the gearbox as described in Chapter 6.

2 Mark the pressure plate cover and flywheel in relation to each other.

3 Using an Allen key unscrew the bolts securing the pressure plate cover to the flywheel in diagonal sequence one turn at a time (photo). If the key handle is pressed towards the centre of the flywheel it should be possible to loosen the bolts while holding the cover stationary by hand. If necessary hold the flywheel stationary using a screwdriver inserted in the starter ring gear teeth.

4 Withdraw the pressure plate assembly and the friction disc from the flywheel. Note that the friction disc hub extension containing the cushion springs faces the pressure plate.

5 Check the clutch components as described in Section 6.

6 Before commencing the refitting procedure a tool must be obtained for centralising the friction disc, otherwise difficulty will be experienced when refitting the gearbox. Unlike the normal arrangement, the gearbox input shaft does not enter a bush or bearing in the rear of the crankshaft. If, however, the friction disc is not centralised the gearbox dowels will not be aligned correctly. If a centralising tool is not available a wooden mandrel may be made to the dimensions shown in Fig. 5.2.

7 Clean the friction faces of the flywheel and pressure plate, then fit the centralising tool to the crankshaft and locate the friction disc on it with the hub extension outwards (photo).

8 Fit the pressure plate assembly to the flywheel (in its original position if not renewed), then insert the bolts and tighten them evenly in diagonal sequence to the specified torque (photo).

9 Check the release bearing as described in Section 7 before refitting the gearbox as described in Chapter 6.

6 Clutch assembly – inspection

1 Examine the surfaces of the pressure plate and flywheel for signs of scoring. Light scoring is normal, but if excessive the pressure plate must be renewed and the flywheel either machined or renewed.

2 Check the pressure plate diaphragm spring fingers for wear caused by the release bearing. If the scoring exceeds the maximum depth given in the Specifications, renew the assembly.

3 Using a straight edge and feeler blade, check that the inward taper of the pressure plate does not exceed the maximum amount given in the Specifications (photo). Also check for loose riveted joints and for any cracks in the pressure plate components.

4 Check the friction disc linings for wear and renew the disc if the linings are worn to within 1.0 mm (0.04 in) of the rivets.

5 Check that the friction disc damper springs and all rivets are secure, and that the linings are not contaminated with oil. Temporarily fit the disc to the gearbox input shaft and check that the run-out does not exceed that given in the Specifications.

6 If the clutch components are contaminated with oil, the leak should be found and rectified. The procedure for renewing the crankshaft oil seal is described in Chapter 1, and the procedure for renewing the gearbox input shaft oil seal is described in Chapter 6.

7 Having checked the clutch disc and pressure plate, it is always worthwhile to check the release bearing with reference to Section 7.

7 Release bearing and shaft – removal, checking and refitting

1 With the gearbox removed, unhook the return spring from the release arm (photo).

2 Turn the release arm to move the release bearing up the guide sleeve, then disengage the two spring clips from the release fork and withdraw the bearing (photos).

3 Note how the springs and clips are fitted then prise the clips from the release bearing.

4 Spin the bearing by hand and check it for roughness, then attempt to move the outer race laterally against the inner race. If any excessive roughness or wear is evident, renew the bearing. Do not wash the bearing in solvent if it is to be re-used.

5 Using a splined socket unbolt and remove the guide sleeve from the clutch housing (photos).

6 Using a narrow drift, drive the release shaft outer bush from the clutch housing. Alternatively prise out the bush.

7 Pull the release shaft from the inner bearing then withdraw the shaft and arm from the housing (photo).

8 Check the bushes and bearing surfaces of the shaft for wear and also check the guide sleeve for scoring. The inner bush may be removed using a soft metal drift and the new bush driven in until flush.

9 Refitting is a reversal of removal, but lubricate all bearing surfaces with a little high melting point grease. Make sure that the release shaft outer bush is correctly sealed with the tab located in the cut-out in the clutch housing (photo).

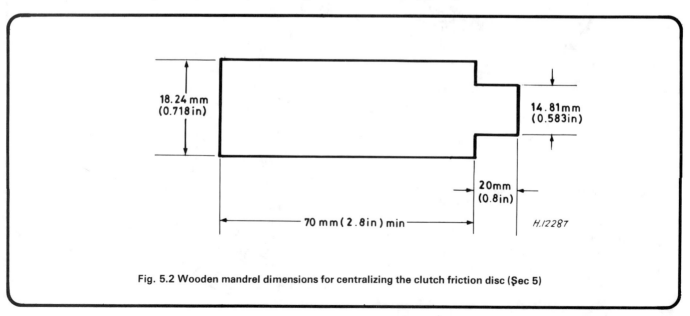

18.24 mm (0.718 in)

14.81 mm (0.583 in)

20 mm (0.8 in)

70 mm (2.8 in) min

H.12287

Fig. 5.2 Wooden mandrel dimensions for centralizing the clutch friction disc (Şec 5)

5.3 Removing the pressure plate bolts

5.7 Showing the friction disc and centralising tool

5.8 Fitting the pressure plate assembly

6.3 Checking the pressure plate for taper

7.1 Clutch release arm return spring

7.2A Showing the release bearing fitted to the arm

7.2B Release bearing showing retaining clips

7.5A Unscrew the splined bolts ...

7.5B ... and withdraw the guide sleeve

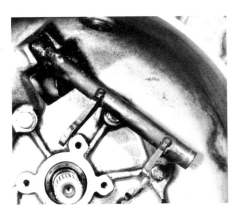

7.7 Removing the release shaft

7.9 Showing the location tab on the release shaft outer bush

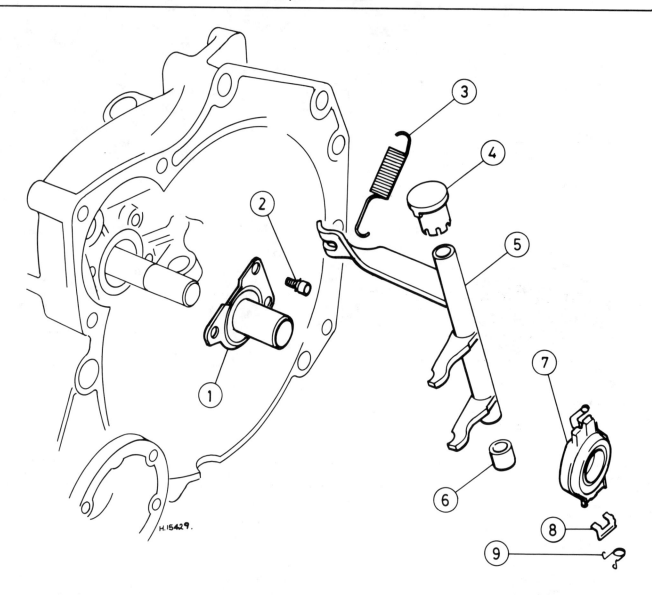

Fig. 5.3 Exploded view of the clutch release bearing and shaft (Sec 7)

1	Guide sleeve	4	Bush	6	Bush	8	Retaining clip
2	Socket head bolt	5	Release shaft	7	Release bearing	9	Retaining spring
3	Release spring						

---

8 Fault diagnosis – clutch

Sympton	Reason(s)
Judder when taking up drive	Loose engine/gearbox mountings Friction bearings worn or contaminated with oil Worn splines on gearbox input shaft and friction disc
Clutch fails to disengage	Incorrect cable adjustment Friction disc sticking on input shaft splines (may be due to rust if car off road for long period)
Clutch slips	Incorrect cable adjustment Friction bindings worn or contaminated with oil
Noise when depressing clutch pedal	Worn release bearing Worn or broken pressure plate diaphragm spring fingers

Chapter 6 Manual gearbox and final drive

For modifications, and information applicable to later models, see Supplement at end of manual

Contents

Specifications

Type	Four forward speeds and reverse, synchromesh on all forward speeds, integral final drive

Code number	084

Code letters

1.05 litre engine	GU
1.1 litre engine (standard)	GW
1.1 litre engine (Formel E)	QS (to 7.82)
	3D (from 8.82)
1.3 litre engine	GU

Ratios (teeth)

	GU	GW	QS	3D
1st	3.45:1 (38:11)	3.45:1 (38:11)	3.45:1 (38:11)	3.45:1 (38:11)
2nd	1.95:1 (41:21)	1.95:1 (41:21)	1.77:1 (39:22)	1.77:1 (39:22)
3rd	1.25:1 (60:48)	1.25:1 (60:48)	1.04:1 (55:53)	1.08:1 (56:52)
4th	0.89:1 (51:57)	0.89:1 (51:57)	0.80:1 (48:60)	0.80:1 (48:60)
Reverse	3.38:1 (44:13)	3.38:1 (44:13)	3.38:1 (44:13)	3.38:1 (44:13)
Final drive	4.27:1 (64:15)	4.57:1 (64:14)	4.06:1 (65:16)	4.06:1 (65:16)
Speedo drive	0.60:1 (12:20)	0.60:1 (12:20)	0.60:1 (12:20)	0.60:1 (12:20)

Oil capacity	3.9 pt (2.2 litre)

Torque wrench settings

	lbf ft	Nm
Gearbox to engine	41	55
Gearshift lever lower housing	11	15
Gearshift lever stop plate	7	10
Shift and clamp bolt	15	20
Shift rod coupling screw	15	20
Bearing cover	18	25
Reverse relay bolt	26	35
Filler and drain plugs	18	25
Reversing light switch	22	30
Clutch housing to gearbox housing	18	25

1 General description

The manual gearbox incorporates four forward speeds and one reverse speed, with synchromesh engagement on all forward gears. Gearshift is by means of a floor mounted lever which pivots in a ball socket, and a shift rod and coupling connected to the gearbox selector rods.

The final drive (differential) is located within the gearbox housings, and the helical gear on the unit is driven by a gear on the end of the output shaft.

Drain and filler plugs are provided, and a magnetic swarf collector is located in the bottom of the gearbox.

When overhauling the gearbox, due consideration should be given to the costs involved, since it is often more economical to obtain a service exchange or good secondhand gearbox rather than fit new parts to the existing gearbox.

2 Gearbox – removal and refitting

The following paragraphs describe how to remove the gearbox leaving the engine in situ. However, if work is necessary on the engine as well, the engine and gearbox can be removed as one unit then separated on the bench as described in Chapter 1.

1 The engine must be supported before the gearbox can be removed and it is recommended that a hoist is used or alternatively a lifting bar as shown in Fig. 6.1. As the gearbox is removed downwards, first position the car over an inspection pit or jack up the front of the car and support on axle stands. Apply the handbrake. Take the weight of the engine with the hoist or lifting bar.
2 Remove the air cleaner as described in Chapter 3.
3 Disconnect the battery earth lead.
4 Remove the windscreen washer bottle and place it to one side.
5 Disconnect the clutch cable from the gearbox with reference to Chapter 5.

6 Unscrew and remove the engine to gearbox bolts that can be reached from the top of the gearbox.
7 Remove the starter with reference to Chapter 9.
8 Loosen the clip securing the support bracket to the coolant pipe at the rear of the engine, remove the upper starter bolt if necessary, and move the bracket away from the gearbox (photo).
9 Remove the left-hand front engine mounting bracket by unscrewing the nuts securing it to the gearbox, removing the mounting bolt, and removing the bolt securing the earth strap.
10 Working beneath the car unbolt and remove the cover plate from the clutch housing (photo).
11 Disconnect the wiring from the reversing light switch and gear-change/consumption indicator switch (photos).
12 Disconnect the inner ends of the driveshafts from the gearbox flanges with reference to Chapter 7 and tie them out of the way.
13 Unscrew the collar and disconnect the speedometer cable from the gearbox.
14 Unscrew and remove the remaining engine to gearbox bolts noting the location of the rear mounting bracket (photos).
15 Unscrew the rear mounting nut and remove the bracket, or leave the mounting on the bracket and remove the mounting bolts (photo).
16 Remove the screw from the shaft rod coupling and ease the coupling from the rod. The screw threads are coated with a liquid locking agent and if difficulty is experienced it may be necessary to heat up the coupling with a blowlamp, *however take the necessary fire precautions.* If required, remove the coupling ball from the adaptor (photos).
17 Support the gearbox on a trolley jack then withdraw it from the engine keeping it in a horizontal position until clear of the clutch. If necessary use a lever to free the gearbox from the locating dowels.
18 Lower the gearbox and remove it from under the car.
19 Refitting is a reversal of removal, but first smear a little molybdenum disulphide based grease on the splines of the input shaft, and make sure that the engine rear plate is correctly located on the dowels. Delay fully tightening the mounting nuts and bolts until the gearbox is in its normal position. Adjust the gearchange if necessary, as described in Section 11.

2.8 Coolant pipe support bracket location

2.10 Clutch housing cover plate

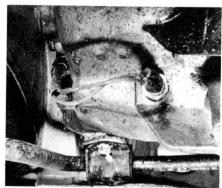

2.11A Reversing light switch location

2.11B Disconnecting the reversing light switch wiring

2.11C Gearchange/consumption indicator switch location

2.14A Engine rear mounting bracket

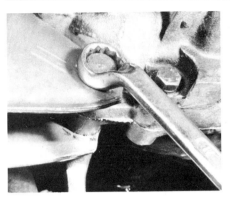

2.14B Removing the rear mounting bracket bolts

2.15 Removing the rear engine mounting and bracket

2.16A Disconnecting the shift rod coupling

2.16B Removing the shift rod coupling

2.16C Shift rod adaptor and bush

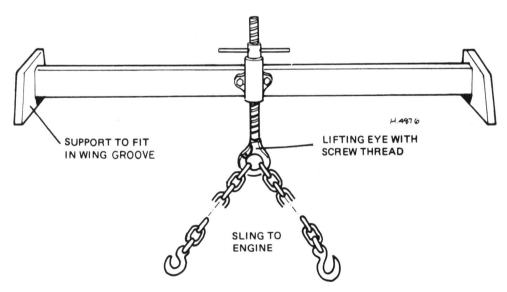

Fig. 6.1 Suggested engine lifting bar (Sec 2)

SUPPORT TO FIT IN WING GROOVE

LIFTING EYE WITH SCREW THREAD

H.4876

SLING TO ENGINE

3 Gearbox – dismantling into major assemblies

1 Unscrew the drain and filler plug using a hexagon key and drain the oil into a suitable container. Refit and tighten the plugs (photos).

2 Remove the clutch release bearing and shaft as described in Chapter 5.

3 Unscrew and remove the reversing light switch, gearchange/consumption indicator switch and pin, and if applicable TDC sensor blanking plug (photos).

4 Temporarily screw two bolts into each drive flange, and using a bar to hold the flange stationary, unscrew each retaining bolt. Identify each flange left and right, then pull them from the differential (photos).

5 Unscrew and remove the bolts securing the clutch housing to the gearbox housing. Make sure that all the bolts are removed from inside the clutch housing.

6 Support the gearbox with the clutch housing uppermost and, using a wooden mallet, tap the clutch housing from the gearbox housing and remove it (photo). If it is difficult to free the housing from the dowels, tap out the dowels first using a soft metal drift.

7 Remove the gasket if applicable and take the magnetic swarf collector from the slot in the bottom of the gearbox housing (photo).

8 Lift the differential from the gearbox housing (photo).

9 Support the gearbox housing with the end cover uppermost.

3.1A Using a key to remove the gearbox drain plug

3.1B Gearbox filler plug location

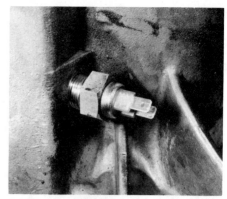

3.3A Removing the reversing light switch

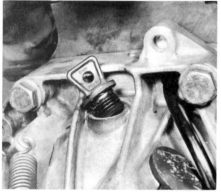

3.3B Removing the TDC sensor blanking plug

3.4A Remove the retaining bolts ...

3.4B ... and pull out the drive flanges

3.6 Removing the clutch housing

3.7 Removing the magnetic swarf collector

3.8 Removing the differential

3.10A Removing the bearing end cover ...

3.10B ... and output bearing shim

3.12A Unscrew the gear detent plugs ...

3.12B ... and extract the sleeves, springs and plungers

3.12C Detent sleeve, spring and plunger

3.13 Reverse relay pivot bolt

3.14A Remove the reverse selector rod ...

3.14B ... and relay lever

3.15 Puller for removing the input shaft bearing

3.17A Fit the puller to the input shaft bearing ...

3.17B ... and pull out the bearing

3.20 Removing the input shaft and 3rd/4th selector rod

10 Unscrew and remove the bolts and remove the bearing end cover. Identify the input and output bearing shims then remove them. Do not interchange the shims otherwise the shaft endfloats will need adjusting on reassembly (photos). Remove the gasket.

11 Using circlip pliers extract the circlip from the end of the input shaft and remove the small shim.

12 Check that the selector rods are in the neutral position then, using an Allen key, unscrew the gear detent plugs with their washers, and extract the sleeves, springs and plungers (photos).

13 Unscrew the reverse relay cross-head bolt next to the detent holes (photo). The bolt is very tight and an impact driver will be required or if not available a cold chisel.

14 Invert the gearbox housing and remove the reverse selector rod and relay lever. The relay lever has slotted ends to engage the pin on the selector rod and the reverse gear (photos).

15 The next stage is the removal of the input and output shafts, and the use of a bearing puller is described in the following paragraphs (photo). However it is possible with some difficulty to remove the shafts

simultaneously by tapping them through the end bearings without the use of a puller. This method is not recommended since damage to the housing may occur and also the synchromesh units can easily come apart causing further damage.

16 Make up a support plate and bolt it to the housing together with packing washers to hold the input shaft stationary (see Fig. 6.3).

17 Support the gearbox with the end bearings uppermost, then using a puller remove the input shaft bearing from the housing (photos).

18 Remove the support plate.

19 Using a large nut or piece of wire retain the selector relay shaft against the spring tension.

20 Move the input shaft away from the output shaft then lift it from the gearbox housing together with the 3rd/4th selector rod and fork (photo). Lift the reverse gear slightly to allow the input shaft 1st gear to pass.

21 Using circlip pliers extract the circlip from the end of the output shaft and remove the small shim (photos).

22 Using the puller press the output shaft from the end bearing and at

3.21A Extract the circlip from the output shaft ...

3.21B ... and remove the small shim

3.22A Pressing the output shaft from the bearing with a puller

3.22B Removing the output shaft and 1st/2nd selector rod

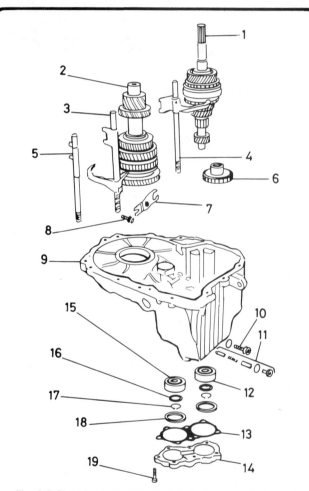

Fig. 6.2 Showing input and output shafts and selector rod locations in the gearbox housing (Sec 3)

1 Input shaft	9 Gearbox housing
2 Output shaft	10 Bolt-relay lever
3 Selector rod and fork, 1st and 2nd gears	11 Gear detent
4 Selector rod and fork, 3rd and 4th gears	12 Input shaft bearing
5 Selector rod, reverse gear	13 Gasket
6 Reverse gear	14 Bearing cover
7 Relay lever	15 Output shaft bearing
8 Pin for relay lever	16 Small shim
	17 Circlip
	18 Large shim
	19 Hexagon bolt

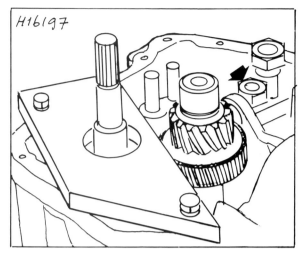

Fig. 6.3 Support plate location when removing the input shaft bearing (Sec 3)

Arrow indicates nut used to retain the selector relay shaft

the same time remove the 1st/2nd selector rod and fork, and the reverse gear. Make sure that the selector rod and reverse gear do not become jammed (photos).

23 Extract the interlock plungers from the gearbox housing.

24 Using a soft metal drift, drive the output shaft bearing from the gearbox housing. Keep both input and output shaft bearings identified.

4 Input shaft – servicing

1 Using circlip pliers extract the circlip from the splined end of the input shaft (photo).

2 Withdraw the 4th gear and needle bearing (photos).

3 Remove the 4th synchro ring (photo).

4 Remove the thrust washer, then using circlip pliers remove the circlip from the 3rd/4th synchro unit (photo). Do not overstretch the circlip.

5 Using a puller beneath the 3rd gear, pull off the 3rd gear together with the 3rd/4th synchro unit (photo). When removed, separate the components and remove the 3rd synchro ring.

6 Remove the 3rd gear needle bearing (photos).

7 Clean the components in paraffin and examine them for wear and damage. Check the gear teeth for pitting and similarly check the needle rollers. Renew the components as necessary.

4.1 Extracting the circlip from the input shaft

4.2A Remove the 4th gear ...

4.2B ... and needle bearing

4.3 Removing the 4th synchro ring

4.4A Remove the thrust washer ...

4.4B ... and circlip

4.5 Pulling off the 3rd gear and 3rd/4th synchro unit

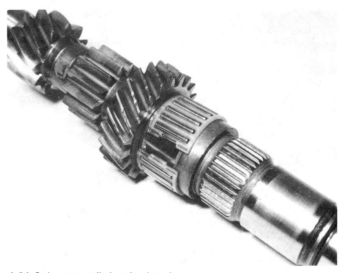

4.6A 3rd gear needle bearing location

4.6B Input shaft with gears removed

8   Check the synchro rings by assembling them on their respective gears and using a feeler gauge to measure the gap between the dogs. If it is less than 0.5 mm (0.02 in), renew the rings (photo).

9   To dismantle the synchro unit first mark the hub and sleeve in relation to each other, then press the hub out of the sleeve and remove the keys and springs. Check the components then slide the sleeve onto the hub so that the marks are aligned. Note that the recesses in the inside of the sleeve must be aligned with the key grooves in the hub, and the dot on the sleeve applied during manufacture must face the same way as the groove on the side of the hub. This groove is on the same side as the longer splines on the hub. Insert the keys and fit the springs with the angled ends located in the keys. Refer to Fig. 6.6 and note that the springs point in opposite directions with the angled ends 120° apart (photos).

10 Commence reassembly by locating the 3rd gear needle bearing on the input shaft. Lubricate it with gear oil.

11 Fit the 3rd gear (photo).

12 Locate the 3rd synchro ring on the 3rd/4th synchro unit with the cut-outs engaged with the keys. Then using a puller, press the synchro unit onto the splines (photos). Alternatively use a metal tube to drive it on. Make sure that the groove on the side of the hub will face the 4th gear position.

13 Fit the circlip in the groove followed by the thrust washer.

4.8 Checking the synchro rings for wear

4.9A Showing recess in synchro sleeve to align with key

4.9B Assembling the synchro sleeve to the hub

4.9C The dot on the synchro sleeve ...

4.9D ... must be on the long spline side of the hub

4.9E Insert the keys ...

4.9F ... and fit the springs

4.9G The assembled synchro unit

4.11 Fitting the 3rd gear on the input shaft

4.12A Fitting the 3rd synchro ring and 3rd/4th synchro unit to the input shaft

4.12B Using a puller to press on the 3rd/4th synchro unit

4.16 Circlip fitted to the 4th gear

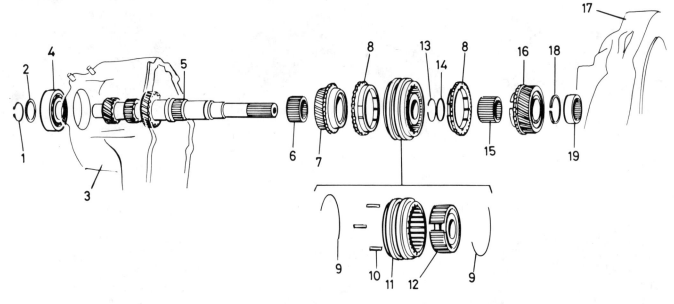

Fig. 6.4 Exploded view of the input shaft (Sec 4)

1 Circlip	7 3rd speed gear
2 Shim	8 Synchro rings for
3 Gearbox housing	3rd and 4th gears
4 Grooved ball bearing	9 Spring
5 Input shaft	10 Key
6 Needle bearing for	11 Sleeve
3rd gear	12 Synchro hub

13 Circlip	16 4th speed gear
14 Thrust washer	17 Clutch housing
15 Needle bearing for	18 Circlip
4th gear	19 Needle bearing

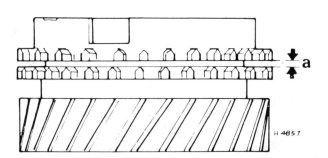

Fig. 6.5 Synchro ring wear checking dimension (Sec 4)

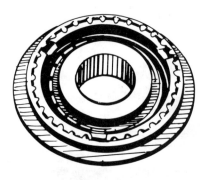

Fig. 6.6 Showing correct fitting of synchro unit springs (Sec 4)

14 Locate the 4th synchro ring on the 3rd/4th synchro unit with the cutouts engaged with the keys.
15 Locate the 4th gear needle bearing on the shaft and lubricate it with gear oil, then fit the 4th gear.
16 Fit the circlip in the groove making sure that it is correctly seated (photo).

5 Output shaft – servicing

1   Using circlip pliers extract the circlip from the end of the output shaft, and remove the thrust washer (photos).
2   Remove the 1st gear and needle roller bearing (photos).
3   Remove the 1st synchro ring (photo).
4   Remove the thrust washer, then using circlip pliers remove the circlip from the 1st/2nd synchro unit (photos). Do not overstretch the circlip.
5   Using a puller beneath the 2nd gear, pull off the 2nd gear together with the 1st/2nd synchro unit. When removed, separate the components and remove the 2nd synchro ring.

6   Remove the 2nd gear needle bearing (photos).
7   Clean the components in paraffin and examine them for wear and damage. Check the gear teeth for pitting and similarly check the needle rollers. Renew the components as necessary. If the 3rd and/or 4th gears require renewal it is recommended that the output shaft is taken to a VW garage as a press is necessary and the new gears must be heated to 120°C (248°F) before fitting. Note that the shoulders on the two gears are adjacent. The gear on the output shaft and the final drive crown wheel are not matched so if necessary the output shaft can be renewed separately.
8   Check the synchro rings and synchro units with reference to Section 4 paragraphs 8 and 9, however there are no grooves or dot.
9   Commence reassembly by locating the 2nd gear needle bearing on the output shaft. Lubricate it with gear oil.
10 Fit the 2nd gear (photo).
11 Locate the 2nd synchro ring on the 1st/2nd synchro unit with the cutouts engaged with the keys. The ring must be fitted on the reverse gear teeth end of the unit (photo).
12 Using a puller press the synchro unit onto the splines (photo). Alternatively use a metal tube to drive it on. When fitted the selector groove must be on the 1st gear end of the unit.

5.1A Remove the circlip ...

5.1B ... and thrust washer from the output shaft

5.2A Remove the 1st gear ...

5.2B ... and needle roller bearing

5.3 Remove the 1st synchro ring

5.4A Remove the thrust washer ...

5.4B ... and circlip

5.6A Remove the 2nd gear needle bearing

5.6B Output shaft with gears removed

5.10 Fitting the 2nd gear on the output shaft

5.11 Fitting the 2nd synchro ring and 1st/2nd synchro unit to the output shaft

5.12 Using a puller to press on the 1st/2nd synchro unit

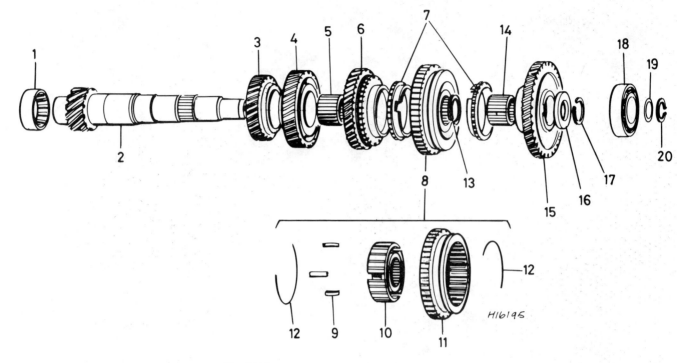

Fig. 6.7 Exploded view of the output shaft (Sec 5)

1	Needle bearing	6	2nd speed gear	10	Hub
2	Output shaft	7	Synchro ring for	11	Sleeve
3	4th speed gear		1st and 2nd gears	12	Spring
4	3rd speed gear	8	Sleeve hub for	13	Circlip
5	Needle bearing for		1st and 2nd gears	14	Needle bearing
	2nd gear	9	Key		for 1st gear

15	1st speed gear
16	Thrust washer
17	Circlip
18	Grooved ball bearing
19	Shim
20	Circlip

13 Fit the circlip in the groove followed by the thrust washer.

14 Locate the 1st synchro ring on the 1st/2nd synchro unit with the cut-outs engaged with the keys.

15 Locate the 1st gear needle bearing on the shaft and lubricate it with gear oil, then fit the 1st gear.

16 Fit the thrust washer and a new circlip making sure that it is correctly seated.

6 Differential unit – servicing

1 Overhaul of the differential unit is not within the scope of the home mechanic as special instrumentation is required including the use of thermo pencils to obtain extremely accurate temperatures. However if the gearbox or clutch housings are renewed, the differential bearing pre-load must be adjusted, and this procedure is included in the following paragraphs for the renewal of the differential taper bearings.

2 Examine the taper bearing rollers and races for pitting and scoring, and if evident renew the bearings as follows. Note that the bearings and races are matched so the new bearings must be fitted with their corresponding races.

3 Using a puller pull the inner races and rollers from each side of the differential.

4 Wipe clean the bearing surfaces on the differential then heat the new inner races and bearings in boiling water and immediately drive them onto the differential using a metal tube on the races only. Make sure that the narrow diameter of the rollers faces away from the differential.

5 Using a metal tube drive the outer races from the clutch and gearbox housings after prising out the oil seals (photos). Drive them out from the outside of the housings then remove the shims. Keep the shim from the gearbox housing as it is 1 mm (0.04 in) thick.

6 Clean the recesses in the housings then fit the 1 mm (0.04 in) shim in the gearbox housing and drive in the new outer race while supporting the housing on a block of wood.

7 Similarly drive the new outer race into the clutch housing *without* a shim.

8 Locate the differential in the gearbox housing then clean the mating faces and fit the clutch housing (together with a new gasket if applicable). Insert the bolts and tighten them to the specified torque in diagonal sequence.

9 Attach a dial gauge to the gearbox and without turning the differential measure the endfloat by pushing the differential in and out – dimension A.

6.5A Prising out the drive flange oil seal from the gearbox housing

6.5B Drive flange oil seal on the clutch housing

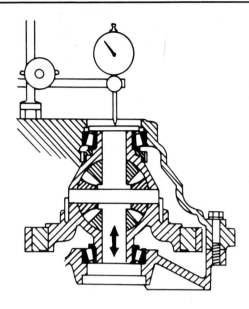

Fig. 6.8 Cross section diagram showing method of checking differential bearing endfloat (Sec 6)

10 The bearing preload is 0.30 mm (0.0118 in) – dimension B. Add dimension A to dimension B to obtain the thickness of the shim to fit in the clutch housing.

Example:

Dimension A   = 1.25 mm (0.0492 in)
Dimension B   = 0.30 mm (0.0118 in)
Shim thickness = 1.55 mm (0.0610 in)

11 Remove the clutch bearing, drive out the outer race, then fit the correct shim and drive in the outer race.

12 Allow any water to dry from the taper roller bearings before the gearbox is reassembled, and fit new oil seals as described in Section 10.

7 Clutch housing – servicing

1 Clean the housing and examine it for damage and cracks. If evident renew it.

2 Prise the seal from the inner shift lever. If the lever is not being removed smear the lip of the new seal with grease then drive it squarely into the housing until flush with the rim of the bush. To remove the lever unscrew and remove the finger then slide out the lever (photos). Using a soft metal drift drive out the lever bush from the housing. Drive

the new bush into position then smear the lever friction surfaces with molybdenum based grease, slide it into the housing, fit the finger and tighten it to the specified torque. Fit the new seal as previously described.

3 Unscrew the speedometer pinion bush and withdraw the pinion (photos). Examine the components for wear and renew them if necessary. Insert the pinion then tighten the bush.

4 Check the starter bush in the housing. If necessary remove it with VW tools 228 b and 204 b, then drive in the new bush with a soft metal drift. Do not grease the bush.

5 Check the output shaft needle roller bearing and if necessary remove it with a puller. Support the housing and drive in the new bearing making sure that the end face with the lettering faces inside the gearbox (photo).

6 Check the input shaft needle roller bearing. To remove it prise out the oil seal then use a soft metal drift from the outside of the gearbox to drive it out. Support the housing and drive in the new bearing flush, making sure that the end face with the lettering faces inside the gearbox (photos). Smear the lip of the new seal with grease then use a metal tube to drive it squarely into the housing as far as it will go. The fitted position of the seal is approximately 2.5 mm (0.098 in) below the housing surface.

7.2A Showing the inner shift lever oil seal location

7.2B Inner shift lever location in the clutch housing

7.3A Speedometer pinion bush in the clutch housing

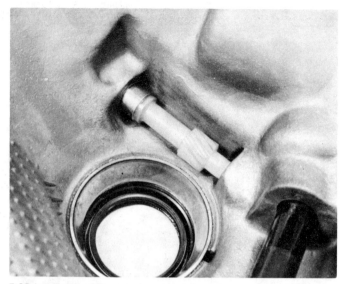

7.3B Inner view of the speedometer pinion

7.5 Output shaft needle roller bearing location in the clutch housing

7.6A Input shaft seal and bearing viewed from engine side of clutch housing

7.6B Input shaft bearing viewed from inside of clutch housing

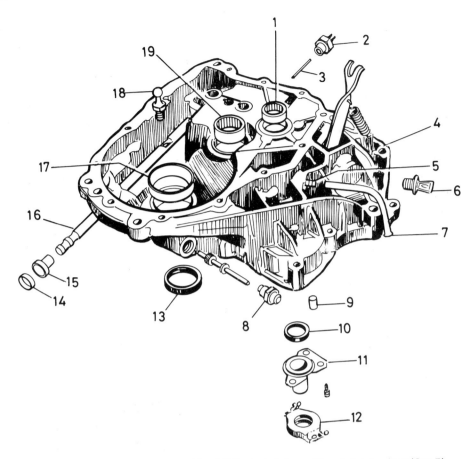

Fig. 6.9 Exploded view of the clutch housing (Sec 7)

1 Needle bearing
2 Switch
3 Extension pin
4 Clutch housing
5 Breather connection
6 Plug
7 Breather pipe
8 Input shaft pinion
9 Starter bush
10 Input shaft seal
11 Guide sleeve
12 Release bearing
13 Drive shaft oil seal
14 Seal
15 Bush
16 Inner shift lever
17 Outer race taper roller bearing
18 Selector finger
19 Needle bearing

8 Gearbox housing – servicing

1 Clean the housing and examine it for damage and cracks. If evident renew it.

2 Check the selector relay shaft for excessive play in the bushes (photo). If evident unscrew the relay lever and withdraw the shaft from inside the housing. Remove the spring and use a soft metal drift to drive out the cap. Also use a drift to drive out the bushes. Drive in the new bushes flush then fit the shaft, insert the relay lever, and tighten it to the specified torque. Insert the spring and drive in the retaining cap.

3 Check the reverse gear shaft and if worn excessively use a soft metal drift to drive the shaft from the housing (photo) – heat the surrounding housing with a blowlamp if difficulty is experienced. Apply a liquid locking agent to the contact end of the shaft then heat up the housing and drive in the shaft from the outside until the inner end is 83.3 mm (3.280 in) from the mating face of the housing.

4 Check the input and output shaft bearings for wear by spinning them, and renew them if there is excessive play or any roughness evident. Also examine the end cover for condition.

5 Examine the selector rods and forks for damage and check the reverse gear for bore wear and chipping or pitting of the teeth. Renew the components as necessary.

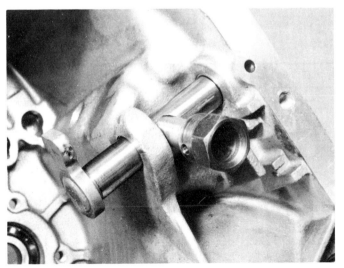

8.2 Selector relay shaft location in the gearbox housing

8.3 Reverse gear shaft location in the gearbox housing

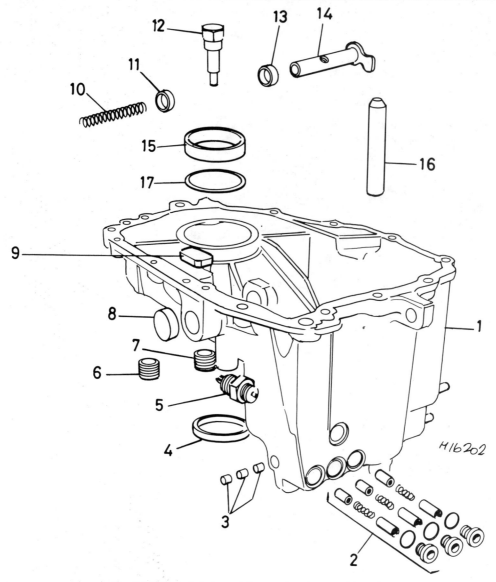

Fig. 6.10 Exploded view of the gearbox housing (Sec 8)

1	Gearbox housing	6	Oil drain plug
2	Gear detents	7	Oil filler plug
3	Interlock plungers	8	Cap
4	Oil seal for left drive flange	9	Magnet
5	Reversing light switch	10	Spring

1 Gearbox housing
2 Gear detents
3 Interlock plungers
4 Oil seal for
   left drive flange
5 Reversing light switch

6 Oil drain plug
7 Oil filler plug
8 Cap
9 Magnet
10 Spring

11 Outer bush for
   selector shaft
12 Relay lever
13 Inner bush for
   selector shaft

14 Selector shaft
15 Outer race taper
   roller bearing
16 Reverse gear shaft
17 Shim

Fig. 6.11 Reverse gear shaft fitting dimension (Sec 8)

$a = 83.3\ mm\ (3.280\ in)$

9 Gearbox – reassembly

Make sure that all components are clean, and during reassembly lubricate all bearings and bearing surfaces with gear oil.

1   Using a metal tube drive the output shaft bearing into the gearbox housing with the closed side of the bearing facing in the gearbox.

2   Grease the interlock plungers and locate them in the housing – use a pen magnet if necessary (photo).

3   Using a large nut or piece of wire retain the selector relay shaft against the spring tension (photo).

4   Locate the 1st/2nd selector rod and fork in the groove of the synchro unit on the output shaft.

5   Locate the reverse gear on its shaft but retain it in a slightly raised position with a piece of wire.

6   Lower the output shaft and selector rod into the gearbox housing and at the same time feed the reverse gear in after the 1st gear (photo).

7   With the output shaft entered fully in its bearing check that the selector rod is in neutral and the reverse gear is free to move.

9.2 Using a pen magnet to insert the interlock plungers

9.3 Using a large nut to hold the selector relay shaft against the spring tension

9.6 Inserting the output shaft and 1st/2nd selector rod in the gearbox housing. Note the wire hooked beneath the reverse gear

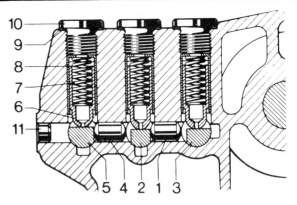

Fig. 6.12 Cross section diagram showing interlock plunger locations (Sec 9)

1	Interlock plunger	7	Spring
2	1st/2nd selector rod	8	Sleeve
3	3rd/4th selector rod	9	Washer
4	Interlock plunger	10	Plug
5	Reverse selector rod	11	Plug
6	Detent plunger		

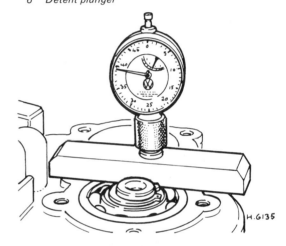

Fig. 6.13 Using a dial gauge to determine the bearing preload shim thickness (Sec 9)

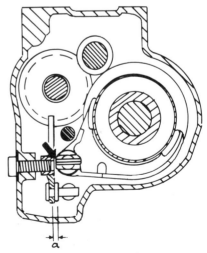

Fig. 6.14 Showing clearance between the reverse relay lever and the 1st/2nd selector rod – arrow shows roll pin flush (Sec 9)

a = 1.3 to 2.8 mm (0.051 to 0.110 in)

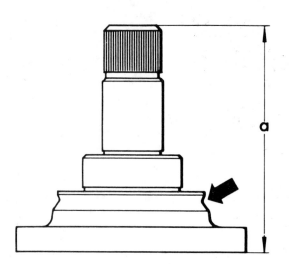
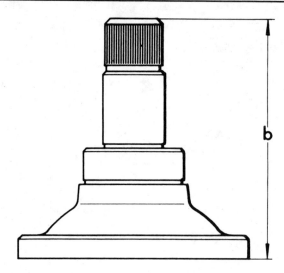

Fig. 6.15 Diagram showing difference between the left and right drive flanges (Sec 9)

a = 86.8 mm (3.417 in) – left-hand drive flange showing groove   *b = 89.6 mm (3.528 in) – right-hand drive flange*

8   If a new bearing, bearing or output shaft has been fitted, determine and fit the bearing preload shims as follows. Fit the circlip and using a feeler gauge determine the clearance between the circlip and bearing inner race (photo). Select a shim to set the clearance to between 0 and 0.05 mm (0 and 0.002 in) then fit the shim beneath the circlip. Using a dial gauge or straight edge and feeler gauge determine the clearance between the housing face (without gasket) and bearing outer race. Add 0.27 to 0.31 mm (0.011 to 0.012 in) to the clearance for the thickness of the large shim to fit against the outer race.
9   Locate the 3rd/4th selector rod and fork in the groove of the synchro unit on the input shaft.
10 Lower the input shaft and selector rod into the gearbox housing and mesh the gears with those on the output shaft. Lift the reverse gear slightly to allow the input shaft 1st gear to pass.
11 Support the output shaft using the plate described in Section 3 then remove the wire from the reverse gear.
12 Using a metal tube drive the input shaft bearing into the gearbox housing and onto the shaft. The closed side of the bearing must face into the gearbox (photo).
13 Refer to paragraph 8 and if necessary determine and fit the small and large shims to the end of the input shaft.
14 Remove the input shaft support plate.
15 Remove the nut or wire from the selector relay shaft.
16 Locate the relay lever on the reverse selector rod then lower them into the housing and engage the lever with the reverse gear. It will be necessary to lift the gears slightly.
17 Position the relay lever approximately 2.0 mm (0.08 in) away from the 1st/2nd selector rod. Make sure that the roll pin on the selector rod is flush with the fork (photo).
18 Screw in the cross-head bolt and washer, and tighten it to the specified torque. Check that the clearance between the relay lever and selector rod is 1.3 to 2.8 mm (0.051 to 0.110 in).

19 Insert the detent plungers, springs and sleeves in the housing apertures followed by the plugs and their washers. Tighten the plugs with an Allen key.
20 Move the relay shaft lever and check that each gear can be engaged easily. Also check that it is not possible to move two adjacent selector rods at the same time.
21 Locate the correct large shims on the input and output shaft bearings then fit the end cover together with a new gasket. Apply a liquid locking agent to the bolt thread then insert the bolts and tighten them to the specified torque in diagonal sequence (photos).
22 Invert the gearbox and insert the differential (photo).
23 Clean the mating faces of the gearbox and clutch housings. If applicable fit a new gasket otherwise apply sealing compound to the faces.
24 Locate the magnetic swarf collector in the gearbox housing slot.
25 Check that the selector rods are in neutral, then lower the clutch housing onto the gearbox housing making sure that the shift lever engages the relay shaft lever.
26 Tap in the dowels, then insert the bolts and tighten them evenly to the specified torque in diagonal sequence (photo).
27 Insert the drive flanges into the differential, insert the bolts, and tighten them to the specified torque. Hold the flanges stationary with a bar between two bolts screwed into adjacent holes (photo). Note that the left and right flanges are different, the left one being 2.8 mm (0.110 in) shorter and also incorporating a groove in the inner shoulder.
28 Insert and tighten the reversing light switch and gearchange/consumption indicator switch and pin (photo).
29 Refit the clutch release shaft and bearing as described in Chapter 5.
30 After refitting the gearbox to the engine, refill the gearbox with the specified oil until the oil just begins to overflow from the filler hole (photo). Refit the filler plug.

9.8 Checking the output shaft bearing endfloat

9.12 Fitting the input shaft bearing to the gearbox housing

9.17 Showing fitted position of the reverse relay lever

9.21A Bearing end cover gasket and large shims located on the bearings

9.21B Apply a liquid locking agent to the bolt threads ...

9.21C ... then insert and tighten the bolts

9.22 Differential located in the gearbox housing

9.26 Tightening the clutch housing to gearbox housing bolts

9.27 Method of tightening the drive flange bolts

9.28 Refitting the reversing light switch

9.30 Refilling the gearbox with oil

11.4 View of the gearchange mechanism housing

10 Drive flange oil seals – renewal

1   Jack up the front of the car and support on axle stands. Apply the handbrake.
2   Detach the inner ends of the driveshafts from the drive flanges with reference to Chapter 7 and tie the driveshafts to one side.
3   Unscrew the bolt from the centre of each drive flange using a bar and two temporarily inserted bolts to hold the flange stationary.
4   Place a container beneath the gearbox then remove the drive flanges and lever out the old oil seals. Identify the flanges side for side.
5   Clean the recesses then drive in the new oil seals using a suitable length of metal tubing.
6   Smear a little grease on the lips of the oil seals, and insert the drive flanges.
7   Insert the bolts and tighten them to the specified torque using the bar and bolts to hold the flanges stationary.

8   Refit the driveshafts with reference to Chapter 7.
9   Check and if necessary top up the gearbox oil level then lower the car to the ground.

11 Gearchange mechanism – removal, refitting and adjustment

1   Jack up the front of the car and support on axle stands. Apply the handbrake.
2   With neutral selected mark the shift rod and coupling in relation to each other, then unscrew the coupling clamp and pull out the shift rod.
3   Working inside the car unscrew the gear knob and remove the gaiter.
4   Unscrew the nuts from the ball housing stop plate, and withdraw the complete gearchange mechanism upwards into the car (photo). Recover the spacers.

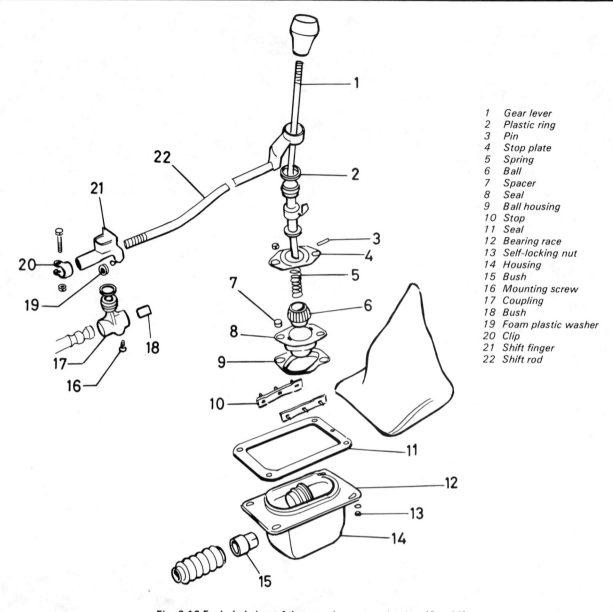

1   Gear lever
2   Plastic ring
3   Pin
4   Stop plate
5   Spring
6   Ball
7   Spacer
8   Seal
9   Ball housing
10 Stop
11 Seal
12 Bearing race
13 Self-locking nut
14 Housing
15 Bush
16 Mounting screw
17 Coupling
18 Bush
19 Foam plastic washer
20 Clip
21 Shift finger
22 Shift rod

Fig. 6.16 Exploded view of the gearchange mechanism (Sec 11)

5 Dismantle the mechanism as necessary and examine the components for wear and damage. Renew as necessary.
6 Lubricate the joints and bearing surfaces with high melting point grease then refit using a reversal of the removal procedure. If a new coupling has been fitted it will be necessary to adjust the coupling position – this is best carried out by a VW garage using tool 3069, but if necessary the following method can be used in an emergency. With the coupling disconnected and the gearbox in neutral have an assistant hold the gear lever in neutral position between 3rd and 4th gear positions (ie half way between front and rear movement and to the right). Engage the shift rod and coupling fully and with the gear lever in the same position, tighten the clamp bolt.

12 Fault diagnosis – manual gearbox and final drive

Symptom	Reason(s)
Ineffective synchromesh	Worn synchro rings
Jumps out of gear	Weak or broken detent spring
	Worn selector forks
	Worn gears and/or synchro sleeves
Noisy operation	Worn bearings
	Worn gears
Difficult engagement of gears	Worn selector components
	Clutch fault

Chapter 7 Driveshafts

Contents

Specifications

Type .... Solid (left) and tubular (right) driveshafts with constant velocity joints at each end.

Outer CV joint diameter
All models except Coupé .... 75 mm (2.95 in)
Coupé .... 81 mm (3.19 in)

Torque wrench settings

	lbf ft	Nm
Driveshaft to flange	33	45
Driveshaft nut	155	210

1 General description

Drive from the differential unit to the roadwheels is provided by two driveshafts. Each driveshaft has a constant velocity joint (CVJ) at each end, the inner joint being flanged and secured to the final drive flange by bolts, and the outer joint being splined to the hub and secured with a nut.

The left-hand driveshaft is of solid construction and is shorter than the tubular right-hand driveshaft.

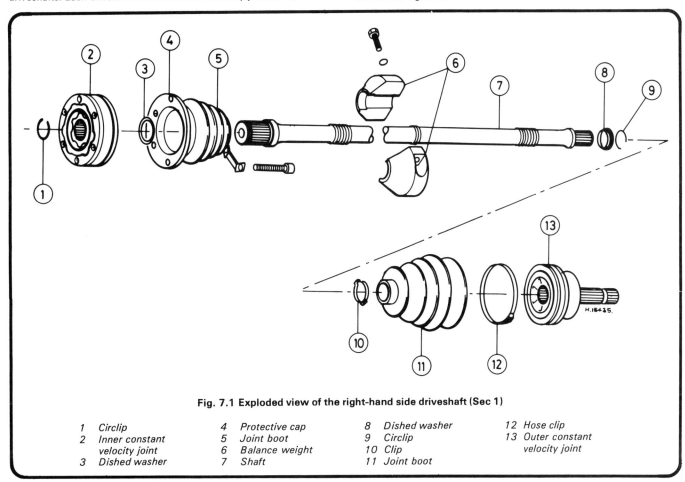

Fig. 7.1 Exploded view of the right-hand side driveshaft (Sec 1)

1 Circlip	4 Protective cap	8 Dished washer	12 Hose clip
2 Inner constant	5 Joint boot	9 Circlip	13 Outer constant
velocity joint	6 Balance weight	10 Clip	velocity joint
3 Dished washer	7 Shaft	11 Joint boot	

2.4 Unscrewing the driveshaft inner flange bolts

2.5 Showing the driveshaft inner joint

2.6 Refitting the driveshaft to the final drive flange

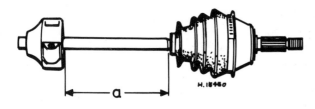

Fig. 7.2 Location of the balance weight on the right-hand side driveshaft (Sec 2)

Dimension a = 151.0 mm (5.95 in)

2 Driveshaft – removal and refitting

1 Remove the wheel trim from the relevant wheel.
2 With the handbrake applied loosen the driveshaft nut. The nut is tightened to a high torque and a socket extension may be required.
3 Jack up the front of the car and support it on axle stands. Remove the roadwheel.
4 Using an Allen key unscrew and remove the bolts securing the inner CV joint to the final drive flange (photo). Note the location of the spacer plates. Support the inner end of the driveshaft on an axle stand.

5 Remove the outer nut and washer, then turn the steering on full lock and tap the driveshaft from the splined hub using a soft head mallet. When removing the right-hand side driveshaft it is advantageous to disconnect the anti-roll bar front mountings and the track control arm from the strut. Do not move the car on its wheels with either driveshaft removed otherwise damage may occur to the wheel bearings (photo).
6 Refitting is a reversal of removal, but first clean the hub and driveshaft splines and the mating faces of the inner CV joint and final drive flange (photo). Smear a little molybdenum based grease on the splines. Fit a new outer nut and tighten it to the specified torque with the car lowered to the ground. Tighten the inner bolts to the specified torque. On the right-hand side driveshaft make sure that the balance weight is located with its conical side facing the gearbox and the opposite side in the groove on the driveshaft. Where there is no groove, locate it on the point mark at the dimension shown in Fig. 7.2.

3 Driveshaft – dismantling and reassembly

If either CV joint is worn excessively it can be renewed in kit form including the rubber boot and a tube of special grease.

Outer joint

1 Loosen the rubber boot clips and release the large diameter end of the boot from the joint.
2 Using a soft faced mallet drive the outer joint from the driveshaft.

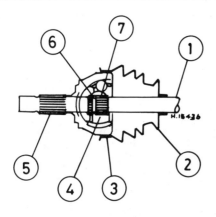

Fig. 7.3 Cross-section diagram of the driveshaft outer joint (Sec 3)

1	Driveshaft	5	Splined shaft
2	Rubber boot	6	Distance washer
3	Worm drive clip	7	Dished washer
4	Bearing race		

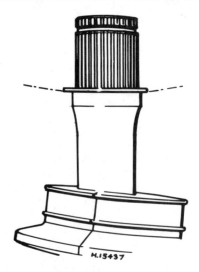

Fig. 7.4 Showing correct fitting of the dished washer (Sec 3)

Fig. 7.5 Removing the cage and hub from the outer joint housing (Sec 3)

Arrow shows rectangular aperture

Fig. 7.6 Removing the outer joint hub from the cage (Sec 3)

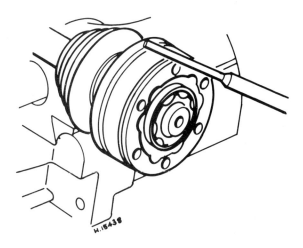

Fig. 7.7 Removing the plastic cap from the inner joint housing (Sec 3)

9 Note that the joint components including the balls form a matched set and must only be fitted to the correct side.

10 Clean the components in paraffin and examine them for wear and damage. Excessive wear will have been evident when driving the car especially when changing from acceleration to overrun. Renew the components as necessary.

11 Commence reassembly by inserting half the amount of special grease (ie 45 g) into the joint housing.

12 Fit the hub to the cage by inserting one of the segments into the rectangular aperture.

13 With the rectangular apertures aligned with the housing fit the hub and cage to the housing in its original position.

14 Swivel the hub and cage and insert the balls from alternate sides.

15 Fit the rubber boot and clips on the driveshaft.

16 Fit the dished washer and spacer (if applicable) to the driveshaft and insert the circlip in the groove.

17 Locate the outer joint on the driveshaft and using a soft faced mallet drive it fully into position until the circlip is engaged.

18 Insert the remaining grease in the joint then locate the boot and tighten the clips.

Inner joint

19 Extract the retaining circlip (photo).

20 Using a small drift drive the plastic cap from the joint housing. Loosen the clip and slide the rubber boot away from the joint.

21 Support the joint over the jaws of a vice and using a soft metal drift drive out the driveshaft.

22 Remove the dished washer from the driveshaft noting that the concave side faces the end of the driveshaft.

23 Slide the rubber boot and clip from the driveshaft.

24 Mark the hub in relation to the cage and joint housing.

25 Turn the hub and cage 90° to the housing and press out the hub and cage (photo).

26 Extract the balls then turn the hub so that one of the track grooves is located on the rim of the cage, and withdraw the hub.

27 Note that the joint components including the balls form a matched set and must only be fitted to the correct side (photo).

28 Clean the components in paraffin and examine them for wear and damage. Excessive wear will have been evident when driving the car

3 Extract the circlip from the driveshaft and remove the spacer (if fitted) and dished washer noting that the concave side faces the end of the driveshaft.

4 Slide the rubber boot and clips from the driveshaft.

5 Mark the hub in relation to the cage and joint housing.

6 Swivel the hub and cage and remove the balls one at a time.

7 Turn the cage until the rectangular apertures are aligned with the housing then withdraw the cage and hub.

8 Turn the hub and insert one of the segments into one of the rectangular apertures, then swivel the hub from the cage.

3.19 The retaining circlip on the driveshaft inner joint

3.25 Removing the joint hub and cage

3.27 Joint hub, cage and housing

Fig. 7.8 Removing the inner joint hub from the cage (Sec 3)

especially when changing from acceleration to overrun. Renew the components as necessary.

29 Commence reassembly by fitting the hub to the cage.

30 Insert the balls into position using the special grease to hold them in place.

31 Press the hub and cage into the housing making sure that the wide track spacing on the housing will be adjacent to the narrow spacing on the hub (see Fig. 7.9) when fully assembled. Note also that the chamfer on the hub splines must face the large diameter side of the housing.

32 Swivel the cage ahead of the hub so that the balls enter their respective tracks then align the hub and cage with the housing.

33 Check that the hub can be moved freely through its operating arc.

34 Fit the rubber boot and clip to the driveshaft followed by the dished washer.

35 Mount the driveshaft in a vice then drive the joint onto the driveshaft using a suitable metal tube on the hub.

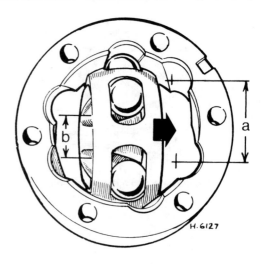

Fig. 7.9 Assembly of the inner joint cage and hub to the housing (Sec 3)

a must be aligned with b

36 Fit the returning circlip in its groove.

37 Insert the remaining grease in the joint then tap the plastic cap into position.

38 With the rubber boot correctly located, tighten the clip.

4 Fault diagnosis – driveshafts

Symptom	Reason(s)
Vibrations and noise on turns	Worn driveshaft joints
Noise on taking up drive	Worn driveshaft joints Worn drive flange and/or driveshaft splines Loose driveshaft bolts or nut

Chapter 8 Braking system

For modifications, and information applicable to later models, see Supplement at end of manual

Contents

Specification

System type .... Hydraulic, dual circuit split diagonally, with discs front and self-adjusting drums on rear, pressure regulator on rear brakes on some models. Cable operated handbrake on rear wheels

Front brakes
Disc thickness (new) .... 10.0 mm (0.394 in)
Disc thickness (minimum .... 8.0 mm (0.315 in)
Maximum disc run-out .... 0.06 mm (0.002 in)
Disc pad thickness – new (including backplate) .... 15.0 mm (0.591 in)
Disc pad thickness – minimum (including backplate) .... 7.0 mm (0.28 in)

Rear brakes
Drum internal diameter (new) .... 180.0 mm (7.087 in)
Drum internal diameter (maximum) .... 181.0 mm (7.126 in)
Maximum drum run-out:
    Radial (at friction surface) .... 0.05 mm (0.002 in)
    Lateral (wheel contact surface) .... 0.2 mm (0.008 in)
Lining thickness:
    Minimum (including shoe) .... 5.00 mm (0.20 in)
    Minimum (excluding shoe) .... 2.5 mm (0.10 in)

General
Master cylinder type ....

	Front	Rear
Master cylinder type	ATE (Teves) or FAG (Shafer)	
Pressure regulator test pressures:		
1st test	50 bar (725 lbf/in^2	27 to 31 bar (392 to 450 lbf/in^2)
2nd test	100 bar (1450 lbf/in^2)	59 to 54 bar (725 to 783 lbf/in^2)

Torque wrench settings	**lbf ft**	**Nm**
Caliper to wheel bearing housing	52	70
Splash plate to strut	7	10
Wheel bolts	81	110
Backplate to rear axle	44	60

1 General description

The braking system is of hydraulic, dual circuit type with discs at the front and self-adjusting drum brakes at the rear. The hydraulic circuit is split diagonally so that with the failure of one circuit, one front and rear brake remain operative. A load sensitive pressure regulator is incorporated in the rear hydraulic circuits on some models to prevent the rear wheels locking in advance of the front wheels during heavy application of the brakes. The regulator proportions the hydraulic pressure between the front and rear brakes according to the load being carried.

The handbrake operates on the rear wheels only and the lever incorporates a switch which illuminates a warning light on the instrument panel when the handbrake is applied. The same warning light is wired into the low hydraulic fluid switch circuit.

2 Routine maintenance

1 Every 10000 miles (15000 km) the front disc pad linings and rear brake shoe linings should be checked for wear and renewed if necessary. At the same time check that the hydraulic fluid in the master cylinder reservoir is between the minimum and maximum level marks. The reservoir is translucent and the check can be made without removing the filler cap. Note that the level will drop slightly as the front disc pad linings wear and it is not necessary to top up the level in this case. However if the level drops significantly the hydraulic circuit should be checked for leakage.

2 Every two years the hydraulic fluid must be renewed. At the same time check the operation of the low level warning switch as follows. Switch on the ignition and release the handbrake lever, then depress the float pin on the top of the fluid reservoir and check that the warning lamps light up on the instrument panel. Also at the same time check the condition of the hydraulic lines and hoses.

3 Disc pads – inspection and renewal

1 The disc pad lining wear can be checked by viewing through a hole in the wheel rim and by using a mirror on the inside of the wheel. The use of a torch may also be necessary. If the thickness of any disc pad is less than the minimum amount given in the Specification, renew the front pads as a set. Where the thickness is more than the minimum amount, 1 mm (0.04 in) of lining will last for approximately 1000 km (600 miles) under severe conditions and therefore due consideration must be made as to whether there is sufficient lining left before the next service.

2 To remove the disc pads first jack up the front of the car and support it on axle stands. Apply the handbrake and remove both front wheels.

3 Extract the spring clip from the inner ends of the retaining pins (photo).

4 Using a small punch drive out the retaining pins and remove the spreader spring (photos).

5 Using a pair of pliers, press each pad outwards from the brake disc in order to push the piston into the caliper and allow the pads to be removed.

6 Pull the inner pad from the caliper (photo). Mark it if it is to be refitted.

7 Press the caliper frame outwards to disengage the frame projection from the recess in the pad backing plate, then remove the outer pad (photos).

8 Brush the dust and dirt from the caliper, piston, disc and pads, but *do not inhale it as it is injurious to health.* Scrape any scale or rust from the disc and pad backing plates.

Fig. 8.1 Checking the disc pad wear through the front wheel (Sec 3)

a = 7 mm (0.28 in) minimum

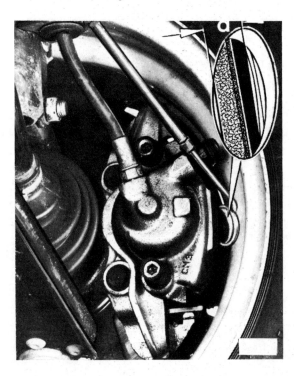

Fig. 8.2 Using a mirror to check the inner disc pad wear (Sec 3)

a = 7 mm (0.28 in) minimum

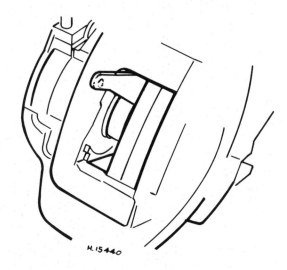

Fig. 8.3 Using a 20° angle gauge to set the caliper piston (Sec 3)

3.3 Removing the disc pad retaining pin spring clip

3.4A Removing the retaining pins ...

3.4B ... and spreader spring

3.6 Removing the inner disc pad

3.7A Removing the outer disc pad

3.7B Showing outer (left) and inner (right) disc pads

3.7C Showing frame projection for engagement with the outer disc pad

3.14 Correct installation of the disc pads

9 Using a piece of wood push the piston back into the caliper, but while doing this check the level of the fluid in the reservoir and if necessary draw off some with a pipette or release some from the caliper bleed screw. Tighten the screw immediately afterwards.

10 Check that the angle of the raised face of the piston is 20° to the upper inner face of the caliper. Make a gauge out of cardboard and if necessary turn the piston to its correct position.

11 Smear a little brake grease on the metal-to-metal contact surfaces of each pad backing plate.

12 Insert the inner pad then pull the caliper frame outwards, insert the outer pad and press in the frame so that the projection engages the pad recess.

13 Position the spreader spring on the pads then insert the retaining pins through the caliper and pad backing plates and tap them fully home.

14 Fit the spring clip to the inner ends of the retaining pins, turning the

pins as necessary with a pair of pliers to align the holes (photo).

15 Repeat the procedure given in paragraphs 3 to 14 on the remaining front brake, then refit the wheels and lower the car to the ground.

16 Depress the footbrake pedal several times to set the pads, then check and if necessary top-up the level of fluid in the master cylinder reservoir.

4 Rear brake shoes – inspection and renewal

1 Jack up the rear of the car and support it on axle stands. Check the front wheels.

2 Working beneath the car remove the rubber plugs from the front of the backplates and check that the linings are not worn below the minimum thickness given in the Specifications. If necessary use a torch. Refit the plugs.

3   To remove the rear brake shoes first remove the wheels.
4   Prise off the hub cap then extract the split pin and remove the locking ring.
5   Unscrew the hub nut and remove the thrust washer and outer wheel bearing.
6   Withdraw the brake drum. If difficulty is experienced, the brake shoes must be backed away from the drum first. To do this, insert a screwdriver through one of the bolt holes and push the automatic adjuster wedge upwards against the spring tension. This will release the shoes from the drum.
7   Brush the dust from the brake drum, brake shoes and backplate, *but do not inhale it as it is injurious to health.* Scrape any scale or rust from the drum. Note that the rear brake shoes should be renewed as a set of four.
8   Using a pair of pliers depress the steady spring cups, turn them through 90° and remove the cups, springs and pins (photo).
9   Note the location of the return springs and strut on the brake shoes, then lever the shoes from the bottom anchor. Unhook and remove the bottom return spring (photos).
10 Disengage the handbrake cable from the lever on the trailing brake shoe.
11 Release the brake shoes from the wheel cylinder, unhook the wedge spring and upper return spring and withdraw the shoes (photo).
12 Grip the strut in a vice and release the shoe, then remove the wedge and spring. The backplate and stub axle may be removed if necessary

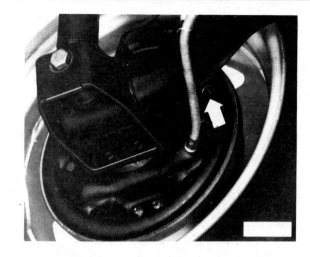

Fig. 8.4 Rear brake shoe lining inspection plug location (arrowed) (Sec 4)

4.8 Location of the rear brake shoe steady springs

4.9A Correct location of the rear brake components

4.9B Rear brake shoe bottom anchor

4.11 Showing the rear wheel cylinder and brake shoes

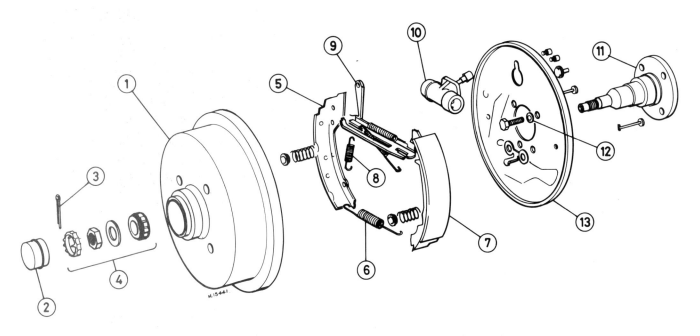

Fig. 8.5 Exploded view of the rear brake shoes and drum (Sec 4)

1	Brake drum	5	Upper return spring	8	Spring for wedge	11	Stub axle
2	Hub cap		assembly	9	Wedge	12	Lock washer
3	Split pin	6	Lower return assembly	10	Wheel (slave) cylinder	13	Backplate
4	Bearing assembly	7	Brake shoe				

by unscrewing the four bolts after removing the wheel cylinder (Section 7). Note the location of the handbrake cable bracket. If the wheel cylinder is being left in position, retain the pistons with an elastic band, Check that there are no signs of fluid leakage and if necessary repair or renew the wheel cylinder as described in Section 7.

13 Fit the new brake shoes using a reversal of the removal procedure, but note that the lug on the wedge faces the backplate. Check the brake drum for wear and damage as described in Section 8. Adjust the wheel

bearings as described in Chapter 10. Finally, fully depress the brake pedal several times in order to set the shoes in their correct position.

5 Disc caliper – removal, inspection and refitting

1 Remove the disc pads as described in Section 3.
2 If available fit a hose clamp to the caliper flexible brake hose.

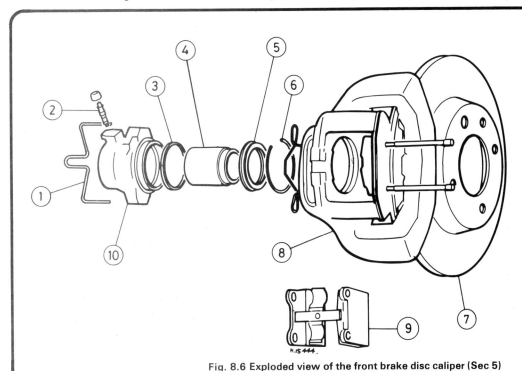

1 Locating spring
2 Bleeder screw
3 Sealing O-ring
4 Piston
5 Dust cap
6 Circlip
7 Brake disc
8 Caliper
9 Brake pads
10 Cylinder

Fig. 8.6 Exploded view of the front brake disc caliper (Sec 5)

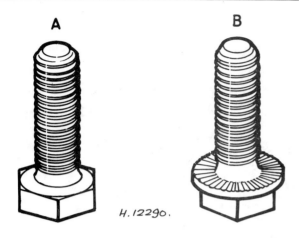

Fig. 8.7 Two types of caliper retaining bolts (Sec 5)

a   Early type   b   Later ribbed type

Fig. 8.8 Showing chamfer modification required when fitting
ribbed type bolts to early calipers (Sec 5)

Alternatively remove the fluid reservoir filler cap and tighten it down
onto a piece of polythene sheet in order to reduce the loss of hydraulic
fluid.
3   Loosen the brake hose union at the caliper.
4   Unscrew the two bolts securing the caliper to the wheel bearing
housing, then unscrew the caliper from the hose.
5   Clean the external surfaces of the caliper with paraffin and wipe dry
– plug the fluid inlet during this operation.
6   Remove the retaining spring then press the mounting frame from
the cylinder and withdraw it from the floating frame.
7   Grip the floating frame in a vice, and using a soft metal drift drive the
cylinder from the frame.
8   Using air pressure from a foot pump in the fluid inlet blow the piston
from the cylinder, but take care not to drop the piston.
9   Prise the sealing ring from the cylinder bore and remove the piston
dust cap and circlip.
10 Clean the components with methylated spirit and allow to dry.
Inspect the surfaces of the piston, cylinder and frames for wear, damage
and corrosion. If evident renew the caliper, but if the components are in
good condition obtain a repair kit of seals.
11 Dip the new sealing ring in brake fluid and locate it in the cylinder
bore groove using the fingers only to manipulate it.
12 Smear the piston with brake fluid, and press it into the cylinder then
fit the dust cap and circlip.
13 Locate the cylinder in the floating frame and drive it fully home using
a soft metal drift.
14 Fit the retaining spring then locate the mounting frame in the
floating frame and press it onto the cylinder.
15 Refer to Section 3 and turn the piston so that its raised face is 20° to
the upper inner face of the caliper.

16 Screw the caliper onto the brake hose so that when the caliper is in
its fitted position the line on the hose is not twisted.
17 Fit the caliper to the wheel bearing housing then insert and tighten
the bolts to the specified torque. Note that early models were fitted with
standard bolts, however locking bolts incorporating ribbed shoulders
were introduced on later models. If the ribbed type bolts are fitted to
early models a 1 mm (0.04 in) wide 45° chamfer must be made in the
mounting frame holes (Fig. 8.8).
18 Tighten the brake hose union.
19 Remove the hose clamp or polythene sheet.
20 Refit the disc pads as described in Section 3.
21 Top up the brake fluid reservoir and bleed the brakes as described in
Section 12.

6   Brake disc – examination, removal and refitting

1   Remove the disc pads as described in Section 3.
2   Rotate the disc and examine it for deep scoring or grooving.
3   Using a dial gauge or metal block and feeler gauges, check that the
disc run-out measured on the friction surface does not exceed the
maximum amount given in the Specifications.
4   Using a micrometer check that the disc thickness is not less than the
minimum amount given in the Specifications.
5   To remove the brake disc, remove the caliper as described in Section
5, but do not disconnect or loosen the brake hose. Locate the caliper on
a stand to prevent straining the hose.
6   Remove the cross-head screw and withdraw the brake disc from the
hub (photo).

6.6 Brake disc retaining screw

7   If necessary the splash plate can be removed from the wheel bearing
housing by unscrewing the three bolts.
8   Refitting is a reversal of removal, but make sure that the mating
faces of the disc and hub are clean. Refer to Section 5 when refitting the
caliper, and Section 3 when refitting the disc pads.

7   Rear wheel cylinder – removal, overhaul and refitting

1   Remove the rear brake shoes as described in Section 4.
2   If available fit a hose clamp to the flexible brake hose. Alternatively
remove the fluid reservoir filler cap and tighten it down onto a piece of
polythene sheet in order to reduce the loss of hydraulic fluid.
3   Unscrew the hydraulic pipe union from the rear of the cylinder, and
plug the end of the pipe (photo).
4   Remove the two screws and withdraw the wheel cylinder from the
backplate.
5   Prise off the dust caps then remove the pistons keeping them
identified for location. If necessary use air pressure from a foot pump in
the fluid inlet.

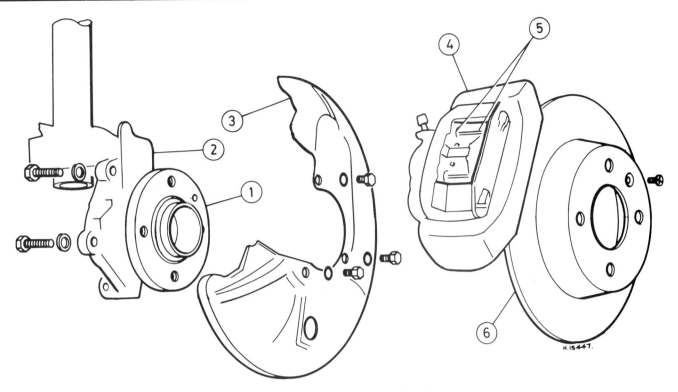

Fig. 8.9 Disc brake components (Sec 6)

1 Wheel hub	3 Splash plate	5 Brake pads	6 Brake disc
2 Wheel bearing housing	4 Brake caliper		

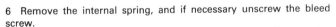

7.3 Rear view of a rear wheel cylinder on the backplate

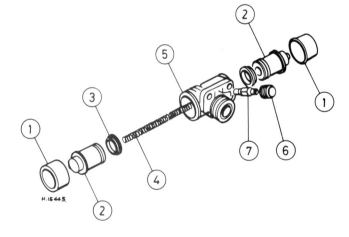

Fig. 8.10 Exploded view of the rear wheel cylinder (Sec 7)

1 Boot	5 Brake cylinder housing
2 Piston	6 Dust cap
3 Cap	7 Bleed screw
4 Spring	

6 Remove the internal spring, and if necessary unscrew the bleed screw.

7 Clean all the components in methylated spirit and allow to dry. Examine the surfaces of the piston and cylinder bore for wear, scoring and corrosion. If evident, renew the complete wheel cylinder. If the components are in good condition, discard the seals and obtain a repair kit.

8 Dip the inner seals in clean brake fluid and fit them to the grooves on the pistons using the fingers only to manipulate them. Make sure that the larger diameter ends face the inner ends of the pistons.

9 Smear brake fluid on the pistons then insert the spring and press the pistons into the cylinder taking care not to damage the seal lips.

10 Locate the dust caps on the pistons and in the grooves on the outside of the cylinder.

11 Insert and tighten the bleed screw.

12 Clean the mating faces then fit the wheel cylinder to the backplate and tighten the screws.

13 Refit the hydraulic pipe and tighten the union. Remove the hose clamp or polythene sheet.

14 Refit the rear brake shoes as described in Section 4.

15 Top up the brake fluid reservoir and bleed the brakes as described in Section 12.

8 Brake drum – examination and renovation

1 Whenever the brake drums are removed, they should be checked for wear and damage. Light scoring of the friction surface is normal, but if excessive the drums must either be renewed as a pair or reground provided that the maximum internal diameter given in the Specifications is not exceeded.
2 After a high mileage the drums may become warped and oval. The run-out can be checked with a dual gauge and if in excess of the maximum amounts given in the Specifications the drums should be renewed as a pair.

9 Master cylinder – removal, overhaul and refitting

1 Disconnect the battery negative lead.
2 Disconnect the wiring from the stop-light and fluid level switches on the master cylinder and fluid reservoir filler cap (photos).
3 Remove the air cleaner as described in Chapter 3.
4 Place a suitable container beneath the master cylinder and place some cloth on the surrounding body to protect it from any spilled brake fluid.
5 Unscrew the unions and disconnect the hydraulic fluid pipes from the master cylinder.

9.2 Brake master cylinder showing stop light and fluid level switch wiring

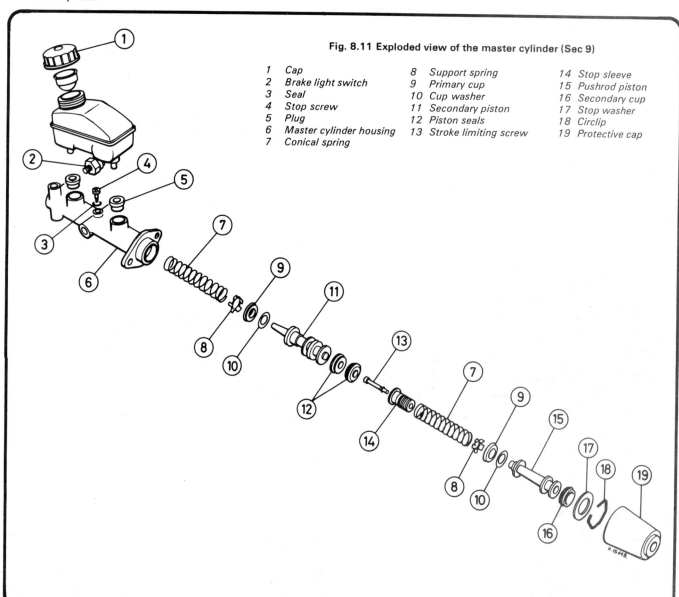

Fig. 8.11 Exploded view of the master cylinder (Sec 9)

1 Cap	8 Support spring	14 Stop sleeve
2 Brake light switch	9 Primary cup	15 Pushrod piston
3 Seal	10 Cup washer	16 Secondary cup
4 Stop screw	11 Secondary piston	17 Stop washer
5 Plug	12 Piston seals	18 Circlip
6 Master cylinder housing	13 Stroke limiting screw	19 Protective cap
7 Conical spring		

6 Unscrew the mounting nuts and withdraw the master cylinder from the bulkhead and away from the pushrod. Remove the spacer and seal where applicable.

7 Remove the master cylinder from the engine compartment taking care not to spill any hydraulic fluid on the body paintwork.

8 Clean the exterior of the master cylinder with paraffin and wipe dry.

9 Note that it is only possible to overhaul master cylinders fitted to early models. On late models the circlip in the mouth of the cylinder cannot be removed and in this case the complete cylinder must be renewed if faulty.

10 Remove the filler cap and filter, and drain the fluid from the reservoir.

11 Unscrew and remove the stop light switch.

12 Pull the reservoir out of the rubber grommets, then prise the grommets from the cylinder.

13 Unscrew the stop screw and remove the washer from the top of the cylinder.

14 Remove the rubber boot from the end of the cylinder.

15 Push the primary piston in slightly then extract the circlip from the mouth of the cylinder.

16 Extract all the components from the cylinder keeping them in their order of removal. If necessary tap the cylinder on a block of wood to remove the secondary piston.

17 Clean all the components in methylated spirit and examine them for wear and damage. In particular check the surfaces of the piston and cylinder bore for wear, scoring and corrosion. If evident, renew the complete master cylinder, but if in good condition discard all the inner components and obtain a repair kit which includes all the components and a special fitting sleeve. Check that all the parts in the cylinder are free and unobstructed.

18 Commence reassembly by smearing fresh brake fluid on the cylinder bore then grip the cylinder in a vice.

19 Insert the fitting sleeve in the cylinder, then using a screwdriver push the entire contents in the cylinder.

20 With the primary piston depressed, insert the stop screw together with a new washer and tighten it. Remove the fitting sleeve.

21 Fit the stop washer and circlip in the mouth of the cylinder then fit the rubber boot.

22 Dip the rubber grommets in brake fluid and press them into the cylinder, then press the reservoir into the grommets.

23 Insert and tighten the stop-light switch.

24 Fit the filter and filler cap.

25 Refitting is a reversal of the removal procedure, but fit a new mounting seal where applicable. Bleed the hydraulic system as described in Section 12.

10 Brake pressure regulator – general

1 A brake pressure regulator is fitted in the rear brake circuit of some models and its purpose is to prevent the rear wheels locking in advance of the first wheels during heavy application of the brakes. The regulator is also load sensitive in order to vary the pressure according to the load being carried.

2 The regulator is located on the under-body, in front of the left-hand rear wheel.

3 Checking of the regulator is best left to a VW garage as special pressure gauges and spring tensioning tools are required. Adjustment is made by varying the spring tension, but this must be carried out by the garage.

4 Removal and refitting are straight forward but after fitting, bleed the hydraulic system as described in Section 12, and have the regulator adjusted by a garage.

11 Hydraulic pipes and hoses – inspection and renewal

1 At the intervals given in Section 2 clean the rigid brake lines and flexible hoses and check them for damage, leakage, chafing and cracks. If the coating on the rigid pipes is damaged or if rusting is apparent they must be renewed. Check the retaining clips for security, and clean away any accumulations of dirt and debris.

2 To remove a rigid brake pipe, unscrew the union nuts at each end and where necessary remove the line from the clips. Refitting is a reversal of removal.

Fig. 8.12 Master cylinder repair kit in special fitting sleeve (Sec 9)

Fig. 8.13 Brake pressure regulator location (Sec 10)

11.3 Brake hydraulic line connection

3 To remove a flexible brake hose, unscrew the union nut securing the rigid brake pipe to the end of the flexible hose and remove the spring clip and hose end fitting from the bracket (photo). Unscrew the remaining end from the component on rigid pipe according to position. Refitting is a reversal of removal.

4 Bleed the complete hydraulic system as described in Section 12 after fitting a rigid brake pipe or flexible brake hose.

12 Hydraulic system – bleeding

1 If any of the hydraulic components in the braking system have been removed or disconnected, or if the fluid level in the master cylinder has been allowed to fall appreciably, it is inevitable that air will have been introduced into the system. The removal of all this air from the

hydraulic system is essential if the brakes are to function correctly, and the process of removing it is known as bleeding.

2   There are a number of one-man, do-it-yourself, brake bleeding kits currently available from motor accessory shops. It is recommended that one of these kits should be used wherever possible as they greatly simplify the bleeding operation and also reduce the risk of expelled air and fluid being drawn back into the system.

3   If one of these kits is not available then it will be necessary to gather together a clean jar and a suitable length of clear plastic tubing which is a tight fit over the bleed screw, and also to engage the help of an assistant.

4   Before commencing the bleeding operation, check that all rigid pipes and flexible hoses are in good condition and that all hydraulic unions are tight. Take great care not to allow hydraulic fluid to come into contact with the vehicle paintwork, otherwise the finish will be seriously damaged. Wash off any spilled fluid immediately with cold water.

5   If hydraulic fluid has been lost from the master cylinder, due to a leak in the system, ensure that the cause is traced and rectified before proceeding further or a serious malfunction of the braking system may occur.

6   To bleed the system, clean the area around the bleed screw at the wheel cylinder to be bled. If the hydraulic system has only been partially disconnected and suitable precautions were taken to prevent further loss of fluid, it should only be necessary to bleed that part of the system. However, if the entire system is to be bled, start at the wheel furthest away from the master cylinder (ie right-hand rear wheel).

7   Remove the master cylinder filler cap and top up the reservoir. Periodically check the fluid level during the bleeding operation and top up as necessary.

8   If a one-man brake bleeding kit is being used, connect the outlet tube to the bleed screw and then open the screw half a turn. If possible position the unit so that it can be viewed from the car, then depress the brake pedal to the floor and slowly release it. The one-way valve in the kit will prevent dispelled air from returning to the system at the end of each stroke. Repeat this operation until clean hydraulic fluid, free from air bubbles, can be seen coming through the tube. Now tighten the bleed screw and remove the outlet tube.

9   If a one-man brake bleeding kit is not available, connect one end of the plastic tubing to the bleed screw and immerse the other end in the jar containing sufficient clean hydraulic fluid to keep the end of the tube submerged. Open the bleed screw half a turn and have your assistant depress the brake pedal to the floor and then slowly release it. Tighten the bleed screw at the end of each downstroke to prevent expelled air and fluid from being drawn back into the system. Repeat this operation until clean hydraulic fluid, free from air bubbles, can be seen coming through the tube. Now tighten the bleed screw and remove the plastic tube.

10 If the entire system is being bled the procedures described above should now be repeated at each wheel, finishing at the wheel nearest to the master cylinder. The correct sequence is as follows:

Right-hand rear wheel
Left-hand rear wheel
Right-hand front wheel
Left-hand front wheel

Do not forget to recheck the fluid level in the master cylinder at regular intervals and top up as necessary.

11 When completed, recheck the fluid level in the master cylinder, top up if necessary and refit the cap. Check the 'feel' of the brake pedal which should be firm and free from any 'sponginess' which would indicate air still present in the system.

12 Discard any expelled hydraulic fluid as it is likely to be contaminated with moisture, air and dirt which makes it unsuitable for further use.

13 Handbrake lever – removal, refitting and adjustment

1   To remove the lever first remove the cover if fitted and fully release the lever.

2   Extract one circlip from the cable pivot and push the pivot from the handbrake lever to release the cable.

3   Unscrew and remove the pivot bolt and withdraw the handbrake lever from the bracket.

4   If required remove the screw from the lever switch, disconnect the wiring, and remove the switch.

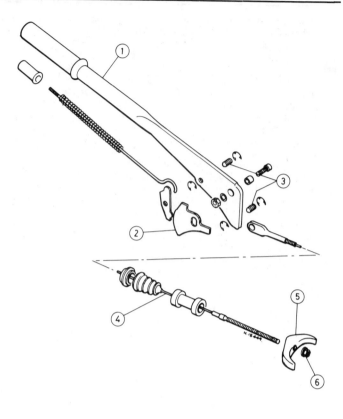

Fig. 8.14 Exploded view of the handbrake lever (Sec 13)

1	*Handbrake lever*	4	*Cable*
2	*Toothed segment*	5	*Compensator bar*
3	*Pivot pins*	6	*Adjusting nut*

5   Extract the circlip and remove the pawl pivot then remove the pawl and rod together with the spring and button.

6   Refitting is a reversal of removal, but smear a little molybdenum disulphide based grease on the pivoting surfaces. Finally adjust the handbrake as follows.

7   Chock the front wheels then jack up the rear of the car and support it on axle stands.

8   Fully release the handbrake then pull the lever onto the second notch.

9   Check that it is just possible to turn each rear wheel by hand. If necessary adjust the handbrake by turning the nut on the rear of the compensator bar beneath the car.

10 Fully release the lever and check that both rear wheels rotate freely, then fully apply the lever and check that both rear wheels are locked.

11 Lower the car to the ground.

14 Handbrake cables – removal and refitting

1   Chock the front wheels then jack up the rear of the car and support it on axle stands. Release the handbrake.

Front cable

2   If fitted, remove the cover from the lever.

3   Extract the circlip from the cable pivot and push the pivot from the lever.

4   Working beneath the car unscrew and remove the adjusting nut from the rear of the compensator bar (photo). Remove the cable from the bar.

5   Release the rubber boot and withdraw the cable from under the car after removing the guides (photo).

6   Refitting is a reversal of removal, but adjust the handbrake as described in Section 13.

14.4 Showing the handbrake cable compensator

14.5 Front handbrake cable and guide

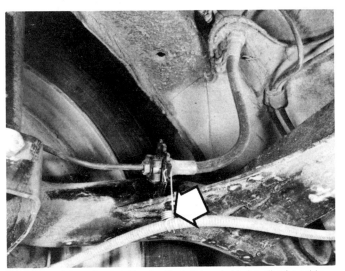

14.9 Mounting spring location for the left-hand side handbrake cable

14.10 Handbrake cable and bracket

Rear cable

7 Remove the rear brake shoes as described in Section 4.
8 Working beneath the car unscrew the adjusting nut from the rear of the compensator bar sufficient to detach the cable.
9 Remove the cross-head screw to release the right-hand side cable clip, and remove the tension spring from the left-hand side cable (photo).
10 Disconnect the cables from the brackets and pull them out from the backplates (photo).
11 Unscrew the nut and remove the cable guide wheel and plate.
12 Refitting is a reversal of removal, but lubricate the guide wheel with a little grease and adjust the handbrake as described in Section 13.

---

15 Footbrake pedal – removal and refitting

---

1 Working inside the car remove the lower trim panel from around the steering column.
2 Prise the clip from the end of the pedal pivot shaft.

3 Unhook the return spring from the pedal.
4 Withdraw the pivot shaft sufficient to remove the pedal, at the same time pull the pushrod from the master cylinder.
5 Extract the clip, remove the pivot, and detach the pushrod from the pedal.
6 If necessary the pedal bracket can be removed after removing the clutch pedal and mounting nuts and bolts, the two nuts being the master cylinder mounting nuts.
7 Clean the pedal and pivot shaft and examine them for wear. If the bushes are worn, they can be removed using a soft metal drift, and the new bushes installed using a vice to press them into position. Check the rubber foot pad and the stop rubber on the bracket, and renew them if necessary.
8 Refitting is a reversal of removal, but apply a little multi-purpose grease to the pivot shaft and bushes. If the clutch pedal was removed, adjust the cable as described in Chapter 5. To adjust the footbrake pedal, fully depress and release the pedal, then check that there is between 2 and 4 mm (0.08 and 0.16 in) free play measured at the foot pad. If necessary loosen the locknut and turn the master cylinder pushrod as required. Tighten the locknut after making the adjustment.

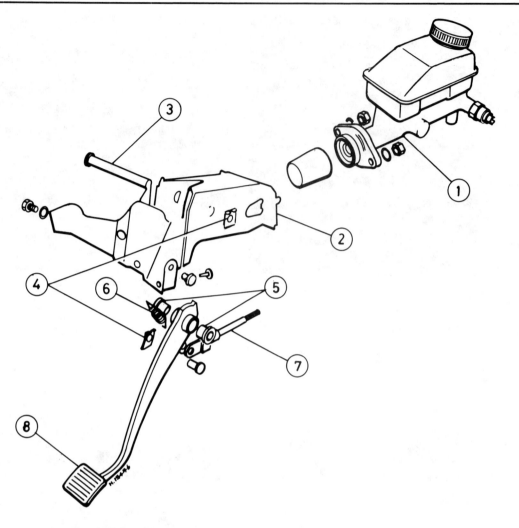

Fig. 8.15 Exploded view of the footbrake pedal and bracket (Sec 15)

1	Brake master cylinder assembly	3 Pivot pin	5 Bush	7 Adjusting pushrod
2	Bracket	4 Clip	6 Return spring	8 Brake pedal

---

16 Fault diagnosis – braking system

Symptom	Reason(s)
Excessive pedal travel	Brake fluid leak Air in hydraulic system Worn rear brake shoes
Uneven braking and pulling to one side	Contaminated linings Seized wheel cylinder or caliper Incorrect and unequal tyre pressures Loose suspension anchor point Different lining material at each wheel
Brake judder	Worn drums and/or discs Loose suspension anchor point Loose rear brake backplate
Brake pedal feels spongy	Air in hydraulic system Faulty master cylinder seals
Excessive effort to stop car	Seized wheel cylinders or calipers Incorrect lining material Contaminated linings New linings not yet bedded-in Excessively worn linings

Chapter 9 Electrical system

For modifications, and information applicable to later models, see Supplement at end of manual

Contents

Specifications

System type
12 volt, negative earth

Battery
Capacity	36 amp hr or 45 amp hr
Minimum voltage (under load)	9.6 volts at 110 amps

Alternator
Type	Bosch or Motorola
Output at 3000 rpm (engine speed)	30 amps (45 amp model) 45 amps (65 amp model)
Regulator voltage	12.5 to 14.5 volts
Minimum brush length	5.0 mm (0.2 in)
Rotor winding resistance:	
45 amp	3.4 to 3.7 ohm
65 amp	2.8 to 3.0 ohm

Starter motor
Minimum brush length	13.0 mm (0.5 in)
Commutator minimum diameter	33.5 mm (1.319 in)
Shaft endplay	0.05 to 0.30 mm (0.002 to 0.012 in)
Commutator run-out	0.03 mm (0.001 in)

Fuses

Number	Component	Rating (amps)
1	Foglights	8
2	Rear foglight	8
3	Left side light and tail light, instrument panel lights	8
4	Right side light and tail light, number plate light, headlight washer	8
5	Left main beam	8
6	Right main beam, main beam warning light	8
7	Left dipped beam	8
8	Right dipped beam	8
9	Horn, idle cut-off solenoid, reversing light	8
10	Direction indicators	8
11	Interior light, cigarette lighter, radio, clock	8
12	Hazard warning lights, stop-lights	8
13	Radiator cooling fan	16
14	Rear wiper, heater blower	16
15	Windscreen wipers, intermittent wiper unit	8
16	Heated rear window	16

Bulbs

	Wattage
Headlamp:	
Standard	45/40
Halogen	60/55
Sidelamp	4
Taillamp	10
Stop-light	21
Direction indicators	21
Foglamp	21
Reversing light	21
Stop/tail light (Classic)	21/5
Boot light (Classic)	5
Interior light	5
Number plate light	4

Torque wrench settings

	lbf ft	Nm
Starter	18	25
Wiper arm	3 to 4	4 to 6
Alternator bracket:		
Engine	33	45
Alternator	22	30

1 General description

The electrical system is of 12 volt negative earth type. The battery is charged by a belt-driven alternator which incorporates a voltage regulator. The starter motor is of pre-engaged type incorporating a solenoid which moves the drive pinion into engagement with the flywheel ring gear before the motor is energised.

Although repair procedures are given in this Chapter, it may well be more economical to renew worn components as complete units.

2 Battery – removal and refitting

1 The battery is located under the bonnet on the right-hand side of the bulkhead (photo).

2 Loosen the battery terminal clamp nuts and disconnect the negative lead followed by the positive lead.

3 Unscrew the bolt and remove the battery retaining clamp.

4 Lift the battery from its platform taking care not to spill any electrolyte on the bodywork.

5 Refitting is a reversal of removal, but make sure that the leads are fitted to their correct terminals, and do not overtighten the lead clamp nuts or the battery retaining clamp bolt. Finally smear a little petroleum jelly on the terminals and clamps.

3 Battery – maintenance

1 Every 10 000 miles (15 000 km) or more frequently in hot climates, check the level of electrolyte in each cell. The battery case is translucent

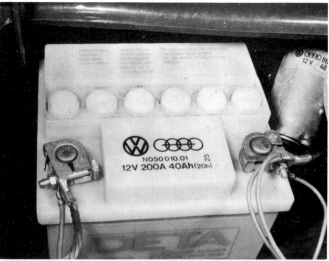

2.1 The battery is located on the bulkhead

and checking is therefore possible without removing the cell caps – the level should be between the minimum and maximum lines.

2 If topping up is necessary the caps can be removed by piercing the notch with a screwdriver then turning the cap (with screwdriver still inserted) to the stop. The caps can then be unscrewed. Add distilled or de-ionized water to each cell as necessary then refit the caps.

3 At the same time wipe clean the battery case with a dry cloth. If there

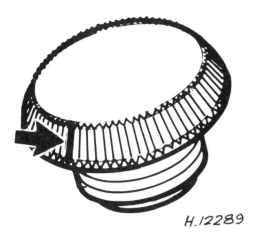

Fig. 9.1 Pierce the battery cap notch with a screwdriver when removing the caps (Sec 3)

is any sign of corrosion on the terminals or lead clamps, disconnect the leads and clean them. Then refit them and smear the outer surfaces with petroleum jelly.

4 Similarly check the battery platform for corrosion and if necessary clean the deposits away. Then treat the affected metal with a propriet-ary anti-rust liquid and paint with the original colour.

5 If topping up the battery becomes excessive check the casing for cracking. If evident it may be possible to repair it with a proprietary compound. Overcharging can also result in excessive topping up and in this case the voltage regulator should be checked.

6 If the battery condition is suspect, the specific gravity of the electrolyte in each cell should be checked using a hydrometer and compared with the following table:

	Ambient temperature above 25°C (77°F)	Ambient temperature below 25°C (77°F)
Fully charged	*1.210 to 1.230*	*1.270 to 1.290*
70% charged	*1.170 to 1.190*	*1.230 to 1.250*
Fully charged	*1.050 to 1.070*	*1.110 to 1.130*

Note that the readings assume an electrolyte temperature of 15°C (60°F); for every 10°C (18°F) below 15°C (60°F) subtract 0.007, or above, add 0.007.

7 A variation of 0.040 or more between any cells indicates loss of electrolyte or deterioration of the internal plates.

8 A further test can be made using a battery heavy discharge meter. The battery should be discharged for a maximum of 15 seconds at a load of three times the ampere-hour capacity. Alternatively, connect a voltmeter across the battery terminals, and spin the engine on the starter with the coil low tension negative lead disconnected and the headlamps, heated rear window and heater blower switched on.

9 If the voltmeter reading remains above 9.6 volts, the battery condition is satisfactory. If the voltmeter reading drops below 9.6 volts and the battery has already been charged as described in Section 5, it is faulty and should be renewed.

4 Battery – electrolyte replenishment

1 If after fully charging the battery one of the cells maintains a specific gravity which is 0.040 or more lower than the others, but the battery also maintains 9.6 volts during the heavy discharge test (Section 3), it is likely that electrolyte has been lost. In this case it will not suffice merely to refill with distilled water. Top up the cell with a mixture of 2 parts sulphuric acid to 5 parts distilled water.

2 When mixing the electrolyte, **never** add water to sulphuric acid – always pour the acid slowly onto the water in a glass container. If water is added to sulphuric acid, it will explode.

3 After topping up the cell with fresh electrolyte, recharge the battery and check the hydrometer readings again.

5 Battery – charging

1 In winter when a heavy demand is placed on the battery, such as when starting from cold and using more electrical equipment, the battery may occasionally require charging from an external source at a rate of 3 to 5 amps. Note that both battery terminal leads must be disconnected before charging and also the cell caps removed.

2 Continue to charge the battery until no further rise in specific gravity is noted over a three hour period.

3 Alternatively a trickle charger, charging at a rate of 1.5 amps, can be safely used overnight.

4 Special rapid boost charges are not recommended unless carried out by a qualified person using a thermostatic control, otherwise serious damage can occur to the battery plates through overheating.

5 While charging the battery, ensure that the temperature of the electrolyte never exceeds 40°C (104°F).

6 Alternator – maintenance and special precautions

1 At the 20 000 mile (30 000 km) service the alternator drivebelt should be checked for wear and damage and its tension adjusted as described in Section 7. At the same time check that the plug is pushed firmly into the terminals on the rear of the alternator.

2 Take extreme care when making electrical circuit connections on the car otherwise damage may occur to the alternator or other electrical components employing semi-conductors. Always make sure that the battery leads are correctly connected. Before using electric-arc welding equipment to repair any part of the car, disconnect the battery leads and alternator multi-plug. Never run the alternator with the multi-plug or a battery lead disconnected.

7 Alternator drivebelt – adjustment

1 The alternator drivebelt should be adjusted every 20 000 miles (30 000 km). To check its tension depress the belt firmly with a finger or thumb midway between the alternator and crankshaft pulleys. The belt should deflect approximately 15 mm (0.6 in) (photo).

2 If adjustment is necessary loosen the nut on the adjusting link under the alternator, then lever the alternator away from the cylinder block until the belt is tensioned correctly, using a lever at the pulley end of the alternator (photo).

3 Tighten the nut after adjusting the drivebelt.

7.1 Checking the alternator drivebelt tension

7.2 Loosening the adjusting link nut to adjust the alternator drivebelt tension

8 Alternator – testing

Accurate testing of the alternator is only possible using specialised instruments and is therefore best left to a qualified electrician. If, however, the alternator is faulty the home mechanic should dismantle it with reference to Section 10 or 11 and check the condition of the brushes, soldered joints etc. If the fault cannot be found, refit the alternator and have it checked professionally.

9 Alternator – removal and refitting

1 Disconnect the battery negative lead.
2 Release the clip and pull the multi-plug from the rear of the alternator (photo).
3 Loosen the pivot and adjustment bolts then push the alternator in towards the engine and slip the drivebelt from the alternator and crankshaft pulleys (photo).
4 Remove the adjustment link nut and washer.
5 Support the alternator then remove the pivot bolt and withdraw the unit from the engine (photo).
6 Refitting is a reversal of removal, but before fully tightening the pivot and adjustment bolts tension the drivebelt as described in Section 7.

10 Alternator (Bosch) – overhaul

1 Wipe clean the exterior surfaces of the alternator.
2 Remove the two screws and withdraw the voltage regulator and brush assembly from the rear of the alternator (photos).
3 Mark the housings and stator in relation to each other, then unscrew the through bolts and tap the drive end housing off.
4 Grip the pulley in a soft jawed vice and unscrew the nut. Tap the rotor shaft through the pulley and remove the spacers and fan noting the direction of rotation arrow on the front of the fan.
5 Using a three-arm puller press the rotor shaft out of the drive end housing. Note that the arms of the pulley must be located on the

9.2 Showing multi-plug on the rear of the alternator

9.3 Loosening the alternator adjusting link inner bolt

9.5 Removing the alternator pivot bolt

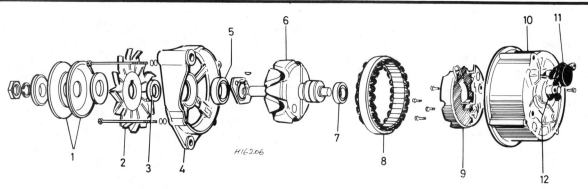

Fig. 9.2 Exploded view of the Bosch alternator (Sec 10)

1 Belt pulley	4 Drive end housing	7 Bearing	10 Housing
2 Fan	5 Bearing	8 Stator	11 Regulator
3 Spacer	6 Rotor	9 Diode plate	12 Regulator brushes

10.2A Voltage regulator location

10.2B Removing the voltage regulator and brush assembly

10.2C View of the slip rings with voltage regulator removed

10.10 Checking the length of the alternator brushes

bearing retainer otherwise damage may occur to the retainer screws.

6   Remove the screws and the retainer and use a soft metal drift to drive out the bearing.

7   Using a puller, remove the bearing from the end of the rotor shaft.

8   If necessary the stator and diode plate can be removed from the end housing after removing the retaining screws.

9   Clean all the components in paraffin or petrol and wipe them dry.

10 Check that the length of the carbon brushes is not less than the minimum amount given in the Specifications (photo). If necessary unsolder the leads and remove the old brushes then clean the housing, insert the new brushes, and solder the new leads into position.

11 The rotor bearings should be renewed as a matter of course.

12 To check the stator first identify the wire positions then unsolder them using long nose pliers to dissipate heat from the diode plate. Check the windings for short circuits by connecting an ohmmeter between each of the three wires (ie between wire 1 and 2, wire 1 and 3, and wire 2 and 3). Each reading should be between 0.18 and 0.20 ohm for the 45 amp alternator and between 0.10 and 0.11 ohm for the 65 amp alternator. Check the windings for insulation by connecting a 12 volt testlamp and leads between each of the wires and the stator ring. If the lamp illuminates, the windings are faulty.

13 Check the rotor windings for continuity by connecting an ohmmeter to the two slip rings. A reading of 3.4 to 3.7 ohm should be obtained for the 45 amp alternator, or 2.8 to 3.0 ohm for the 65 amp alternator. Check

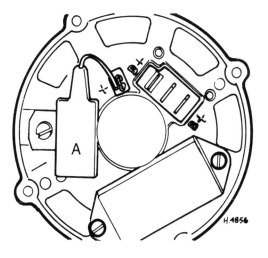

Fig. 9.3 Location of suppression condenser (A) on the rear of the alternator (Sec 10)

the windings for insulation by connecting a 12 volt testlamp and leads between each of the slip rings and the winding core. If the lamp illuminates, the windings are faulty.

14 The diodes can be checked by connecting an ohmmeter across them. The reading should be between 50 and 80 ohm in one direction and at or near infinity in the other direction (ie with lead positions reversed).

15 Clean the slip rings with fine glasspaper and wipe clean with a fuel moistened cloth.

16 Reassemble the alternator using a reversal of the dismantling procedure. When fitting the bearing to the rotor shaft, drive it on with a metal tube located on the inner race. If the diode plate has been renewed, a suppression condenser should be fitted to the rear of the alternator as shown in Fig. 9.3.

11 Alternator (Motorola) – overhaul

1 The procedure is similar to that described in Section 10, and the exploded diagrams of the 45 amp and 65 amp alternators are shown in Figs. 9.4 and 9.5. Identify the regulator wires for position before disconnecting them.

2 The 45 amp stator windings may be of two types, the early type can be recognised by having single wires soldered to the terminals whereas the later type has double wires on each terminal. The resistance of the early 45 amp windings should be between 0.27 and 0.3 ohm, the later 45 amp windings between 0.09 and 0.11 ohm, and the 65 amp windings between 0.13 and 0.15 ohm.

3 The resistance of the rotor windings should be between 3.8 and 4.2 ohm on both types of alternator, and the diode resistance between 50 and 80 ohm, the same as on the Bosch alternator.

4 On the 65 amp version the DT wire must be routed as shown in Fig. 9.6.

12 Starter motor – testing in the car

1 If the starter motor fails to operate, first check the condition of the battery by switching on the headlamps. If they glow brightly, then gradually dim after a few seconds, the battery is in an uncharged condition.

2 If the battery is in good condition, check the wiring connections on the starter for security and also check the earth wire between the gearbox and body.

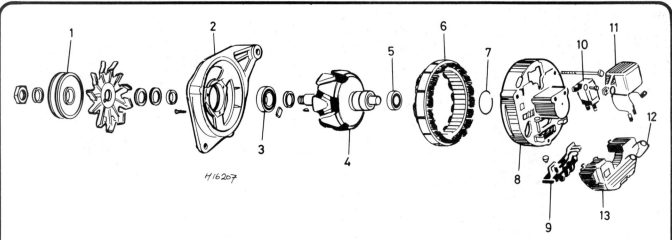

Fig. 9.4 Exploded view of the Motorola 45 amp alternator (Sec 11)

1	Belt pulley	5	Bearing (slip ring	8	Housing	11	Regulator
2	Endplate		end)	9	Diode plate	12	Wire clip
3	Drive end bearing	6	Stator	10	Brush holder	13	Cover
4	Rotor	7	O-ring				

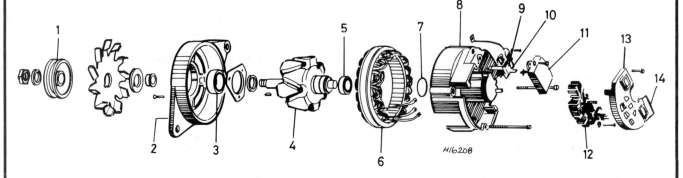

Fig. 9.5 Exploded view of the Motorola 65 amp alternator (Sec 11)

1	Belt pulley	5	Bearing (slip ring end)	9	Brush holder	12	Diode plate
2	Endplate	6	Stator	10	D + connecting plate	13	Cover
3	Bearing (drive end)	7	O-ring	11	Regulator	14	Wire clip
4	Rotor	8	Housing				

Fig. 9.6 Showing the correct routing of the D+ wire on the 65 amp Motorola alternator (Sec 11)

13.7A Starter retaining bolts showing exhaust bracket location

3   If the starter still fails to turn, use a voltmeter or 12 volt testlamp and leads to check that current is reaching the main terminal (terminal 30) on the starter solenoid.

4   With the ignition switched on and the ignition key in the start position check that current is reaching the remaining terminals on the solenoid. Also check that an audible click is heard as the solenoid operates indicating that the internal contacts are closed and that current is available at the field windings terminal.

5   Failure to obtain current at terminal 50 indicates a faulty ignition switch.

6   If current at the correct voltage is available at the starter motor, yet it does not operate, the unit is faulty and should be removed for further investigation.

13 Starter motor – removal and refitting

1   Remove the windscreen washer bottle and if necessary remove the air cleaner with reference to Chapter 3.

2   Disconnect the battery negative lead.

3   Identify the wiring for position then disconnect it from the solenoid.

4   Jack up the front of the car and support it on axle stands. Apply the handbrake.

5   Unscrew the bolt securing the exhaust pipe to the support strap beneath the starter.

6   Where applicable unscrew the nuts and bolts and remove the support bracket from the cylinder block.

7   Unscrew and remove the retaining bolts, then unbolt the exhaust bracket and withdraw the starter (photos).

8   Refitting is a reversal of removal, but tighten the bolts to the specified torque. Where a support bracket is fitted, do not fully tighten the nuts and bolts until the bracket is correctly located and free of any tension.

14 Starter motor – overhaul

1   Wipe clean the exterior surfaces of the starter motor.

2   Unscrew the terminal nut and disconnect the field windings lead from the solenoid.

3   Unscrew the bolts and withdraw the solenoid from the housing, then unhook the solenoid core from the operating lever.

4   Remove the screws and lift off the end cap, then prise out the circlip and remove the shims.

5   Unscrew the through bolts and remove the end cover.

6   Lift the springs and remove the carbon brushes from the brush holder, then withdraw the holder.

7   Remove the field coil housing from the end housing.

8   Using a metal tube drive the stop ring towards the pinion, then remove the circlip and stop ring.

9   Slide the armature from the pinion, and withdraw the pinion.

10 Prise the rubber pad from the end housing.

11 Unscrew and remove the pivot bolt and withdraw the operating lever.

12 Clean all the components in paraffin and wipe dry. Check the pinion teeth for wear and pitting and check that the one-way clutch only allows

13.7B Removing the starter motor

the pinion to turn in one direction. Clean the commutator with a fuel moistened cloth and if necessary use fine glasspaper to remove any carbon deposits. If the commutator is worn excessively it can be machined provided that the diameter is not less than the amount given in the Specifications.

13 If the brushes are less than the minimum length given in the Specifications they must be renewed. To do this crush the old brushes with a pair of pliers and clean the leads. Insert the leads into the new brushes and splay out the ends. Solder the wires in position but grip the wire next to the brush with long nosed pliers in order to prevent the solder penetrating the flexible section of the wire. File off any surplus solder.

14 Check the bush in the end cover and if necessary drive it out with a soft metal drift. Soak the end cover in hot oil for five minutes before driving the new bush into it.

15 Assemble the starter motor in reversal of the dismantling procedure but note that the unit must be sealed with suitable sealant on the surfaces shown in Fig. 9.8. Lubricate the pinion drive with a little molybdenum disulphide grease. Make sure that the stop ring is fitted from the inside of the circlip with the annular groove facing outwards, and also make sure that the stop ring turns freely on the shaft. Lubricate the solenoid and operating lever with a little molybdenum disulphide grease. When fitting the brush holder, the springs may be held in a raised position by using two lengths of bent wire.

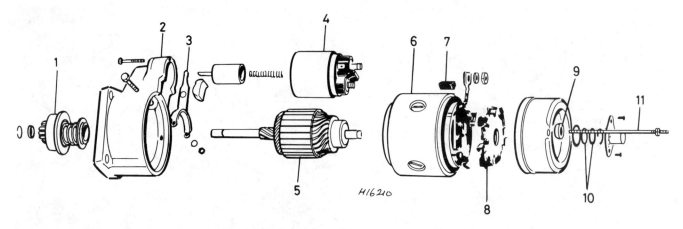

Fig. 9.7 Exploded view of the starter motor (Sec 14)

1	Pinion	4	Solenoid	7	Carbon brushes	10	Spacers
2	Mounting bracket	5	Armature	8	Brush plate	11	Housing bolt
3	Operating lever	6	Housing with windings	9	Bush		

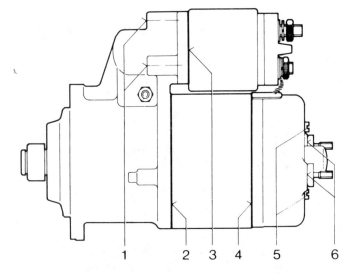

Fig. 9.8 Surfaces to be sealed when reassembling the starter motor (Sec 14)

1	Solenoid securing screws	4	Starter/end cap joint
2	Stator/mounting surface	5	Through bolts
3	Solenoid joint	6	Shaft cover joint and screws

15 Fuses – general

1   The fuses are located beneath the bonnet on the left-hand side of the plenum chamber. Access is gained by squeezing the sides of the plastic lid at the top and bottom. Take care not to damage the seal (photo).

2   The fuse circuits are given in the Specifications and the fuses are numbered in a clockwise sequence starting at the top left.

3   Blown fuses are easily recognised by the metal strip being burnt apart in the centre. Make sure that new fuses are firmly held between the terminals.

4   Always renew a fuse with one of identical rating, and never renew it more than once without finding the source of the trouble (usually a short circuit).

16 Direction indicator and hazard flasher system – general

1   The flasher unit is located next to the fusebox beneath the bonnet.

2   To remove the unit first disconnect the battery negative lead, then

15.1 Removing the plastic lid from the fuse box

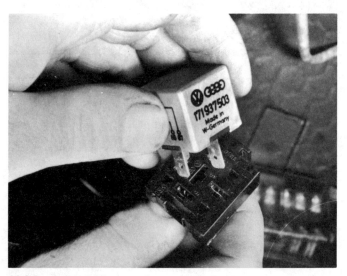

16.2 Removing the flasher unit

slide out the plastic holder and pull out the flasher unit (photo). Make sure that the new unit is fully entered in the holder.

3 Should the flashers become faulty in operation, check the bulbs for security and make sure that the contact surfaces are not corroded. Check all the relevant wiring and terminals. If the flashers are still faulty and the relevant fuse has not blown, renew the flasher unit. If the fuse has blown, a short circuit may be the cause of the failure.

17 Ignition switch/steering column lock – removal and refitting

The procedure is described in Chapter 10 for the removal and refitting of the steering lock.

18 Combination switches – removal and refitting

1 Remove the steering wheel as described in Chapter 10.
2 Disconnect the battery negative lead.
3 Remove the screws and withdraw the steering column lower shroud.
4 Remove the three screws securing the combination switch (photo).
5 Disconnect the multi-plugs and withdraw the combination switch (photos).
6 If necessary the direction indicator switch can be separated from the windscreen wiper switch (photo).
7 If the wiper switch is not fitted with an intermittent relay, this can be fitted with reference to the relevant wiring diagram. It will be necessary to remove the wedge from the switch.
8 Refitting is a reversal of removal, with reference to Chapter 10 when refitting the steering wheel.

19 Facia switches – removal and refitting

1 Disconnect the battery negative lead.
2 Prise the switch from the facia (photo). If difficulty is experienced

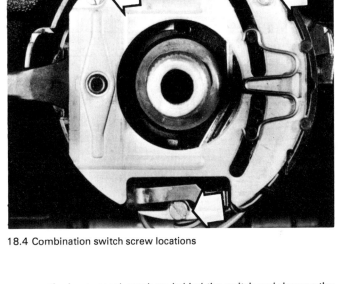

18.4 Combination switch screw locations

remove the lower panel, reach up behind the switch and depress the spring clips in order to withdraw the switch.
3 Disconnect the multi-plug and remove the switch (photo).
4 Refitting is a reversal of removal.

20 Cigarette lighter – removal and refitting

1 Disconnect the battery negative lead.
2 Remove the lower facia panel then reach up and disconnect the wiring from the cigarette lighter.

18.5A Disconnecting the multi-plugs from the combination switch

18.5B The combination switch

18.6 The direction indicator and windscreen wiper switches separated

19.2 Removing the foglight switch

19.3 Heated rear window switch with multi-plug removed

3 Remove the retaining ring and withdraw the cigarette lighter from the facia.
4 Refitting is a reversal of removal.

21 Courtesy light switch – removal and refitting

1 Disconnect the battery negative lead.
2 Open the door and unscrew the cross-head screw from the switch (photo).
3 Withdraw the switch and disconnect the wiring. Tie a loose knot in the wire to prevent it dropping into the door pillar.
4 Check the switch seal for condition and renew it if necessary.
5 Refitting is a reversal of removal.

22 Speedometer cable – removal and refitting

1 Open the bonnet and then reach down behind the engine and unscrew the speedometer cable nut from the gearbox.
2 Withdraw the instrument panel sufficient to disconnect the cable with reference to Section 23 (photo).
3 Remove the air cleaner as described in Chapter 3.
4 Pull the speedometer cable through the bulkhead and withdraw it from the engine compartment.
5 Refitting is a reversal of removal. Make sure that the grommet is correctly fitted in the bulkhead and that there are no sharp bends in the cable. Do not grease the cable ends.

23 Instrument panel – removal and refitting

1 Disconnect the battery negative lead.

2 For better access remove the steering wheel as described in Chapter 10.
3 Unscrew the cross-head screws located above the instrument panel (photo). Remove the facia switches as described in Section 19 and withdraw the instrument panel surround.
4 Unscrew the cross-head retaining screws and swivel the panel forwards sufficient to disconnect the speedometer cable and multi-plug (photos).
5 Withdraw the instrument panel from the facia (photos).
6 Refitting is a reversal of removal (photo).

24 Voltage stabiliser – testing and renewal

1 The voltage stabiliser is located on the rear of the instrument panel and its purpose is to provide constant voltage to the fuel and temperature gauges, and the temperature warning lamp (photo).
2 To check the voltage stabiliser remove the instrument panel as described in Section 23 then reconnect the multi-plugs. Connect a voltmeter between the + out terminal (+A) and the central earth terminal, then switch on the ignition. The voltage should be between 9.5 and 10.5 volts. If not, renew it as follows.
3 With the battery negative lead disconnected, unscrew the retaining screw and disconnect the pressed wires from the printed circuit.
4 Refitting is a reversal of removal.

25 Headlamp bulbs and headlamps – removal and refitting

1 To remove a headlamp bulb first open the bonnet and pull the connector from the rear of the headlamp (photo).
2 Prise off the rubber cap (photo).

21.2 Courtesy light switch location

22.2 Showing the instrument panel end of the speedometer cable

23.3 Removing the instrument panel surround screws

23.4A Instrument panel retaining screw location

23.4B Disconnecting the multi-plug from the instrument panel

23.5A Front view of the instrument panel

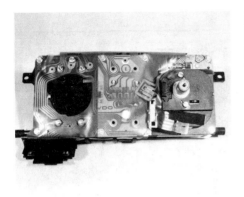

23.5B Rear view of the instrument panel

23.6 Instrument panel in fitted position

24.1 Voltage stabilizer location

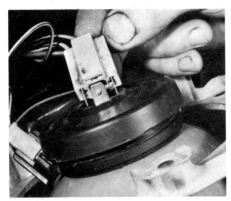

25.1 Pull off the connector ...

25.2 ... prise off the rubber cap ...

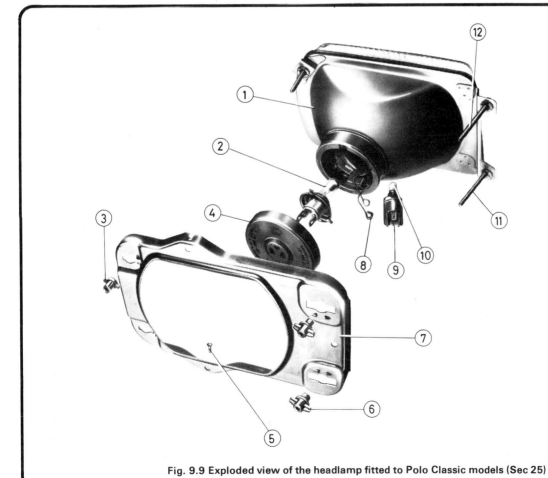

1 Headlight unit
2 Halogen bulb
3 Plastic holder
4 Cap
5 Securing screw
6 Plastic holder
7 Support plate
8 Wire clip
9 Sidelight bulbholder
10 Sidelight bulb
11 Adjusting screw
   (vertical setting)
12 Adjusting screw
   (horizontal setting)

Fig. 9.9 Exploded view of the headlamp fitted to Polo Classic models (Sec 25)

25.3A ... remove the retaining ring ...

25.3B ... and remove the headlamp bulb

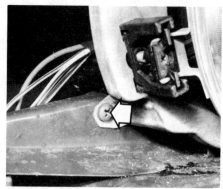
25.6A Headlamp carrier plate retaining screw

25.6B Showing the headlamp and carrier plate removed

25.6C Showing a headlamp beam adjuster with unit removed

3 On Polo and Polo Coupe models turn the retaining ring anti-clockwise and remove the bulb (photos). On Polo Classic models squeeze the spring clips together and release it from the bulb, then remove the bulb.

4 Refitting is a reversal of removal, but make sure that the locating plug on the bulbholder engages the recess in the reflector.

5 To remove the headlamp unit first remove the radiator grille as described in Chapter 11.

6 With the headlamp bulb removed, unscrew the screws securing the carrier plate to the front panel, and withdraw the unit (photos).

7 Refitting is a reversal of removal, but check and if necessary adjust the beam alignment as described in Section 26.

26.5 Headlamp lower adjusting screw for vertical movement

26 Headlamps – alignment

1 The headlamp beam alignment should be checked and if necessary adjusted every 10 000 miles (15 000 km).

2 It is recommended that the alignment is carried out by a VW garage using modern beam setting equipment. However in an emergency the following procedure will provide an acceptable light pattern.

3 Position the car on a level surface with tyres correctly inflated, approximately 10 metres (33 feet) in front of, and at right-angles to, a wall or garage door.

4 Draw a horizontal line on the wall or door at headlamp centre height. Draw a vertical line corresponding to the centre line of the car, then measure off a point either side of this, on the horizontal line, corresponding with the headlamp centres.

5 Switch on the main beam and check that the areas of maximum illumination coincide with the headlamp centre marks on the wall. If not, turn the upper cross-head adjustment screw to adjust the beam laterally, and the lower screw to adjust the beam vertically (photo).

27 Lamp bulbs – renewal

Note: *Lamp bulbs should always be renewed with ones of similar type and rating as listed in the Specifications.*

Sidelights

1 Open the bonnet and pull the connector from the sidelight bulbholder located beneath the headlamp bulb.

2 Turn the bulbholder anti-clockwise and remove it from the reflector (photo).

3 Depress and twist the bulb to remove it (photo).

Rear lights

4 Open the tailgate or bootlid as applicable and pull the connector from the bulbholder (photo).

27.2 Removing the sidelight bulbholder

27.3 Sidelight bulb and bulbholder

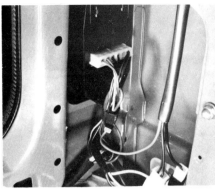

27.4 Showing rear light wiring connector

27.5 Depress the clips to remove the rear light bulbholder

27.6 Showing rear light bulbs in the bulbholder

27.7 Removing the front indicator lamp lens

27.8 Removing the front indicator lamp bulb

27.9 Removing the front indicator lamp

27.11 Removing the number plate light lens and cover

5 Release the bulbholder from the lamp unit by prising out or depressing the clips as applicable (photo).
6 Depress and twist the relevant bulb to remove it (photo).

Front indicator lights
7 Remove the cross-head screws and withdraw the lens (photo).
8 Depress and twist the bulb to remove it (photo).
9 If necessary the lamp unit can be withdrawn from the bumper and the wiring disconnected (photo).
10 When refitting the lens make sure that the gasket is correctly located.

Number plate light
11 Remove the cross-head screws and withdraw the lens and cover (photo).
12 Depress and twist the bulb to remove it.
13 When refitting the lens and cover make sure that the lug is correctly located.

Interior light
14 Using a screwdriver depress the spring clip then withdraw the light from the roof (photos).
15 Release the festoon type bulb from the spring terminals.
16 When fitting the new bulb make sure that the terminals are tensioned sufficient to retain the bulb. The switch end of the light should be inserted into the roof first.

Foglight
17 Remove the lower screw and withdraw the insert.
18 Disconnect the bulb wiring, then release the spring clip and remove the bulb.
19 When fitting the new bulb make sure that the locating lug is correctly positioned.

Instrument panel light
20 Remove the instrument panel as described in Section 23.

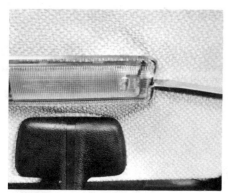
27.14A Depress the spring clip ...

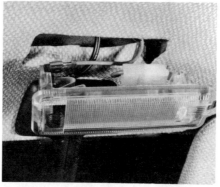
27.14B ... and withdraw the interior light

27.21 Removing an instrument panel light bulb

27.23A Removing the bulb from the hazard warning switch

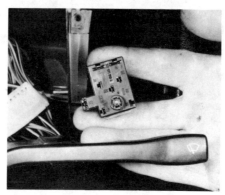
27.23B Showing the lighting switch connector and illumination bulb

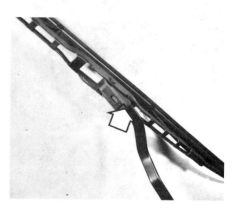
28.1A Depress the clip ...

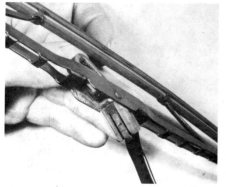
28.1B ... and slide the wiper blade from the arm

29.2 Location of wiper arm retaining nut

30.3 Windscreen wiper motor and pull rods

21 Twist the bulbholder through 90° to remove it then pull out the bulb (photo).

Facia switch lights

22 Remove the relevant facia switch as described in Section 19.
23 Remove the bulb from the switch or connector as applicable (photos).

28 Wiper blades – renewal

1 To remove a wiper blade pull the arm from the windscreen/rear window as far as possible, then depress the plastic clip and slide the blade from the arm (photos).
2 If necessary the wiper rubber may be renewed separately. To do this

use pliers to compress the rubber so that it can be removed from the blade.
3 Refitting is a reversal of removal.

29 Wiper arms – removal and refitting

1 Make sure that the wiper arms are in their parked position then remove the wiper blade as described in Section 28.
2 Lift the hinged cover and unscrew the nut (photo).
3 Ease the wiper arm from the spindle taking care not to damage the paintwork.
4 Refitting is a reversal of removal. In the parked position, the end of the wiper arm (ie middle of the blade), should be 43 mm (1.69 in) from the bottom of the windscreen for the passenger side wiper or 37 mm (1.46 in) for the driver's side wiper. On the rear window the dimension is 25 mm (1 in).

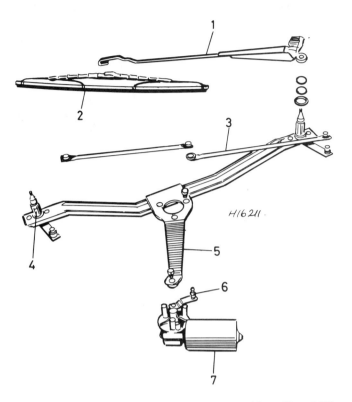

Fig. 9.10 Windscreen wiper motor and linkage (Secs 30 and 32)

1 Wiper arm	5 Windscreen wiper frame
2 Wiper blade	6 Parking position
3 Pull rods	7 Wiper motor
4 Wiper bearing	

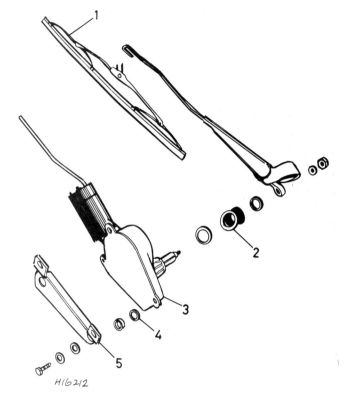

Fig. 9.11 Exploded view of the rear window wiper motor (Sec 31)

1 Wiper blade	4 Spacer washer
2 Outer spacer	5 Securing plate
3 Rear wiper motor	

30 Windscreen wiper motor – removal and refitting

1 Open the bonnet and disconnect the battery negative lead.
2 Pull the weatherstrip from the front of the plenum chamber and remove the plastic cover.
3 Unscrew the nut and remove the crank from the motor spindle (photo).
4 Disconnect the wiring multi-plug.
5 Unscrew the bolts and withdraw the wiper motor from the frame.
6 Refitting is a reversal of removal, but when fitting the crank to the spindle (motor in parked position) make sure that the marks are aligned.

31 Rear window wiper motor – removal and refitting

1 Disconnect the battery negative lead.
2 Open the tailgate and prise off the inner trim panel.
3 Remove the wiper arm as described in Section 29, and unscrew the outer nut. Remove the spacers.
4 Remove the mounting bracket cross-head screws and withdraw the motor sufficient to disconnect the wiring plug (photo). Note the location of any spacers.
5 Refitting is a reversal of removal.

32 Windscreen wiper linkage – removal and refitting

1 Disconnect the battery negative lead.
2 Remove the wiper arms as described in Section 29, then unscrew the bearing nuts and remove the spacers.
3 Pull the weatherstrips from the front of the plenum chamber and remove the plastic cover.

31.4 Rear window wiper motor location in the tailgate

4 Disconnect the wiring multi-plug.
5 Unscrew the frame mounting bolt, then withdraw the assembly from the bulkhead.
6 Prise the pull rods from the motor crank and bearing levers.
7 Unbolt the wiper motor from the frame.
8 Refitting is a reversal of removal, but lubricate the bearing units and pull rod joints with molybdenum disulphide grease.

33.4A Front view of the horn and mounting bolt

33.4B Rear view of the horn

33 Horn – removal and refitting

1   The horn is located behind the radiator grille.
2   To remove the horn first disconnect the battery negative lead.
3   Remove the radiator grille as described in Chapter 11.
4   Unscrew the mounting bolt, disconnect the wires, and withdraw the horn (photos).
5   If the horn emits an unsatisfactory sound it may be possible to adjust it by removing the sealant from the adjusting screw and turning it one way or the other.
6   Refitting is a reversal of removal.

34 Windscreen washer system – general

1   The windscreen washer fluid reservoir is located on the left-hand side of the engine compartment, and the pump and motor is fitted to the side of the reservoir (photo).
2   The reservoir should be regularly topped up with the recommended washer fluid.
3   To adjust the jets for the windscreen washer, use a needle to direct the spray into the centre of the wiped area. A special tool (VW tool 3019 A) is necessary to direct the headlight washer spray to the centre of the headlights although a needle may be used as an alternative.

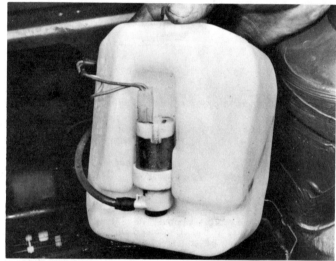

34.1 Showing windscreen washer fluid reservoir and pump

35 Radios and tape players – installation

A radio or tape player is an expensive item to buy; and will only give its best performance if fitted properly. It is useless to expect concert hall performances from a unit that is suspended from the dashpanel by string with its speaker resting on the back seat or parcel shelf! If you do not wish to do the installation yourself there are many in-car entertainment specialists who can do the fitting for you.

Make sure the unit purchased is of the same polarity as the vehicle. Ensure that units with adjustable polarity are correctly set before commencing installation.

It is difficult to give specific information with regard to fitting, as final positioning of the radio/tape player, speakers and aerial is entirely a matter of personal preference. However, the following paragraphs give guidelines to follow, which are relevant to all installations.

Radios

Most radios are a standardised size of 7 inches wide, by 2 inches deep – this ensures that they will fit into the radio aperture provided in most cars. If your car does not have such an aperture, then the radio must be fitted in a suitable position either in, or beneath, the dashpanel. Alternatively, a special console can be purchased which will fit between

the dashpanel and the floor, or on the transmission tunnel. These consoles can also be used for additional switches and instrumentation if required. Where no radio aperture is provided, the following points should be borne in mind before deciding exactly where to fit the unit.

(a)   *The unit must be within easy reach of the driver wearing a seatbelt.*
(b)   *The unit must not be mounted in close proximity to a tachometer, the ignition switch and its wiring, or the flasher unit and associated wiring.*
(c)   *The unit must be mounted within reach of the aerial lead, and in such a place that the aerial lead will not have to be routed near the components detailed in the preceding paragraph 'b'.*
(d)   *The unit should not be positioned in a place where it might cause injury to the car occupants in an accident; for instance, under the dashpanel above the driver's or passenger's legs.*
(e)   *The unit must be fitted really securely.*

Some radios will have mounting brackets provided together with instructions: others will need to be fitted using drilled and slotted metal strips, bent to form mounting brackets – these strips are available from most accessory stores. The unit must be properly earthed, by fitting a separate earth lead between the casing of the radio and the vehicle frame.

Use the radio manufacturer's instructions when wiring the radio into the vehicle's electrical system. If no instructions are available, refer to the relevant wiring diagram to find the location of the radio 'feed' connection in the vehicle's wiring circuit. A 1–2 amp 'in-line' fuse must be fitted in the radio's 'feed' wire – a choke may also be necessary (see next Section).

The type of aerial used, and its fitted position is a matter of personal preference. In general the taller the aerial, the better the reception. It is best to fit a fully retractable aerial – especially, if a mechanical car-wash is used or if you live in an area where cars tend to be vandalised. In this respect electric aerials which are raised and lowered automatically when switching the radio on or off, are convenient, but are more likely to give trouble than the manual type.

When choosing a site for the aerial the following points should be considered:

(a) *The aerial lead should be as short as possible; this means that the aerial should be mounted at the front of the vehicle.*

(b) *The aerial must be mounted as far away from the distributor and HT leads as possible.*

(c) *The part of the aerial which protrudes beneath the mounting point must not foul the roadwheels, or anything else.*

(d) *If possible the aerial should be positioned so that the coaxial lead does not have to be routed through the engine compartment.*

(e) *The plane of the panel on which the aerial is mounted should not be so steeply angled that the aerial cannot be mounted vertically (in relation to the 'end-on' aspect of the vehicle). Most aerials have a small amount of adjustment available.*

Having decided on a mounting position, a relatively large hole will have to be made in the panel. The exact size of the hole will depend upon the specific aerial being fitted, although, generally, the hole required is of ¾ inch diameter. On metal bodied cars, a 'tank-cutter' of the relevant diameter is the best tool to be used for making the hole. This tool needs a small diameter pilot hole drilled through the panel, through which, the tool clamping bolt is inserted. On GRP bodied cars, a 'hole saw' is the best tool to use. Again, this tool will require the drilling of a small pilot hole. When the hole has been made the raw edges should be de-burred with a file and then painted, to prevent corrosion.

Fit the aerial according to the manufacturer's instructions. If the aerial is very tall, or if it protrudes beneath the mounting panel for a considerable distance it is a good idea to fit a stay between the aerial and the vehicle frame. This stay can be manufactured from the slotted and drilled metal strips previously mentioned. The stay should be securely screwed or bolted in place. For best reception it is advisable to fit an earth lead between the aerial body and the vehicle frame – this is essential on fibre glass bodied vehicles.

It will probably be necessary to drill one, or two holes through bodywork panels in order to feed the aerial lead into the interior of the car. Where this is the case ensure that the holes are fitted with rubber grommets to protect the cable, and to stop possible entry of water.

Positioning and fitting of the speaker depends mainly on its type. Generally, the speaker is designed to fit directly into the aperture already provided in the car (usually in the shelf behind the rear seats, or in the top of the dashpanel). Where this is the case, fitting the speaker is just a matter of removing the protective grille from the aperture and screwing or bolting the speaker in place. Take great care not to damage the speaker diaphragm whilst doing this. It is a good idea to fit a 'gasket' between the speaker frame and the mounting panel in order to prevent vibration – some speakers will already have such a gasket fitted.

If a 'pod' type speaker was supplied with the radio, the best acoustic results will normally be obtained by mounting it on the shelf behind the rear seat. The pod can be secured to the mounting panel with self-tapping screws.

When connecting a rear mounted speaker to the radio, the wires should be routed through the vehicle beneath the carpets or floor mats preferably through the middle, or along the side of the floorpan, where they will not be trodden on by passengers. Make the relevant connections as directed by the radio manufacture.

By now you will have several yards of additional wiring in the car; use PVC tape to secure this wiring out of harm's way. Do not leave electrical leads dangling. Ensure that all new electrical connections are properly made (wires twisted together will not do) and completely secure.

The radio should now be working, but before you pack away your tools it will be necessary to 'trim' the radio to the aerial. Follow the radio manufacturer's instructions regarding this adjustment.

Tape players

Fitting instructions for both cartridge and cassette stereo tape players are the same and in general the same rules apply as when fitting a radio. Tape players are not usually prone to electrical interference like radio – although it can occur – so positioning is not so critical. If possible the player should be mounted on an 'even-keel'. Also, it must be possible for a driver wearing a seatbelt to reach the unit in order to change, or turn over, tapes.

For the best results from speakers designed to be recessed into a panel, mount them so that the back of the speaker protrudes into an enclosed chamber within the vehicle (eg; door interiors or the boot cavity).

To fit recessed type speakers in the front doors first check that there is sufficient room to mount the speaker in each door without it fouling the latch or window winding mechanism. Hold the speaker against the skin of the door, and draw a line, around the periphery of the speaker. With the speaker removed draw a second 'cutting' line, within the first, to allow enough room for the entry of the speaker back but at the same time providing a broad seat for the speaker flange. When you are sure that the 'cutting-line' is correct, drill a series of holes around its periphery. Pass a hacksaw blade through one of the holes and then cut through the metal between the holes until the centre section of the panels falls out.

De-burr the edges of the hole and then paint the raw metal to prevent corrosion. Cut a corresponding hole in the door trim panel ensuring that it will be completely covered by the speaker grille. Now drill a hole in the door edge and a corresponding hole in the door surround. These holes are to feed the speaker leads through – so fit grommets. Pass the speaker leads through the door trim, door skin and out through the holes in the side of the door and door surround. Refit the door trim panel and then secure the speaker to the door using self-tapping screws. **Note:** If the speaker is fitted with a shield to prevent water dripping on it, ensure that this shield is at the top.

'Pod' type speakers can be fastened to the shelf behind the rear seat, or anywhere else offering a corresponding mounting point on each side of the car. If the 'pod' speakers are mounted on each side of the shelf behind the rear seat, it is a good idea to drill several large diameter holes through to the trunk cavity, beneath each speaker – this will improve the sound reproduction. 'Pod' speakers sometimes offer a better reproduction quality if they face the rear window – which then acts as a reflector – so it is worthwhile experimenting before finally fixing the speakers.

36 Radios and tape players – suppression of interference (general)

To eliminate buzzes, and other unwanted noises, costs very little and is not as difficult as sometimes thought. With a modicum of common sense and patience and following the instructions in the following paragraphs, interference can be virtually eliminated.

The first cause for concern is the generator. The noise this makes over the radio is like an electric mixer and the noise speeds up when you rev up the engine (if you wish to prove this, you can remove the fanbelt and try it). The remedy for this is simple; connect a 1.0 mf–3.0 mf capacitor between earth, probably the bolt that holds down the generator base, and the *output* terminal on the alternator. This is most important, for if you connect it to the other terminal you will probably damage the generator permanently (see Fig. 9.12).

A second common cause of electrical interference is the ignition system. Here a 1.0 mf capacitor must be connected between earth and the SW or + terminal on the coil (see Fig 9.13). This may stop the tick-tick sound that comes over the speaker. Next comes the spark itself.

There are several ways of curing interference from the ignition HT system. One is the use of carbon-cored HT leads as original equipment. Where copper cable is substituted then you must use resistive spark plug caps (see Fig. 9.14) of about 10 000 ohm to 15 000 ohm resistance. If, due to lack of room, these cannot be used, an alternative is to use 'in-line' suppressors – if the interference is not too bad, you may get away with only one suppressor in the coil to distributor line. If the interference does continue (a 'clacking' noise) then modify all HT leads.

At this stage it is advisable to check that the radio is well earthed, also the aerial and to see that the aerial plug is pushed well into the set and that the radio is properly trimmed (see preceding Section). In addition, check that the wire which supplies the power to the set is as short as possible and does not wander all over the car. At this stage it is

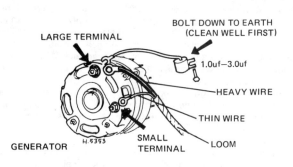

Fig. 9.12 The correct way to connect a capacitor to the alternator
(Sec 36)

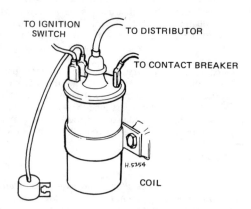

Fig. 9.13 The capacitor must be connected to the ignition switch
side of the coil

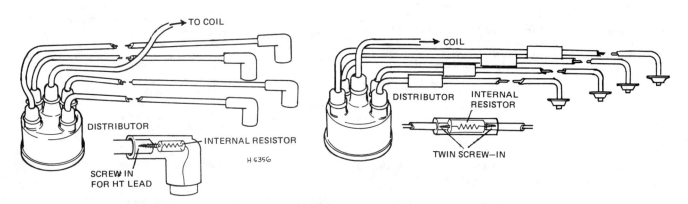

Fig. 9.14 Ignition HT lead suppressors

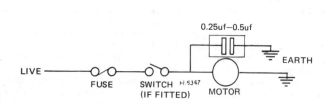

Fig. 9.15 Correct method of suppressing electric motors

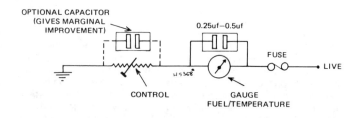

Fig. 9.16 Method of suppressing gauges and their control units

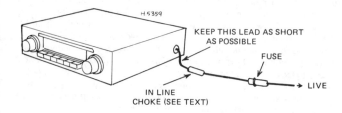

Fig. 9.17 An 'in-line' choke should be fitted into the drive supply
lead as close to the unit as possible

a good idea to check that the fuse is of the correct rating. For most sets this will be about 1 to 2 amps.

At this point the more usual causes of interference have been suppressed. If the problem still exists, a look at the cause of interference may help to pinpoint the component generating the stray electrical discharges.

The radio picks up electromagnetic waves in the air; now some are made by regular broadcasters, and some, which we do not want, are made by the car itself. The home made signals are produced by stray electrical discharges floating around in the car. Common producers of these signals are electrical motors, ie, the windscreen wipers, electric screen washers, electric window winders, heater fan or an electric aerial if fitted. Other sources of interference are flashing turn signals and instruments. The remedy for these is shown in Fig. 9.15 for an electric motor whose interference is not too bad and Fig. 9.16 for instrument suppression. Turn signals are not normally suppressed. In recent years, radio manufacturers have included in the line (live) of the radio, in addition to the fuse, an 'in-line' choke. If your circuit lacks one of these, put one in as shown in Fig. 9.17.

All the foregoing components are available from radio stores or accessory stores. If you have an electric clock fitted this should be suppressed by connecting a 0.5 mf capacity directly across it as shown for a motor in Fig. 9.15.

If after all this, you are still experiencing radio interference, first assess how bad it is, for the human ear can filter out unobtrusive unwanted noises quite easily. But if you are still adamant about eradicating the noise, then continue.

As a first step, a few 'experts' seem to favour a screen between the radio and the engine. This is OK as far as it goes – literally! – for the whole set is screened anyway and if interference can get past that then a small piece of aluminium is not going to stop it.

A more sensible way of screening is to discover if interference is coming down the wires. First, take the live lead; interference can get between the set and the choke (hence the reason for keeping the wires short). One remedy here is to screen the wire and this is done by buying screened wire and fitting that. The loudspeaker lead could be screened also to prevent 'pick-up' getting back to the radio although this is unlikely.

Without doubt, the worst source of radio interference comes from the ignition HT leads, even if they have been suppressed. The ideal way of suppressing these is to slide screening tubes over the leads themselves. As this is impractical, we can place an aluminium shield over the majority of the lead areas. In a vee- or twin-cam engine this is relatively easy but for a straight engine, the results are not particularly good.

Now for the really impossible cases, here are a few tips to try out. Where metal comes into contact with metal, an electrical disturbance is caused which is why good clean connections are essential. To remove interference due to overlapping or butting panels you must bridge the join with a wide braided earth strap (like that from the frame to the engine/transmission). The most common moving parts that could create noise and should be strapped are, in order of importance:

(a) Silencer to frame
(b) Exhaust pipe to engine block and frame
(c) Air cleaner to frame
(d) Front and rear bumpers to frame
(e) Steering column to frame
(f) Bonnet and boot lids to frame
(g) Hood frame to body frame on soft tops

These faults are most pronounced when (1) the engine is idling, (2) labouring under load. Although the moving parts are already connected with nuts, bolts, etc, these do tend to rust and corrode, thus creating a high resistance interference source.

If you have a 'ragged' sounding pulse when mobile, this could be wheel or tyre static. This can be cured by buying some anti-static powder and sprinkling inside the tyres.

If the interference takes the shape of a high pitched screeching noise that changes its note when the car is in motion and only comes now and then, this could be related to the aerial, especially if it is of the telescopic or whip type. This source can be cured quite simply by pushing a small rubber ball on top of the aerial as this breaks the electric field before it can form; but it would be much better to buy yourself a new aerial of a reputable brand. If, on the other hand, you are getting a loud rushing sound every time you brake, then this is brake static. This effect is most prominent on hot dry days and is cured only by fitting a special kit, which is quite expensive.

In conclusion, it is pointed out that it is relatively easy, and therefore cheap, to eliminate 95 per cent of all noise, but to eliminate the final 5 per cent is time and money consuming. It is up to the individual to decide if it is worth it. Please remember also, that you cannot get a concert hall performance out of a cheap radio.

Finally, players and eight track players are not usually affected by car noise but in a very bad case, the best remedies are the first three suggestions plus using a 3–5 amp choke in the 'live' line and in incurable cases screen the live and speaker wires.

Note: If your car is fitted with electronic ignition, then it is not recommended that either the spark plug resistors or the ignition coil capacitor be fitted as these may damage the system. Most electronic ignition units have built-in suppression and should, therefore, not cause interference.

37 Gearchange and consumption gauge – general

1 On Formel E models a gearchange and consumption gauge is fitted in the instrument panel in place of the coolant temperature gauge.

2 The gearchange indicator lights up in all gears except top gear, when better economy without loss of power can be obtained by changing up to a higher gear. The indicator does not operate during acceleration or deceleration, or with the choke knob pulled out.

3 The consumption gauge operates only in top gear and it indicates the actual fuel consumption in mpg.

4 The gearchange and consumption gauge is operated by a switch on the gearbox and a sender in the vacuum line to the distributor (photos).

37.4A Fuel consumption gauge sender unit

37.4B Disconnecting the wiring from the fuel consumption gauge sender unit

38 Fault diagnosis – electrical system

Symptom	Reason(s)
Starter fails to turn engine	Battery discharged or defective Battery terminal and/or earth leads loose Starter motor connections loose Starter solenoid faulty Starter brushes worn or sticking Starter commutator dirty or worn Starter field coils earthed
Starter turns engine very slowly	Battery discharged Starter motor connections loose Starter brushes worn or sticking
Starter noisy	Pinion or flywheel ring gear badly worn Mounting bolts loose
Battery will not hold charge	Battery defective Electrolyte level too low Battery terminals loose Alternator drivebelt slipping Alternator or regulator faulty Short circuit in wiring
Ignition light stays on	Alternator faulty Alternator drivebelt faulty
Ignition light fails to come on	Warning bulb blown Alternator faulty
Fuel and temperature readings increase with engine speed	Voltage stabiliser faulty
Lights inoperative	Fuse blown Bulb blown Switch faulty Connections or wiring faulty
Failure of component motor	Commutator dirty or burnt Armature faulty Brushes sticking or worn Armature bearings seized Fuse blown
Failure of individual component	Wiring loose or broken Fuse blown Switch faulty Component faulty

Key to Fig. 9.18

Designation		In current track
A	– Battery	5
B	– Starter	9-11
C	– Alternator	6-8
C1	– Voltage regulator	6-8
D	– Ignition/starter switch	11-13
E9	– Fresh air blower switch	39-41
E22	– Intermittent wiper switch	30-33
F1	– Oil pressure switch	46
F4	– Reversing light switch	21
F9	– Handbrake warning system switch	43
F12	– Choke warning system contact	45
F34	– Brake fluid level warning contact	42
G	– Fuel gauge sender	47
G1	– Fuel gauge	47
G2	– Coolant temperature gauge sender	48
G3	– Coolant temperature gauge	48
G5	– Rev. counter	12
H	– Horn control	25
H1	– Horn (Dual horns)*	22, 23
J4	– Dual tone horn relay*	22-25
J6	– Voltage stabiliser	50
J30	– Rear window wiper/washer relay	33, 34
J31	– Intermittent wash/wiper relay	31, 32
J39	– Headlight washer system relay	1-4
K1	– Main beam warning lamp	51
K2	– Generator warning lamp	44
K3	– Oil pressure warning lamp	46
K5	– Turn signal warning lamp	52
K14	– Handbrake warning lamp	43
K15	– Choke warning lamp	45
K28	– Coolant temperature warning lamp (overheating, red)	49
M17	– Reversing light bulb, right	21
N	– Coil	14
N3	– By-pass air cut-off valve	20
N6	– Resistance wire	14
N23	– Series resistance for fresh air blower	39
N52	– Heat resistance (part throttle channel heating/carburettor)	18
O	– Ignition distributor	14-17
P	– Spark plug connector	15-17
Q	– Spark plugs	15-17
S1, S2, S9, S10 S14, S15	– Fuses in relay plate/fuse box	
T1	– Connector, single, near carburettor	
T1a	– Connector, single, in passenger compartment, front left	

Designation		In current track
T1b	– Connector, single, near carburettor	
T1c	– Connector, single, in engine compartment, centre	
T1f	– Connector, single, near carburettor	
T1g	– Connector, single, behind instrument panel	
T1h	– Connector, single, in plenum chamber, near fuse box	
T2b	– Connector, 2 point, behind radiator grille, right	
T2c	– Connector, 2 point, in tailgate near wiper motor	
T2d	– Connector, 2 point, in tailgate near wiper motor	
T2f	– Connector, 2 point, in luggage boot, rear centre	
T8/	– Connector, 8 point on fuse box	
T12/	– Connector, 12 point, in plenum chamber, near fuse box	
T14/	– Connector, 14 point, on dash panel insert	
T20	– Connector, 20 point, on fuse box	
T20a/	– Connector, 20 point, on fuse box	
T29/	– Connector, 29 point, behind instrument panel	
T32/	– Connector, 32 point, on fuse box	
V	– Windscreen wiper motor	28-31
V2	– Fresh air blower	41
V5	– Windscreen washer pump	37
V11	– headlight washer pump	4
V12	– Rear wiper motor	34, 35
V13	– Rear washer pump motor	36
①	– Earthing strap, from battery via body to gearbox	
②	– Earthing strap, from engine to body	
⑩	– Earthing point, on taillight, left	
⑪	– Earthing point, under rear seat	
⑬	– Earthing point, on fuel pump	
⑮	– Earthing point, in wiring loom insulating hose, engine compartment, left	
⑯	– Earthing point, in wiring loom insulating hose, engine compartment, right	
⑰	– Earthing point, bound with insulating tape, in instrument panel loom	
⑧	– Earthing point, bound with insulating tape, in instrument panel loom	

*GL model only

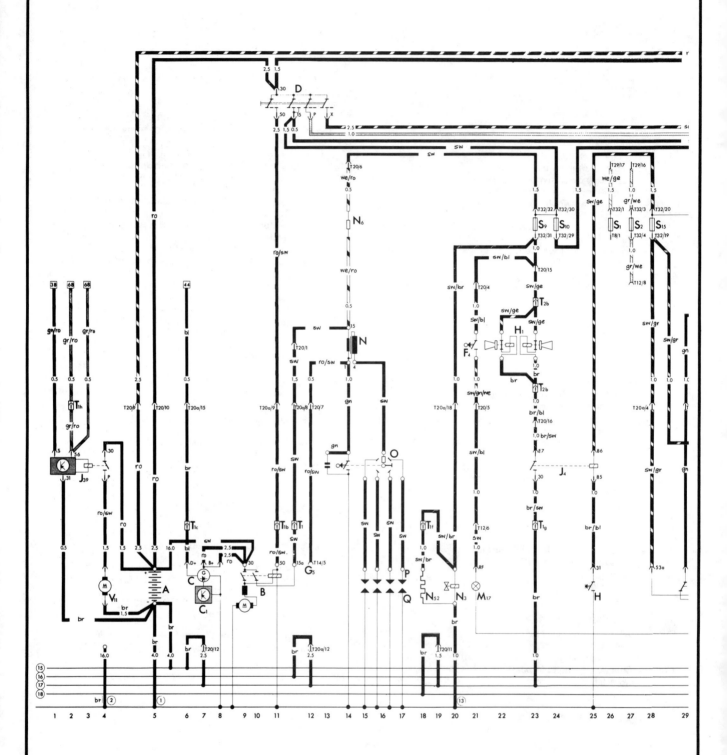

Fig. 9.18 Wiring diagram for 1982 CL and GL models

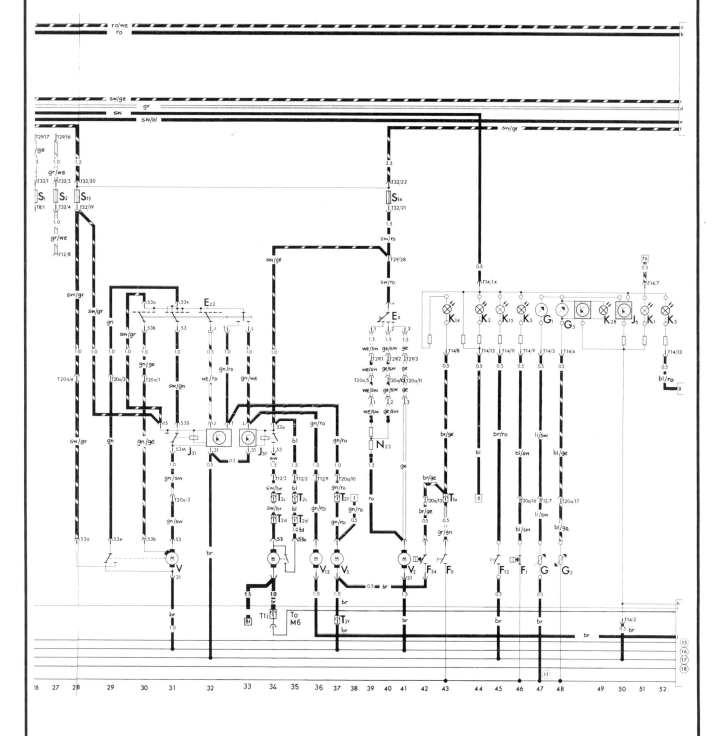

Fig. 9.18 Wiring diagram for 1982 CL and GL models (continued)

NB: Refer to Fig. 12.35 in Chapter 12 for an amendment to this diagram

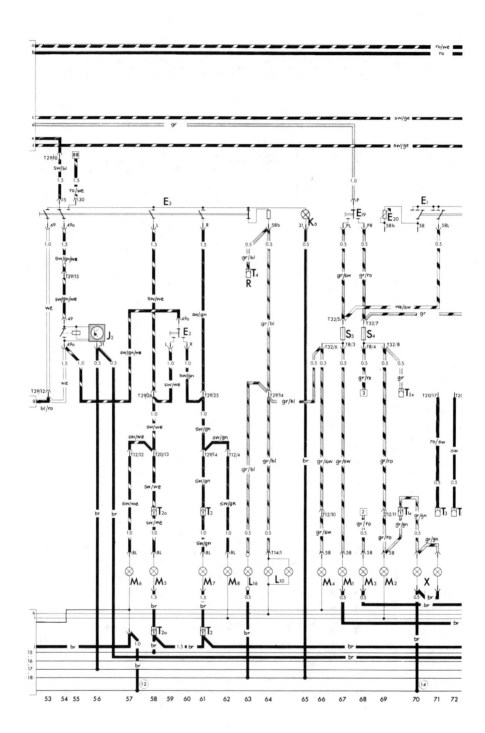

Fig. 9.18 Wiring diagram for 1982 CL and GL models (continued)

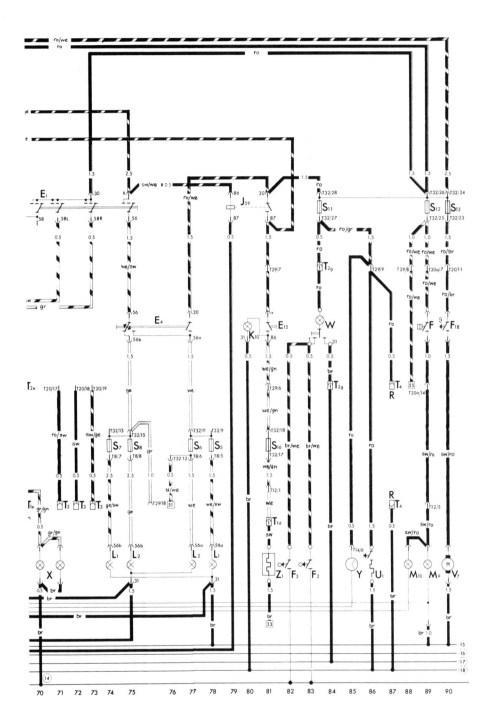

Fig. 9.18 Wiring diagram for 1982 CL and GL models (continued)

Key to Fig. 9.18 (continued)

Designation		In current track
E1	– Lighting switch	69-75
E2	– Turn signal switch	59, 60
E3	– Emergency light switch	53-65
E4	– Headlight dimmer/flasher switch	75-77
E15	– Heated rear window switch	81
E19	– Parking light switch (in turn signal switch)	67, 68
E20	– Instrument/instrument panel lighting control	69
F	– Brake light switch	89
F2	– Front left door contact switch	83
F3	– Front right door contact switch	82
F18	– Radiator fan thermo switch	90
J2	– Emergency light relay	54-56
J59	– Relief relay (for X contact)	79-81
K6	– Emergency light system warning lamp	65
K10	– Heated rear window warning lamp	80
L1	– 2 filament headlight bulb, left	74, 78
L2	– 2 filament headlight bulb, right	75, 77
L10	– Instrument panel insert light	64
L16	– Fresh air controls light	63
M1	– Side light, left	67
M2	– Tail light, right	69
M3	– Side light, right	68
M4	– Tail light, left	66
M5	– Front left turn signal	58
M6	– Rear left turn signal	57
M7	– Front right turn signal	61
M8	– Rear right turn signal	62
M9	– Brake light, left	89
M10	– Brake light, right	88
R	– Radio connection	63
S3-S8		
S11-S13	– Fuses in relay plate/fuse box	
S16		
T1d	– Connector, single, in luggage boot rear left	
T1e	– Connector, single, on rear apron	
T2	– Connector, 2 point, in engine compartment, right, near headlight	
T2a	– Connector, 2 point, in engine compartment, left, near headlight	
T2e	– Connector, 2 point, in plenum chamber, near fuse box	
T2g	– Connector, 2 point, on A pillar, left, near fuse box	
T3	– Connector, 3 point, in plenum chamber, near fuse box	
T4	– Connector, 4 point, behind instrument panel	
T8/	– Connector, 8 point, on fuse box	
T12/	– Connector, 12 point, behind instrument panel	
T14/	– Connector, 14 point, on instrument panel insert	
T20/	– Connector, 20 point, on fuse box	
T20a/	– Connector, 20 point, on fuse box	
T29/	– Connector, 29 point, behind instrument panel	
T32/	– Connector, 32 point, on fuse box	
U1	– Cigarette lighter	86
V7	– Radiator fan	90
W	– Interior light, front	83, 84
X	– Number plate light	70, 71
Y	– Clock	85
Z1	– Heated rear window	81
⑫	– Earthing point on rear apron, left	
⑭	– Earthing point, on tailgate lock carrier	
⑮	– Earthing point in wiring loom insulating hose, engine compartment, left	
⑯	– Earthing point in wiring loom insulating hose, engine compartment, right	
⑰	– Earthing point, bound with insulating tape, in instrument panel loom	
⑱	– Earthing point, bound with insulating tape, in instrument panel loom	

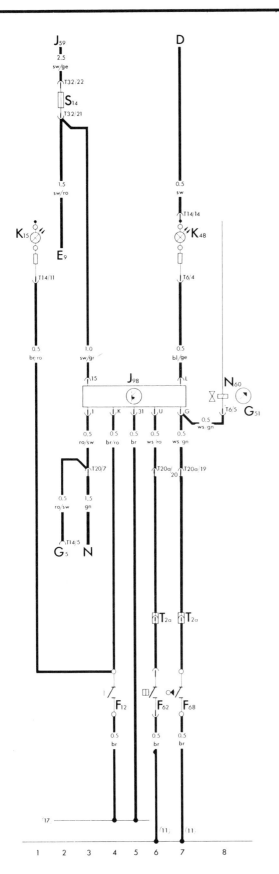

Key to Fig. 9.19

Designation		In current track
D	– to ignition switch, terminal 15	7
E9	– to fresh air blower switch	2
F12	– Contact for choke warning lamp	4
F62	– Vacuum switch for gearchange indicator	6
F68	– Gear switch for GC1	7
G5	– Connection for rev counter	2
G51	– Consumption indicator	8
J59	– to relief relay (for X contact)	2
J98	– Control unit for gearchange indicator	3-7
K15	– Choke warning lamp	1
K48	– Gearchange indicator lamp	7
N	– to ignition coil, terminal 1	3
N60	– Solenoid valve for consumption indicator	8
S14	– Fuse in fuse box	
T2a	– Connector 2 pin, on right in engine compartment	
T6/	– Connector 6 pin on dash insert	
T14/	– Connector 14 pin on dash insert	
T20/	– Connector 20 pin on fuse box	
T20a/	– Connector 20 pin on fuse box	
T32/	– Connector 32 pin on fuse box	

⑪ Earth point on thermostat housing

⑰ Earth point bound with insulating tape in dash loom

Wire colours

br –	brown
ro –	red
sw –	black
gn –	green
ge –	yellow
ws –	white
gr –	grey
bl –	blue

Fig. 9.19 Additional wiring diagram for gearchange and consumption indicator on Formel E models
October 1981 to December 1983

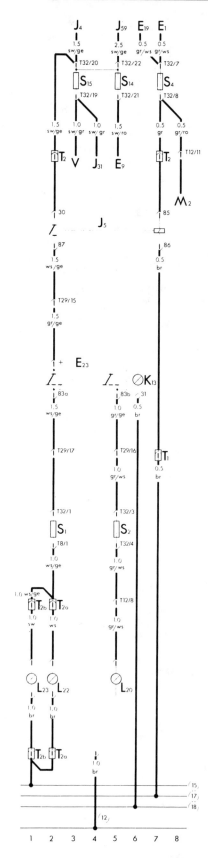

Key to Fig. 9.20

Designation		In current track
E1	– to light switch, terminal 58R	7
E9	– to fresh air blower switch	5
E19	– to parking light switch, terminal PR	6
E23	– Fog and rear fog light switch	2–5
J4	– to dual horn relay	3
J5	– Fog light relay	2–7
J31	– Wash-wiper intermittent relay, terminal 15	4
J59	– to relief relay (for X contact)	5
K13	– Rear fog light warning lamp	6
L20	– Rear fog light	5
L22	– Fog light left	2
L23	– Fog light right	1
M2	– to taillight right	8
S1, S2, S4	– Fuses in fuse box	
S14, S15		
T1	– Connector single, behind dash	
T2	– Connector 2 pin, behind dash	
T2a	– Connector 2 pin, engine compartment front left	
T2b	– Connector 2 pin, engine compartment front right	
T8/	– Connector 8 pin, on fuse box	
T12/	– Connector 12 pin, behind dash	
T29/	– Connector 29 pin, behind dash	
T32/	– Connector 32 pin, on fuse box	
V	– to wiper motor	3

⑫ Earth point, on rear apron left

⑮ Earth point, in insulating sleeve of engine compartment loom left

⑰ Earth point, bound with insulating tape in dash loom

⑱ Earth point, bound with insulating tape in instrument loom

Wire colours

sw = black
ge = yellow
gr = grey
ro = red
ws = white
br = brown

**Fig. 9.20 Additional wiring diagram for fog lights
October 1981 to July 1983**

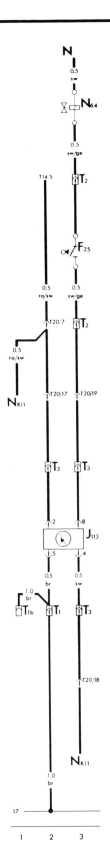

Key to Fig. 9.21

Designation		In current track
F25	– Throttle valve switch	3
J113	– Speed switch for spark control	2, 3
N	– to ignition coil terminal 1, 15	1, 3
N64	– Two way valve for spark control	3
T1	– Connector, single in plenum chamber near fuse box	
T1b	– Connector, single in plenum chamber near fuse box	
T2	– Connector, 2 pin, in centre of engine compartment on partition	
T3	– Connector, 3 pin, in plenum chamber near fuse box	
T14/	– Connector, 14 pin, on dash insert	
T20/	– Connector, 20 pin, on fuse box	
⑰	– Earth point, bound with insulating tape in dash loom	

Wire colours

sw – black
ge – yellow
ro – red
br – brown

Fig. 9.21 Additional wiring diagram for spark control on the
1.05 litre engine

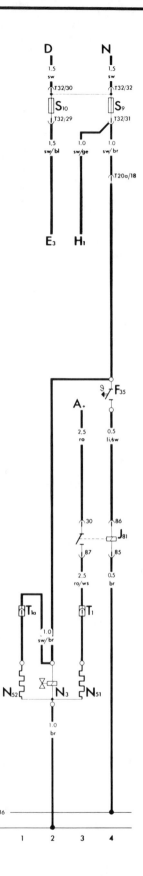

Key to Fig. 9.22

Designation		In current track
A	– to battery	3
D	– to ignition switch, terminal 15	2
E3	– to emergency light switch, terminal 15	2
E35	– Thermoswitch for intake manifold preheating	4
H1	– to double horn	3
J81	– Relay for intake manifold preheating	3, 4
N	– to ignition coil, terminal 15	4
N3	– Bypass air cut-off valve	2
N51	– Heater element for intake manifold preheating	3
N52	– Heater element (Part throttle drilling heating – carburetor)	1
S9, S10,	– Fuses in fuse box	
T1	– Connector single, in engine compartment near intake manifold	
T1a	– Connector single, in engine compartment on right near bypass air cut-off valve	
T20a/	– Connector, 20 pin on fuse box	
T32/	– Connector, 32 pin on fuse box	
⑯	– Earth point in insulating sleeve of engine compartment loom right	

Wire colours

sw =	black
bl =	blue
ge =	yellow
br =	brown
ro =	red
ws =	white
li =	lilac

Fig. 9.22 Additional wiring diagram for inlet manifold preheating on the 1.05 litre engine

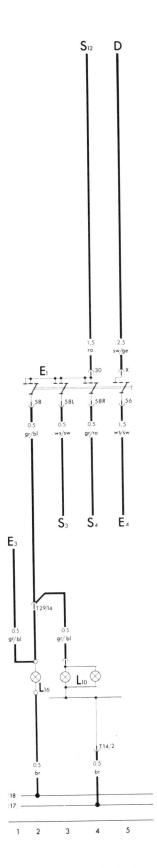

Key to Fig. 9.23

Note:
The wiring of the instrument lights shown in Fig. 9.18 (current tracks 63, 64 and 66) is replaced by this diagram.

Designation		In current track
D	– to ignition switch terminal X	6
E1	– Light switch	2-6
E3	– to emergency light switch, terminal 58b	1
E4	– to headlight dip/flasher switch terminal 56	6
L10	– Instrument light	3, 4
L16	– Fresh air control light	2
S3, S4, S12	– Fuses in fuse box	
T14/	– Connector, 14 pin, on dash insert	
T29/	– Connector, 29 pin, behind dash	

17 – Earth point bound with insulating tape in dash loom

18 – Earth point bound with insulating tape in instrument loom.

Wire colours

ro = red
sw = black
ge = yellow
gr = grey
bl = blue
ws = white
br = brown

Fig. 9.23 Additional wiring diagram for instrument lighting

Key to Fig. 9.24

Designation		in current track
A	Battery	2
B	Starter	6,7
C	Alternator	4,5
C1	Voltage regulator	4,5
D	Ignition/starter switch	7-10
E9	Fresh air blower switch	39-41
E22	Intermittent wiper switch	29-34
F1	Oil pressure switch (1.8 bar)	47
F4	Reversing light switch	17
F9	Handbrake warning system switch*	42
F12	Choke warning system contact	44
F22	Oil pressure switch (0.3 bar)	48
F34	Brake fluid level warning contact*	43
G	Fuel gauge sender	50
G1	Fuel gauge	50
G2	Coolant temperature gauge sender or gearchange/consumption sensors	51
G3	Coolant temperature gauge or gearchange/consumption gauge	51
H	Horn plate	19
H1	Horn	19
J6	Voltage stabiliser	53
J30	Rear window wiper/washer relay	34,35
J31	Intermittent wash/wipe relay	30-33
J114	Oil pressure monitor control unit	46-48
K1	Main beam warning lamp	54
K2	Generator warning lamp	45
K3	Oil pressure warning lamp	49
K5	Turn signal warning lamp	55
K14	Handbrake warning lamp*	43
K15	Starting device warning lamp	44
K28	Coolant temp. warning lamp (overheating, red)	52
L9	Lighting switch bulb	25
M17	Reversing light bulb right	17
N	Ignition coil	11
N3	By-pass air cut-off valve	16
N6	Resistance/resistance wire	21
N23	Series resistance for fresh air blower	39,40
N52	Heat resistance (part throttle channel heating/carburettor)	14
O	Ignition distributor	12,13
P	Spark plug connector	12,13
Q	Spark plugs	12,13

S1,S2,S9,S10,S14,S15 - Fuses in relay plate/fuse box

T1	Connector, single, in engine compartment, centre	
T1a	Connector, single, near carburettor	
T1b	Connector, single, behind instrument panel	

Designation		in current track
T1c	Connector, single, in luggage boot, rear left	
T1f	Connector, single, in passenger compartment, front left	
T2	Connector, 2 point, near carburettor	
T2a	Connector, 2 point, in engine compartment, front left	
T2b	Connector, 2 point, behind instrument panel	
T2c	Connector, 2 point, in tailgate near wiper motor	
T2d	Connector, 2 point, in tailgate near wiper motor	
T2f	Connector, 2 point, in luggage boot, rear right	
T2g	Connector, 2 point behind instrument panel	
T3	Connector, 3 point, behind instrument panel	
T8/	Connector, 8 point, on relay plate/fuse box	
T12/	Connector, 12 point, behind instrument panel	
T14/	Connector, 14 point, on instrument panel insert	
T20/	Connector, 20 point, on relay plate/fuse box	
T20a/	Connector, 20 point, on relay plate/fuse box	
T29/	Connector, 29 point, behind instrument panel	
T32/	Connector, 32 point, on relay plate/fuse box	
V	Windscreen wiper motor	26-30
V2	Fresh air blower	41
V5	Windscreen washer pump	35,36
V12	Rear wiper motor	35,36
V13	Rear washer pump motor	37

① Earthing strap from battery to gearbox via body

② Earthing strap from engine to body

⑩ Earthing via, steering gear

⑪ − Earthing point, under rear seat

⑬ − Earthing point, fuel pump

⑭ Earthing point, left hand tail light

⑮ Earthing point, in insulating hose of left hand engine compartment wiring loom

⑯ Earthing point, in insulating hose of right hand engine compartment wiring loom

⑰ Earthing point, bound up with insulating tape in instrument panel wiring loom

⑱ Earthing point, bound up with insulating tape in instrument panel wiring loom

* CL and GL models only

Key to Fig. 9.24 (continued)

Designation		in current track
E1	Lighting switch	77-81
E2	Turn signal switch	62,63
E3	Emergency light switch	56-67
E4	Headlight dimmer/flasher switch	81-83
E15	Heated rear window switch	88
E19	Parking light switch	73,74
E20	Instrument/instrument panel lighting control	75
F	Brake light switch	98
F2	Front left door contact switch	90
F3	Front right door contact switch	89
F18	Radiator fan thermo-switch	99
J2	Emergency light relay	57-59
J59	Relief relay (for X contact)	85-88
K6	Emergency light system warning lamp	71
K10	Heated rear window warning lamp	87
L1	2 filament bulb, left	80,84
L2	2 filament bulb, right	81,83
L10	Instrument panel insert light bulb	68,69
L16	Fresh air controls light bulb	66
L39	Heated rear window switch bulb	86
M1	Side light bulb, left	73
M2	Tail light bulb, right	75
M3	Side light bulb, right	74
M4	Tail light bulb, left	72
M5	Front left turn signal bulb	61
M6	Rear left turn signal bulb	60
M7	Front right turn signal bulb	64
M8	Rear right turn signal bulb	65
M9	Brake light bulb, left	98
M10	Brake light bulb, right	96
R	Radio connection	

S3-S8,S11-S13,S16 - Fuses in relay plate/fuse box

T1e	Connector, single, on rear apron	
T1g	Connector, single, in luggage boot left	
T2b	Connector, 2 point, in plenum chamber, near fuse box	
T2e	Connector, 2 point, in engine compartment, left, near headlight	

Designation		in current track
T2h	Connector, 2 point, in engine compartment, right, near headlight	
T2i	Connector, 2 point, "A" pillar left, near fuse box	
T3	Connector, 3 point, behind instrument panel	
T4	Connector, 4 point, behind instrument panel	
T8/	Connector, 8 point, on relay plate/fuse box	
T12/	Connector, 12 point, behind instrument panel	
T14/	Connector, 14 point, behind instrument panel insert	
T20/	Connector, 20 point, on relay plate/fuse box	
T20a/	Connector, 20 point, on relay plate/fuse box	
T29/	Connector, 29 point, behind instrument panel	
T32	Connector, 32 point, on relay plate/fuse box	
U1	Cigarette lighter**	94
V7	Radiator fan	99
W	Interior light, front	90-92
X	Number plate light	77,78
Y	Clock*	93
Z1	Heated rear window	88

⑫ Earthing point on rear apron

⑭ Earthing point on luggage boot lock carrier plate

⑮ Earthing point in insulation hose of wiring loom in engine compartment left

⑯ Earthing point in insulation hose of wiring loom in engine compartment, right

⑰ Earthing point bound up with insulating tape in instrument panel wiring loom

⑱ Earthing point bound up with insulating tape in instrument panel wiring loom

* CL and GL models only

** GL models only

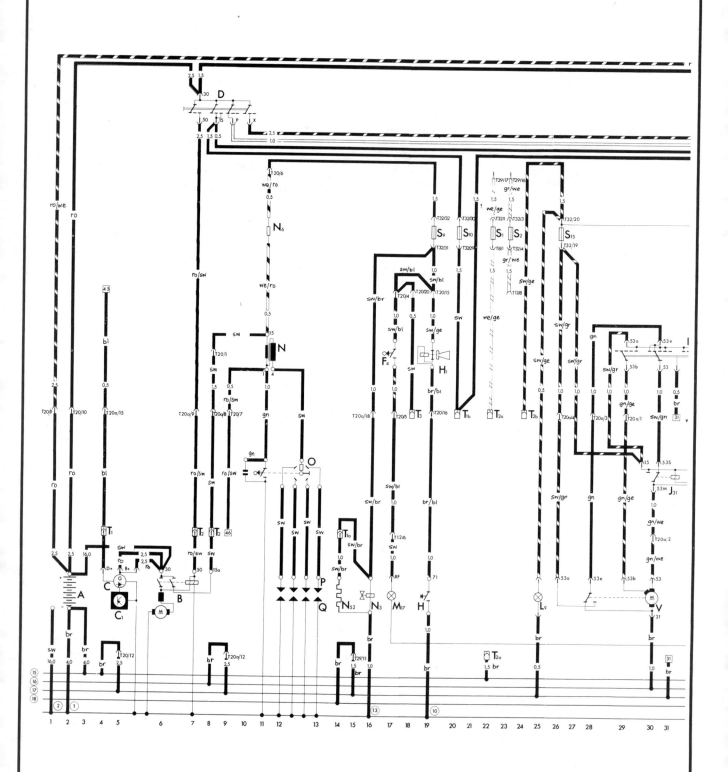

Fig. 9.24 Wiring diagram for 1983 and 1984 C, CL, GL and Coupe models

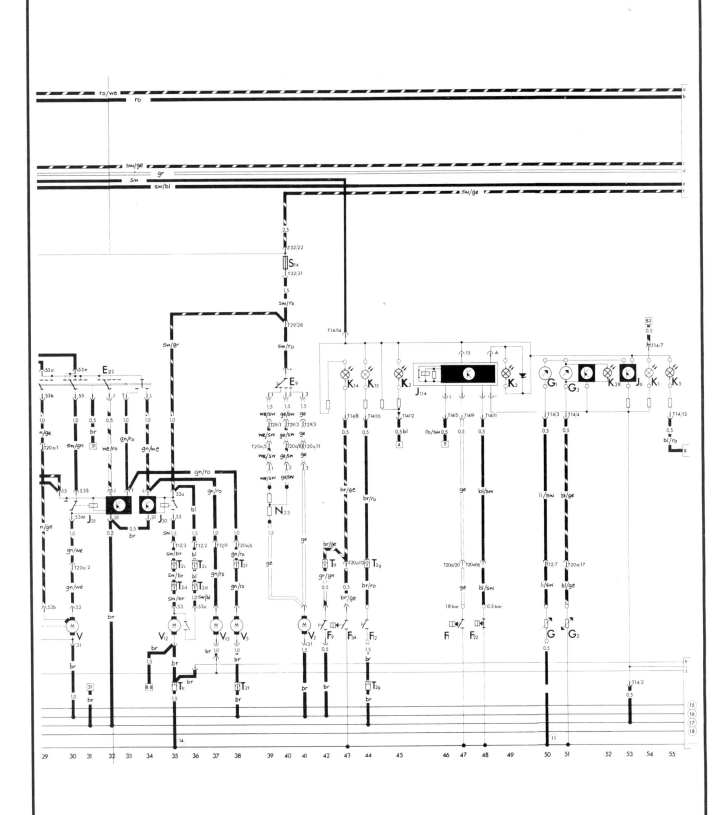

Fig. 9.24 Wiring diagram for 1983 and 1984 C, CL, GL and Coupe models (continued)

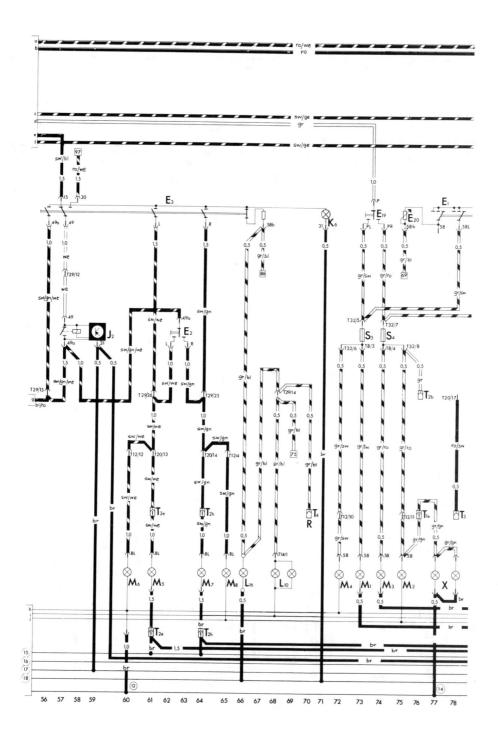

Fig. 9.24 Wiring diagram for 1983 and 1984 C, CL, GL and Coupe models (continued)

155

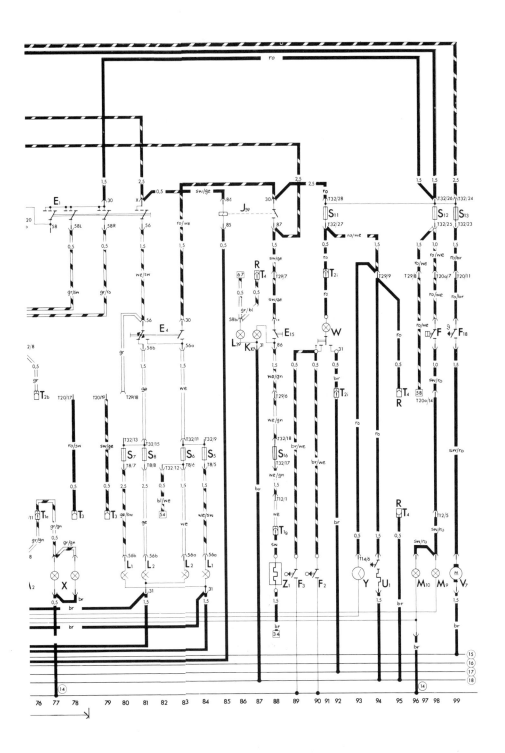

Fig. 9.24 Wiring diagram for 1983 and 1984 C, CL, GL and Coupe models (continued)

Chapter 10 Suspension and steering

For modifications, and information applicable to later models, see Supplement at end of manual

Contents

Specifications

Front suspension

Type .... Independent with spring struts, lower track control arms, and anti-roll bar. Telescopic shock absorbers incorporated in struts

Rear suspension

Type .... Semi-independent incorporating torsion axle beam, trailing arms, and spring struts/shock absorbers

Steering

Type	Rack and pinion with safety column coupling
Steering roll radius	Negative 4.17 mm (0.164 in)
Steering wheel turns lock to lock	3.66
Steering ratio	17.6 to 1

Front wheel alignment

Total toe	0° ± 10′ (0 ± 1 mm/0.04 in)
Camber	+20′ ± 30′
Maximum difference side to side	30′
Castor	2° 20′ ± 30′
Maximum difference side to side	1°

Rear wheel alignment

	To chassis number 86 – CW 028 390	From chassis number 86 – CW 028 391
Total toe	+20′ ± 40′	+25′ ± 15′
Camber	−30′ ± 35′	−1° 40′ ± 20′
Maximum difference side to side	30′	30′

Wheels

Type	Pressed steel disc or alloy
Size:	
Polo, Polo Classic	4½J × 13
Polo Coupé	5½J × 13

Tyres

	Standard	Optional
Size		
Polo, Polo Classic		
29 kW engine	135 SR 13	155/70 SR 13
37 and 44 kW engine	145 SR 13	155/70 SR 13
Polo Coupé	165/65 SR 13	
Pressures – bar (lbf/in²)	Front	Rear
135 SR 13 – half load	1.7 (25)	1.7 (25)
135 SR 13 – full load	1.9 (28)	2.2 (32)
All other sizes – half load	1.6 (23)	1.6 (23)
All other sizes – full load	1.7 (25)	2.1 (30)

Torque wrench settings

	lbf ft	Nm

Front suspension

	lbf ft	Nm
Strut to body	44	60
Shock absorber rod to top mounting	37	50
Strut cap	110	150
Steering knuckle	37	50
Track control arm to body	41	55
Anti-roll bar to control arm	55	75
Anti-roll bar to body	22	30
Anti-roll bar mounting	89	120

Rear suspension

Trailing arm to trunnion	30	40
Trunnion to body	89	120
Stub axle	44	60
Shock absorber to trailing arm	33	45
Shock absorber to body	15	20

Steering

Tie-rod (outer)	26	35
Flange tube	18	25
Column tube	15	20
Steering wheel	30	40
Steering gear	18	25
Tie-rod inner	22	30
Tie-rod carrier	30	40
Tie-rod locknut	30	40

1 General description

The front suspension is of independent type with spring struts, lower track control arms and an anti-roll bar. Each strut incorporates a telescopic shock absorber which can be renewed separately in the event of failure. The track control arms are attached to the wheel bearing housings by balljoints. The pivot points of the struts are positioned to give a negative roll in the interests of steering stability. The anti-roll bar which stabilises the car when cornering, also acts as a radius arm for each track control arm. The front wheel hubs are mounted in twin track ball bearings in the front bearing housings.

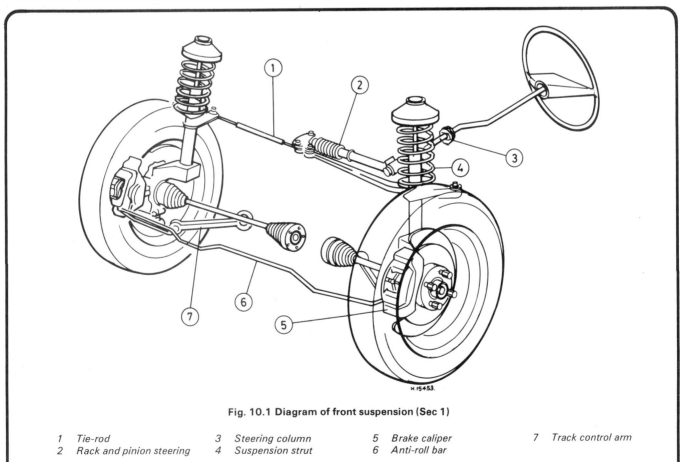

Fig. 10.1 Diagram of front suspension (Sec 1)

1 Tie-rod	3 Steering column	5 Brake caliper	7 Track control arm
2 Rack and pinion steering	4 Suspension strut	6 Anti-roll bar	

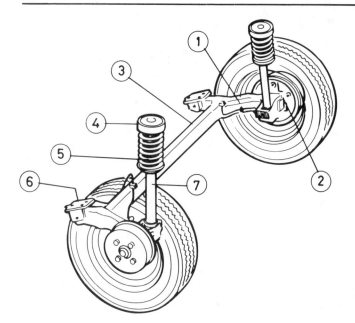

Fig. 10.2 Diagram of rear suspension (Sec 1)

1	Trailing arm	5	Suspension strut
2	Stub axle	6	Trunnion with bonded
3	Axle beam		rubber bush
4	Suspension strut mounting	7	Shock absorber

The rear suspension is of semi-independent type with trailing arms located at each end of the torsion axle beam. The shock absorbers are an integral part of the spring struts. The axle beam is attached to the trailing arms behind the pivot points.

The steering is of rack and pinion type mounted on the front of the bulkhead, and the column coupling consists of two pins which automatically disengage in the event of a severe front end impact.

2 Routine maintenance

1 Every 10000 miles (15000 km) check the tie-rod end balljoints for wear and the dust caps for condition (photo). Renew the balljoints if any play is evident.
2 At the same time check the suspension balljoints for wear and condition of the dust caps. Also check the steering gear bellows.
3 Check the tyres for condition and tread depth.

3 Front suspension strut – removal and refitting

1 Remove the wheel trim from the relevant wheel.
2 With the handbrake applied loosen the driveshaft nut (photo). The nut is tightened to a high torque and a socket extension may be required.
3 Jack up the front of the car and support it on axle stands. Remove the roadwheel.
4 Remove the brake disc and splash plate with reference to Chapter 8.
5 Unscrew the nut securing the tie-rod end to the strut then use a balljoint separator to release the tie-rod.
6 Remove the anti-roll bar as described in Section 8.
7 Unscrew and remove the bolt securing the track control arm to the wheel bearing housing noting that the bolt head faces forward.
8 Push the control arm down to disconnect the balljoint then move the strut sideways.
9 Pull the strut out and at the same time tap the driveshaft through the hub with a mallet.
10 Working in the engine compartment prise the cap from the top of the strut then unscrew the self-locking nut while supporting the strut from below (photos). If necessary hold the shock absorber rod stationary with a spanner.

2.1 Check the tie-rod and balljoint dust caps regularly

3.2 Showing the driveshaft nut

3.10A Removing the front suspension strut top cap

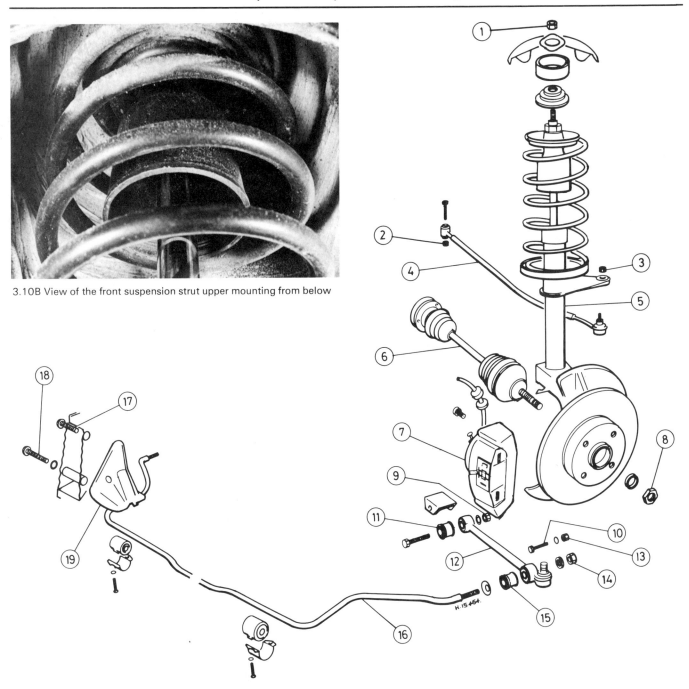

3.10B View of the front suspension strut upper mounting from below

Fig. 10.3 Exploded view of front suspension components (Sec 3)

1	Self-locking nut	6	Driveshaft	11	Inner wishbone bush	16	Anti-roll bar
2	Self-locking nut	7	Brake caliper	12	Wishbone	17	Hexagon bolt
3	Self-locking nut	8	Self-locking nut	13	Self-locking nut	18	Hexagon bolt
4	Tie-rod	9	Self-locking nut	14	Self-locking nut	19	Anti-roll bar locating
5	Suspension strut	10	Hexagon bolt	15	Outer wishbone bush		bracket

11 Lower the strut from under the car.

12 If necessary remove the cups and rubber mountings from the body panel.

13 Refitting is a reversal of removal, but renew the upper rubber mountings if necessary. Refer to Section 8 when refitting the anti-roll bar, Chapter 8 when refitting the brake disc and Chapter 7 when tightening the driveshaft nut. Finally check and if necessary adjust the front wheel tracking as described in Section 21. If difficulty is experienced fitting the upper rubber mounting first dust it with talcum powder.

4 Front coil spring – removal and refitting

1 Remove the front suspension strut as described in Section 3.

2 Using a spring compression tool compress the coil spring until it is clear of the upper retainer. *Do not attempt to use anything other than a purpose made spring compressor tool.*

3 Unscrew the slotted nut from the shock absorber rod and withdraw the spring retainer, washer, bump stop, boot, and coil spring. If a special tool to engage the slotted nut is not available, use a pair of grips.

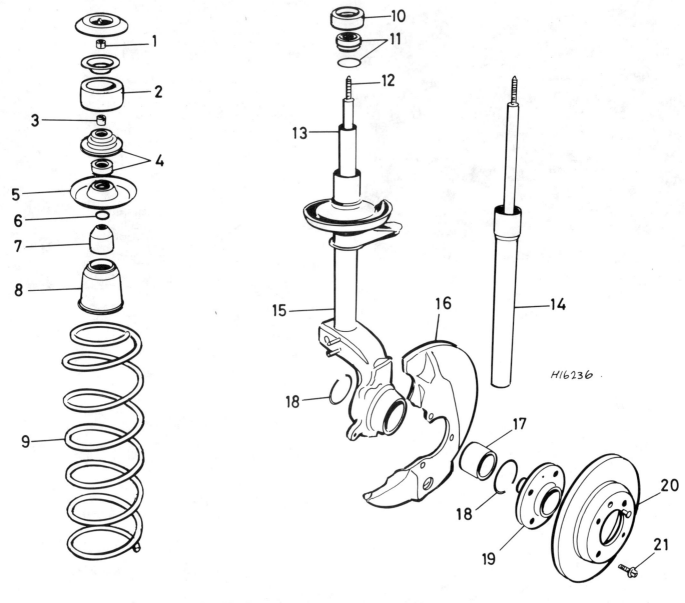

Fig. 10.4 Exploded view of front suspension strut (Sec 4)

1	Self-locking nut	7	Bump stop
2	Damping ring	8	Boot
3	Slotted nut	9	Coil spring
4	Suspension strut bearing	10	Screw cap
5	Spring retainer	11	Piston rod guide seal
6	Washer		

12	Shock absorber	17	Wheel bearing
13	Wet type shock absorber	18	Circlip
14	Shock absorber cartridge	19	Wheel hub
15	Wheel bearing housing	20	Brake disc
16	Splash plate	21	Wheel bolt

4   Remove the compressor tool.

5   Refitting is a reversal of removal with reference to Section 3. Tighten the slotted nut to the specified torque.

5   Front shock absorber – removal and refitting

1   A faulty shock absorber will normally make a knocking noise as the car is driven over rough surfaces. Note that it is normal for a small amount of fluid to be present on the exterior of the shock absorber.

2   To remove the shock absorber first remove the front coil spring as described in Section 4.

3   Using VW tool 40–201 A unscrew the screw cap from the top of the strut and remove the piston rod guide and seal. If necessary first mount the strut in a vice.

4   Pull the shock absorber out of the strut then pour the remaining fluid out and discard it. Clean the inside of the strut with paraffin and wipe dry.

5   Replacement shock absorbers are supplied as dry type cartridges, the wet type are only fitted by the factory when new.

6   With the new shock absorber upright, operate it fully several times and check that the resistance is even without any tight spots.

7   Insert the shock absorber in the strut and fit the guide together with a new seal.

8   Fit the screw cap and tighten it to the specified torque.

9   Refit the coil spring as described in Section 4.

6   Front wheel bearings – testing and renewal

1   Jack up the front of the car and support on axle stands. With neutral selected, spin the wheel. A rumbling noise will be evident if the

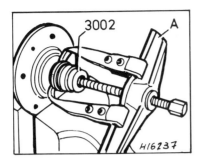

Fig. 10.5 Using a puller to remove the outer wheel bearing race from the hub (Sec 6)

bearings are worn and excessive play will be apparent when the wheel is rocked, however check that the lower balljoint is not responsible for the play.

2 To renew the wheel bearings first remove the suspension strut as described in Section 3.

3 Support the outside of the strut, then using a suitable metal tube, drive the hub from the wheel bearing. The outer bearing race will be forced from the bearing during this procedure and therefore it is not possible to re-use the bearing.

4 Mount the hub in a vice and use a suitable puller to remove the race.

5 Extract the circlips then support the strut again and use a suitable metal tube to drive out the wheel bearing.

6 Clean the inside of the bearing housing in the strut.

7 Fit the outer circlip to the strut.

8 Support the strut then smear a little grease on the bearing contact surfaces and drive in the bearing using a metal tube on the outer race only. Fit the inner circlip.

9 Place the hub upright on the bench and smear a little grease on the bearing contact area.

10 Locate the strut horizontally on the hub, then using a metal tube on the bearing inner race drive the bearing fully onto the hub.

11 Refit the suspension strut as described in Section 3.

7 Front track control arm and balljoint – removal and refitting

1 Jack up the front of the car and support on axle stands. Apply the handbrake and remove the roadwheel.

2 Unscrew the nut and remove the bolt securing the control arm balljoint to the strut. Press the control arm down from the strut. Note that the bolt head faces forward.

3 Unscrew the nut and remove the bolt from the inner end of the control arm. Note that the bolt head faces forward, and also mark its position on the bracket.

4 Press the control arm down from the bracket, then unscrew the nut from the end of the anti-roll bar and pull off the control arm.

5 If the balljoint is worn excessively, renew the complete control arm. Check the condition of the bushes and if necessary press them out using a metal tube, nut and bolt, and washers. Fit the new bushes using the same method, but first dip them in soapy water.

6 Refitting is a reversal of removal, but delay fully tightening the inner pivot bolt and the anti-roll bar nut until the full weight of the car is on the roadwheels. Note that where camber angle adjustment has been made, the bolt hole in the bracket may have been elongated and in this case it is imperative that the bolt is refitted in its original position otherwise the adjustment must be repeated.

8.3 View of an anti-roll bar front mounting from above (engine removed from car)

8 Front anti-roll bar – removal and refitting

1 Jack up the front of the car and support with axle stands. Remove both wheels and apply the handbrake.

2 Note that with the anti-roll bar correctly fitted, the bend in the front of the bar faces upwards.

3 Unscrew the bolts and remove the mounting clamps securing the front of the bar to the underbody (photo).

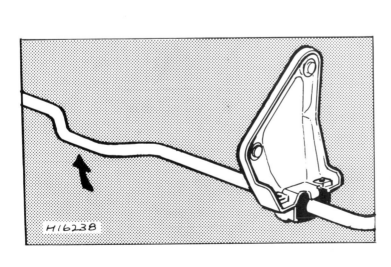

Fig. 10.6 Correct fitting of the anti-roll bar (Sec 8)

Arrow shows bend facing upwards

4   Unscrew and remove the nuts and washers from the ends of the anti-roll bar.

5   Pull the anti-roll bar from the control arms and withdraw it from under the car. If difficulty is experienced temporarily jack up the control arms to give a little extra width for the removal of the bar.

6   Check the bar and rubber bushes for wear and deterioration and renew as necessary. If the bush in the control arm is worn, renew it with reference to Section 7.

7   Refitting is a reversal of removal, but delay fully tightening the nuts and bolts until the full weight of the car is on the roadwheels. Note that the castor angle is determined by the position of the control arms on the anti-roll bar, therefore any adjustment washers should be refitted in their original locations.

9   Rear suspension strut/shock absorber – removal and refitting

1   Check the front wheels then jack up the rear of the car and support on axle stands. Remove the rear wheel.

2   Working inside the rear of the car, remove the parcel tray then remove the cap from the top of the strut by twirling it anti-clockwise (photo).

3   Support the trailing arm with a trolley jack.

4   Unscrew the nut from the top of the shock absorber rod, if necessary holding the rod stationary with a spanner. Remove the cup and upper buffer.

5   Working beneath the car remove the lower mounting bolt, then

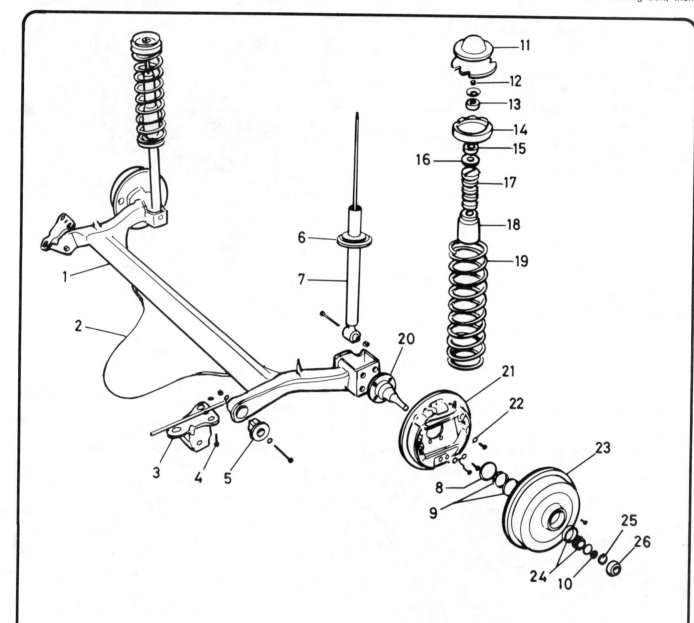

Fig. 10.7 Exploded view of the rear suspension components (Sec 9)

1 Axle beam	8 Seal	15 Lower buffer	21 Backplate complete
2 Handbrake cable	9 Inner wheel bearing	16 Washer	22 Lock ring
3 Bracket	10 Hexagon nut	17 Bump stop	23 Brake drum
4 Collar screw	11 Cover for strut mounting	18 Bellows	24 Outer wheel bearing
5 Bonded rubber bush	12 Hexagon nut	19 Coil spring	25 Slotted ring
6 Spring retainer	13 Upper buffer	20 Stub axle	26 Brake drum cap
7 Shock absorber	14 Spring seat		

9.2 Removing the cap from the top of the rear suspension strut

9.5A Rear suspension strut lower mounting bolt

9.5B View of the rear suspension strut upper mounting from below

lower the trailing arm as far as possible and withdraw the strut/shock absorber. Keep the coil spring, seat and bump stop components in their fitted positions on the strut (photos).

6   Remove the upper spring seat, coil spring, lower buffer, washer, bump stop and bellows and, if the unit is to be renewed, the lower spring retainer.

7   If the shock absorber is faulty it will normally make a knocking noise as the car is driven over rough surfaces, however with the unit removed uneven resistance tight spots will be evident as the central rod is operated. Check the condition of the buffers, bump stop and bellows and renew them if necessary. Before fitting the strut/shock absorber operate it fully several times in an upright position and check that the resistance is even and without any tight spots.

8   Refitting is a reversal of removal, but make sure that the coil spring is correctly located in the seats. Delay tightening the lower mounting bolt until the full weight of the car is on the roadwheels.

10 Rear stub axle – removal and refitting

1   Remove the rear brake shoes and wheel cylinder as described in Chapter 8.

2   Unscrew the bolts and remove the brake backplate followed by the stub axle.

3   Clean the stub axle and check it for distortion using a try-square and vernier calipers as shown in Fig. 10.8. Compare the readings at a minimum of three points and if the difference between the maximum and minimum readings exceeds 0.01 in (0.25 mm), renew the stub axle.

4   Refitting is a reversal of removal, but make sure that all mating faces

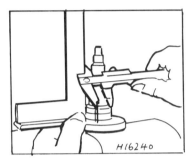
Fig. 10.8 Checking the rear wheel stub axle for distortion (Sec 10)

are clean and tighten the bolts to the specified torque. Refer to Chapter 8 as necessary and adjust the wheel bearings as described in Section 11.

11 Rear wheel bearings – testing, renewal and adjustment

1   Check the front wheels, then jack up the rear of the car and support on axle stands. Release the handbrake.

2   Spin the wheel. A rumbling noise will be evident if the bearings are worn in which case they must be renewed.

3   Remove the wheel then prise off the hub cap and extract the split pin. Remove the locking ring (photos).

11.3A Removing the rear wheel hub cap

11.3B Showing the rear wheel bearing split pin and locking ring

11.4A Showing the rear wheel bearing thrust washer

11.4B Removing the rear wheel outer bearing

11.16 Checking the rear wheel bearing adjustment with a screwdriver

4   Unscrew the hub nut and remove the thrust washer and outer wheel bearing (photos).
5   Withdraw the brake drum. If difficulty is experienced, the brake shoes must be backed away from the drum first. To do this, insert a screwdriver through one of the bolt holes and push the automatic adjuster wedge upwards against the spring tension. This will release the shoes from the drum.
6   Prise the seal from the inside of the drum with a screwdriver.
7   Remove the inner bearing, then using a soft metal drift, drive out the bearing outer races.
8   Clean the components in paraffin, wipe them dry, then examine them for wear and deterioration. Check the rollers and races for signs of pitting. Renew the bearings as necessary and obtain a new oil seal. Wipe clean the stub axle.
9   Using a suitable metal tube, drive the outer races into the drum/hub.
10 Lubricate the bearings with lithium based grease then locate the inner bearing in its race.
11 Smear the lips of the new seal with a little grease. Using a block of wood drive the seal squarely into the drum/hub with the lips facing inwards.
12 Refit the drum and locate the outer bearing on the stub axle.
13 Fit the thrust washer and hub nut, and tighten the nut hand tight.
14 Refit the wheel.
15 With the hub cap, split pin, and locking ring removed tighten the hub nut firmly while turning the wheel in order to settle the bearings.
16 Back off the nut then tighten it until it is just possible to move the thrust washer laterally with a screwdriver under finger pressure. Do not twist the screwdriver or lever it (photo).
17 Fit the locking ring together with a new split pin, then tap the hub cap into the drum with a mallet.
18 Lower the car to the ground.

12 Rear axle beam – removal and refitting

Note: *If the axle beam is suspected of being distorted it should be checked in position by a VW garage using an optical alignment instrument.*
1   Remove the rear stub axles as described in Section 10.
2   Support the weight of the trailing arms with axle stands then disconnect the struts/shock absorbers by removing the lower mounting bolts.
3   Remove the tail section of the exhaust system with reference to Chapter 3.
4   Disconnect the handbrake cables from the axle beam and from the left-hand side underbody bracket with reference to Chapter 8.
5   Remove the brake fluid reservoir filler cap and tighten it down onto a piece of polythene sheet in order to reduce the loss of hydraulic fluid.
6   Lower the axle beam and disconnect the brake hydraulic hoses with reference to Chapter 8.
7   Support the weight of the axle beam with axle stands then unscrew and remove the pivot bolts and lower the axle beam to the ground. Note that the pivot bolt heads face outwards (photo).
8   If the bushes are worn renew them as described in Section 13. If necessary the trunnion brackets can be removed by unscrewing the bolts. Discard the bolts.
9   Refit the trunnion brackets if necessary, but coat the new bolt threads with locking compound before tightening them to the specified torque.
10 Refitting is a reversal of removal, but delay tightening the strut/shock absorber lower mounting bolts and the axle beam pivot bolts to the specified torques until the full weight of the car is on the roadwheels. Bleed the brake hydraulic system as described in Chapter 8.

13 Rear axle beam pivot bushes – renewal

1   Check the front wheels then jack up the rear of the car and support on axle stands. Release the handbrake and remove the rear wheels.
2   Remove the tail section of the exhaust system with reference to Chapter 3.
3   Disconnect the handbrake cables from the underbody brackets with reference to Chapter 8.

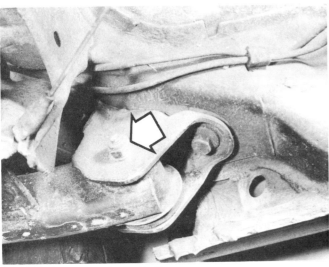

12.7 Showing a rear axle pivot bolt

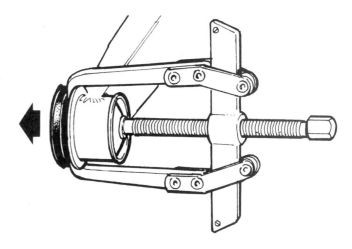

Fig. 10.9 Using a puller to remove the rear axle beam pivot bushes
(Sec 13)

4   Unscrew and remove the pivot bolts and lower the axle beam onto axle stands making sure that the flexible brake hoses are not strained.
5   Using a two-arm puller, force the bushes from the axle beam. Dip the new bushes in soapy water before pressing them in from the outside with the puller.
6   Refit the pivot bolts, handbrake cables, exhaust and rear wheels using a reversal of the removal procedure, but delay tightening the pivot bolt nuts to the specified torque until the full weight of the car is on the roadwheels.

14 Steering wheel – removal and refitting

1   Set the front wheels in the straight-ahead position.
2   Prise the cover from the centre of the steering wheel, note the location of the wires and disconnect them from the terminals on the cover (photos).
3   Mark the steering wheel and inner column in relation to each other, then unscrew the nut and withdraw the steering wheel. Remove the washer (photo).
4   Refitting in a reversal of removal, but make sure that the turn signal lever is in its neutral position otherwise damage may ocur to the cancelling arm. Tighten the nut to the specified torque.

14.2A Prise the cover from the steering wheel ...

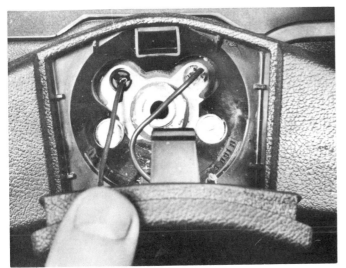

14.2B ... and disconnect the wires

14.3 Removing the steering wheel nut and washer

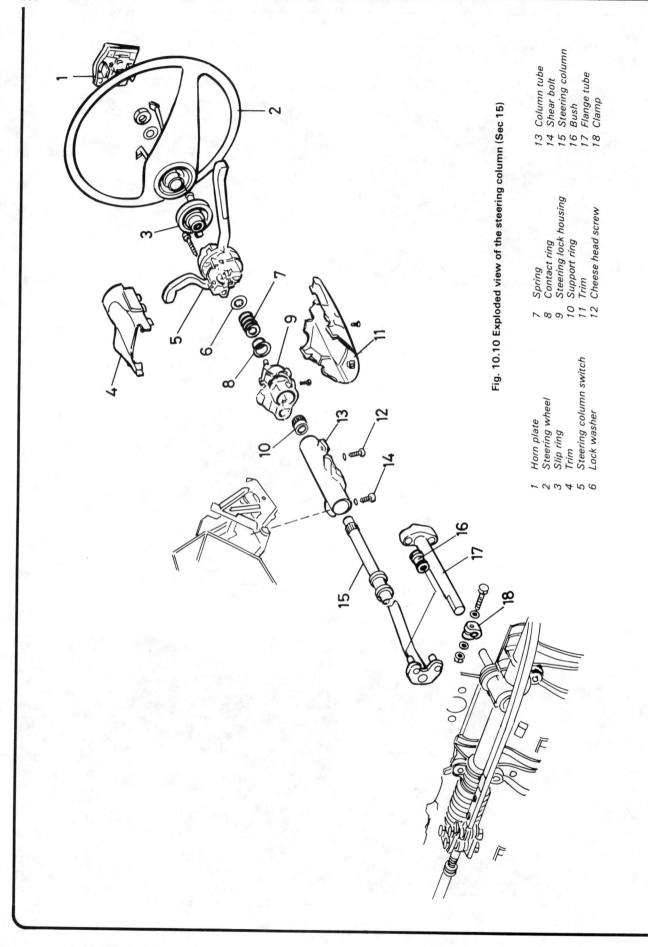

Fig. 10.10 Exploded view of the steering column (Sec 15)

1 Horn plate
2 Steering wheel
3 Slip ring
4 Trim
5 Steering column switch
6 Lock washer
7 Spring
8 Contact ring
9 Steering lock housing
10 Support ring
11 Trim
12 Cheese head screw
13 Column tube
14 Shear bolt
15 Steering column
16 Bush
17 Flange tube
18 Clamp

15.3 Removing the steering column lower shroud

15 Steering column – removal and refitting

1   Disconnect the battery negative lead.
2   Remove the steering wheel as described in Section 14.
3   Remove the screws and withdraw the steering column lower shroud (photo).
4   Remove the three screws and withdraw the combination switch. Disconnect the wiring plug.
5   Remove the screws and withdraw the lower facia trim panel.
6   Remove the column mounting bolts. An Allen key is required to unscrew one bolt, but the remaining bolt is a shear bolt and therefore its head must be drilled out using an 8.5 mm (0.335 in) diameter drill.
7   Lower the steering column and push it downwards to release the two pins from the flange tube, then withdraw the column from the car. Disconnect the ignition switch wiring plug.
8   Check the condition of the flange tube bushes and if necessary renew them. Lever the old bushes out with a screwdriver then press in the new bushes after dipping them in soapy water. Unscrew the old shear bolt and obtain a new one.
9   Refitting is a reversal of removal, but make sure that the column is correctly positioned before tightening the shear bolt until its head is broken off.

16 Steering lock – removal and refitting

1   Disconnect the battery negative lead.
2   Remove the steering wheel as described in Section 14.
3   Remove the screws and withdraw the steering column lower shroud.

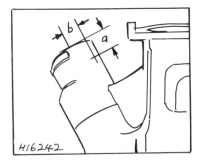

Fig. 10.11 Showing drilling position when removing steering lock cylinder (Sec 16)

a = 12 mm (0.472 in)   b = 10 mm (0.394 in)

4   Remove the three screws and withdraw the combination switch. Disconnect the wiring plug.
5   Using an Allen key unscrew the clamp bolt securing the steering lock.
6   Prise the lockwasher from the inner column and remove the spring and contact ring.
7   Disconnect the wiring plug and withdraw the steering lock from the top of the column together with the upper shroud. Note that the ignition key must be inserted to ensure that the lock is in its released position.
8   Remove the screw and withdraw the switch from the lock housing.
9   To remove the lock cylinder, drill a 3.0 mm (0.118 in) diameter hole in the location shown in Fig. 10.11, depress the spring pin, and extract the cylinder.
10 Refitting is a reversal of removal, but renew the inner column lockwasher and press it fully onto the stop while supporting the lower end of the column.

17 Steering column – dismantling and reassembly

1   With the steering column removed as described in Section 15, prise the lockwasher from the inner column and remove the spring and contact ring.
2   Using an Allen key unscrew the clamp bolt securing the steering lock and withdraw the lock. Note that the ignition key must be inserted and the lock released.
3   Withdraw the inner column from the outer columns and remove the support ring.
4   Clean the components and examine them for wear. Renew them as necessary.
5   Reassembly is a reversal of dismantling, but lubricate bearing surfaces with multi-purpose grease and renew the inner column lockwasher.

18 Tie-rods and balljoints – removal and refitting

1   If the steering tie-rod and balljoints are worn, play will be evident as the roadwheel is rocked from side to side, and the balljoint must then be renewed. On RHD models the left-hand tie-rod is adjustable and the balljoint on this tie-rod can be renewed separately, however the right-hand tie-rod must be renewed complete. On LHD models the tie-rods are vice versa.
2   If the complete tie-rod is to be removed unscrew the centre bolt with the weight of the car on the wheels otherwise the rubber bush may be damaged (photo).
3   Jack up the front of the car and support on axle stands. Apply the handbrake and remove the front wheel(s).

18.2 Steering tie-rod centre bolts

18.4A Unscrew the nut ...

18.4B ... and then use a balljoint separator tool ...

18.4C ... and release the tie-rod

4 Unscrew the balljoint nut then use a balljoint separator tool to release the joint from the strut (photos).

5 Withdraw the tie-rod or if applicable loosen the locknut and unscrew the tie-rod end.

6 Refitting is a reversal of removal, but tighten the nuts to the specified torque and check the front wheel alignment as described in Section 21.

19 Steering gear bellows – renewal

1 Remove the air cleaner as described in Chapter 3.

2 Unscrew and remove the clamp bolt from the end of the steering gear rack. Note that the bolt engages a groove on the side of the rack. Separate the bracket from the rack.

3 Loosen the clip and withdraw the bellows from the steering gear together with the retaining ring.

4 Smear a little steering gear grease on the rack then fit the new bellows together with the inner clip. Locate the bellows on the housing and tighten the clip.

5 Push on the retaining ring and locate the bellows in the outer groove.

6 Fit the bracket then insert the bolt so that it engages the groove and tighten the nut.

7 Refit the air cleaner with reference to Chapter 3.

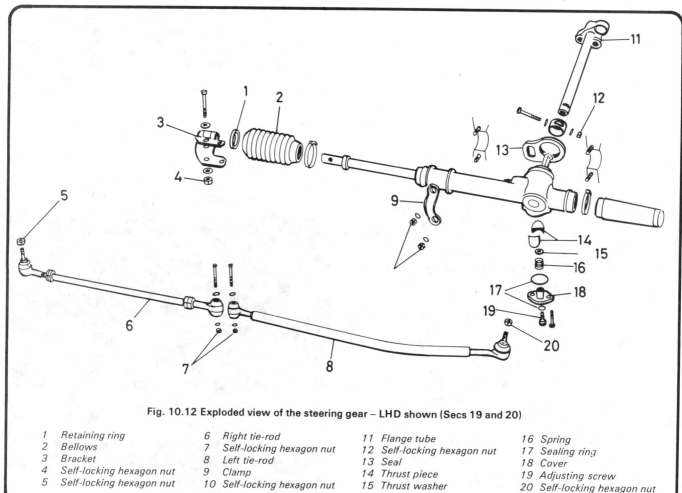

Fig. 10.12 Exploded view of the steering gear – LHD shown (Secs 19 and 20)

1 Retaining ring	6 Right tie-rod	11 Flange tube	16 Spring
2 Bellows	7 Self-locking hexagon nut	12 Self-locking hexagon nut	17 Sealing ring
3 Bracket	8 Left tie-rod	13 Seal	18 Cover
4 Self-locking hexagon nut	9 Clamp	14 Thrust piece	19 Adjusting screw
5 Self-locking hexagon nut	10 Self-locking hexagon nut	15 Thrust washer	20 Self-locking hexagon nut

20.5 Showing the clutch cable hole in the steering gear housing

20.10A Steering gear location (engine removed from car)

20 Steering gear – removal, refitting and adjustment

1 Disconnect the battery negative lead.
2 Remove the air cleaner as described in Chapter 3.
3 Lift out the windscreen washer bottle and place it to one side.
4 Remove the screws and withdraw the lower facia panel shelf from around the steering column.
5 Where applicable remove the clutch cable with reference to Chapter 5 (photo).
6 Set the front wheels in the straight-ahead position then unscrew the clamp bolt securing the flange tube to the steering gear pinion.
7 Prise the flange tube up from the pinion. Do not bend the clamp open.
8 Unscrew and remove the tie-rod centre bolts and move the tie-rods to one side.
9 Jack up the front of the car and support on axle stands. Apply the handbrake and remove the front wheels.
10 Unscrew the nuts and remove the mounting clamps (photos).
11 Withdraw the steering gear upwards from the car. Remove the sealing gasket.
12 Refitting is a reversal of removal, but do not fully tighten the mounting clamp nuts until the steering gear is correctly aligned.
13 With the front of the car supported on axle stands turn the steering from lock to lock and check that there are no tight spots or excessive play. If necessary turn the self-locking adjusting screw on the bottom of the steering gear in to reduce play or out to reduce tight spots. Turn the screw in 20° stages and initially make the adjustment with the front wheels in the straight ahead position.

20.10B Showing right-hand side mounting clamp on the steering gear

necessary remove the steering wheel and reposition it on the inner column splines.
6 Camber and castor angles can be checked by a garage having a special optical alignment gauge.

21 Wheel alignment – checking and adjusting

1 Accurate wheel alignment is essential for good steering and slow tyre wear. Before checking it, make sure that the car is only loaded to kerbside weight and the tyres correctly inflated.
2 Place the car on level ground with the wheels in the straight-ahead position, then roll the car backwards 12 ft (4 m) and forwards again.
3 Using a wheel alignment gauge, check that the front wheel toe-in dimension is as given in the Specifications.
4 If adjustment is necessary, loosen the locknuts on the adjustable tie-rod, turn the tie-rod as necessary, then tighten the locknuts.
5 After making an adjustment give the car a test run and check that the steering wheel spokes are horizontal when travelling straight ahead. If

22 Roadwheels and tyres – general

1 Clean the insides of the roadwheels whenever they are removed. If necessary, remove any rust and repaint them.
2 At the same time remove any flints or stones which may have become embedded in the tyres. Examine the tyres for damage and splits. Where the depth of tread is down to the legal minimum renew them.
3 The wheels should be rebalanced half way through the life of the tyres to compensate for loss of rubber.
4 Check and adjust the tyre pressures regularly and make sure that the dust caps are correctly fitted. Do not forget the spare tyre.

Fault diagnosis overleaf

23 Fault diagnosis – suspension and steering

Sympton	Reason(s)
Excessive play in steering	Worn steering gear or tie-rod balljoints and bushes Worn lower control arm balljoints
Wanders or pulls to one side	Incorrect wheel alignment Worn tie-rod balljoints and bushes Worn lower control arm balljoints Uneven tyre pressures Faulty shock absorber
Heavy or stiff steering	Seized balljoint Incorrect wheel alignment Low tyre pressures Lack of lubricant in steering gear
Wheel wobble and vibration	Roadwheels out of balance Roadwheels damaged Worn shock absorbers Worn wheel bearings
Excessive tyre wear	Incorrect wheel alignment Worn shock absorbers Incorrect tyre pressures Roadwheels out of balance

Chapter 11 Bodywork and fittings

For modifications, and information applicable to later models, see Supplement at end of manual

Contents

1 General description

The body is of all-steel unit construction with impact-absorbing front and rear crumple zones which take the brunt of any accident, leaving the passenger compartment with minimum distortion. The front wings are bolted in position and are easily removed should renewal be necessary after a front end collision.

2 Maintenance – bodywork and underframe

1 The general condition of a vehicle's bodywork is the one thing that significantly affects its value. Maintenance is easy but needs to be regular. Neglect, particularly after minor damage, can lead quickly to further deterioration and costly repair bills. It is important also to keep watch on those parts of the vehicle not immediately visible, for instance the underside, inside all the wheel arches and the lower part of the engine compartment.

2 The basic maintenance routine for the bodywork is washing – preferably with a lot of water, from a hose. This will remove all the loose solids which may have stuck to the vehicle. It is important to flush these off in such a way as to prevent grit from scratching the finish. The wheel arches and underframe need washing in the same way to remove any accumulated mud which will retain moisture and tend to encourage rust. Paradoxically enough, the best time to clean the underframe and wheel arches is in wet weather when the mud is thoroughly wet and soft. In very wet weather the underframe is usually cleaned of large accumulations automatically and this is a good time for inspection.

3 Periodically, it is a good idea to have the whole of the underframe of the vehicle steam cleaned, engine compartment included, so that a thorough inspection can be carried out to see what minor repairs and renovations are necessary. Steam cleaning is available at many garages and is necessary for removal of the accumulation of oily grime which sometimes is allowed to become thick in certain areas. If steam cleaning facilities are not available, there are one or two excellent grease solvents available which can be brush applied. The dirt can then be simply hosed off.

4 After washing paintwork, wipe off with a chamois leather to give an unspotted clear finish. A coat of clear protective wax polish will give added protection against chemical pollutants in the air. If the paintwork sheen has dulled or oxidised, use a cleaner/polish combination to restore the brilliance of the shine. This requires a little effort, but such dulling is usually caused because regular washing has been neglected. Always check that the door sill drain holes and pipes are completely clear so that water can be drained out (photos). Bright work should be treated in the same way as paintwork. Windscreens and windows can be kept clear of the smeary film which often appears, by adding a little ammonia to the water. If they are scratched, a good rub with a proprietary metal polish will often clear them. Never use any form of wax or other body or chromium polish on glass.

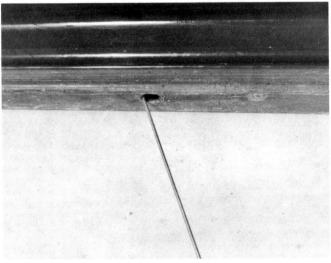

2.4A Clearing a door drain hole

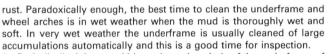

2.4B Clearing a sill drain hole

3 Maintenance – upholstery and carpets

Mats and carpets should be brushed or vacuum cleaned regularly to keep them free of grit. If they are badly stained remove them from the vehicle for scrubbing or sponging and make quite sure they are dry before refitting. Seats and interior trim panels can be kept clean by wiping with a damp cloth. If they do become stained (which can be more apparent on light coloured upholstery) use a little liquid detergent and a soft nail brush to scour the grime out of the grain of the material. Do not forget to keep the headlining clean in the same way as the upholstery. When using liquid cleaners inside the vehicle do not over-wet the surfaces being cleaned. Excessive damp could get into the seams and padded interior causing stains, offensive odours or even rot. If the inside of the vehicle gets wet accidentally it is worthwhile taking some trouble to dry it out properly, particularly where carpets are involved. *Do not leave oil or electric heaters inside the vehicle for this purpose.*

4 Minor body damage – repair

The photographic sequences on pages 174 and 175 illustrate the operations detailed in the following sub-sections.

Note: *For more detailed information about bodywork repair, the Haynes Publishing Group publish a book by Lindsay Porter called* The Car Bodywork Repair Manual. *This incorporates information on such aspects as rust treatment, painting and glass fibre repairs, as well as details on more ambitious repairs involving welding and panel beating.*

Repair of minor scratches in bodywork

If the scratch is very superficial, and does not penetrate to the metal of the bodywork, repair is very simple. Lightly rub the area of the scratch with a paintwork renovator, or a very fine cutting paste, to remove loose paint from the scratch and to clear the surrounding bodywork of wax polish. Rinse the area with clean water.

Apply touch-up paint to the scratch using a fine paint brush; continue to apply fine layers of paint until the surface of the paint in the scratch is level with the surrounding paintwork. Allow the new paint at least two weeks to harden: then blend it into the surrounding paintwork by rubbing the scratch area with a paintwork renovator or a very fine cutting paste. Finally, apply wax polish.

Where the scratch has penetrated right through to the metal of the bodywork, causing the metal to rust, a different repair technique is required. Remove any loose rust from the bottom of the scratch with a penknife, then apply rust inhibiting paint to prevent the formation of rust in the future. Using a rubber or nylon applicator fill the scratch with bodystopper paste. If required, this paste can be mixed with cellulose thinners to provide a very thin paste which is ideal for filling narrow scratches. Before the stopper-paste in the scratch hardens, wrap a piece of smooth cotton rag around the top of a finger. Dip the finger in cellulose thinners and then quickly sweep it across the surface of the stopper-paste in the scratch; this will ensure that the surface of the stopper-paste is slightly hollowed. The scratch can now be painted over as described earlier in this Section.

Repair of dents in bodywork

When deep denting of the vehicle's bodywork has taken place, the first task is to pull the dent out, until the affected bodywork almost attains its original shape. There is little point in trying to restore the original shape completely, as the metal in the damaged area will have stretched on impact and cannot be reshaped fully to its original contour. It is better to bring the level of the dent up to a point which is about $\frac{1}{8}$ in (3 mm) below the level of the surrounding bodywork. In cases where the dent is very shallow anyway, it is not worth trying to pull it out at all. If the underside of the dent is accessible, it can be hammered out gently from behind, using a mallet with a wooden or plastic head. Whilst doing this, hold a suitable block of wood firmly against the outside of the panel to absorb the impact from the hammer blows and thus prevent a large area of bodywork from being 'belled-out'.

Should the dent be in a section of the bodywork which has a double skin or some other factor making it inaccessible from behind, a different technique is called for. Drill several small holes through the metal inside the area – particularly in the deeper section. Then screw long self-tapping screws into the holes just sufficiently for them to gain a good purchase in the metal. Now the dent can be pulled out by pulling on the protruding heads of the screws with a pair of pliers.

The next stage of the repair is the removal of the paint from the damaged area, and from an inch or so of the surrounding 'sound' bodywork. This is accomplished most easily by using a wire brush or abrasive pad on a power drill, although it can be done just as effectively by hand using sheets of abrasive paper. To complete the preparation for filling, score the surface of the bare metal with a screwdriver or the tang of a file, or alternatively, drill small holes in the affected area. This will provide a really good 'key' for the filler paste.

To complete the repair see the Section on filling and re-spraying.

Repair of rust holes or gashes in bodywork

Remove all paint from the affected area and from an inch or so of the surrounding 'sound' bodywork, using an abrasive pad or a wire brush on a power drill. If these are not available a few sheets of abrasive paper will do the job just as effectively. With the paint removed you will be able to gauge the severity of the corrosion and therefore decide whether to renew the whole panel (if this is possible) or to repair the affected area. New body panels are not as expensive as most people think and it is often quicker and more satisfactory to fit a new panel than to attempt to repair large areas of corrosion.

Remove all fittings from the affected area except those which will act as a guide to the original shape of the damaged bodywork (eg headlamp shells etc). Then, using tin snips or a hacksaw blade, remove all loose metal and any other metal badly affected by corrosion. Hammer the edges of the hole inwards in order to create a slight depression for the filler paste.

Wire brush the affected area to remove the powdery rust from the surface of the remaining metal. Paint the affected area with rust inhibiting paint; if the back of the rusted area is accessible treat this also.

Before filling can take place it will be necessary to block the hole in some way. This can be achieved by the use of aluminium or plastic mesh, or aluminium tape.

Aluminium or plastic mesh is probably the best material to use for a large hole. Cut a piece to the approximate size and shape of the hole to be filled, then position it in the hole so that its edges are below the level of the surrounding bodywork. It can be retained in position by several blobs of filler paste around its periphery.

Aluminium tape should be used for small or very narrow holes. Pull a piece off the roll and trim it to the approximate size and shape required, then pull off the backing paper (if used) and stick the tape over the hole; it can be overlapped if the thickness of one piece is insufficient. Burnish down the edges of the tape with the handle of a screwdriver or similar, to ensure that the tape is securely attached to the metal underneath.

Bodywork repairs – filling and re-spraying

Before using this Section, see the Sections on dent, deep scratch, rust holes and gash repairs.

Many types of bodyfiller are available, but generally speaking those proprietary kits which contain a tin of filler paste and a tube of resin hardener are best for this type of repair. A wide, flexible plastic or nylon applicator will be found invaluable for imparting a smooth and well contoured finish to the surface of the filler.

Mix up a little filler on a clean piece of card or board – measure the hardener carefully (follow the maker's instructions on the pack) otherwise the filler will set too rapidly or too slowly.

Using the applicator apply the filler paste to the prepared area; draw the applicator across the surface of the filler to achieve the correct contour and to level the filler surface. As soon as a contour that approximates to the correct one is achieved, stop working the paste – if you carry on too long the paste will become sticky and begin to 'pick up' on the applicator. Continue to add thin layers of filler paste at twenty-minute intervals until the level of the filler is just proud of the surrounding bodywork.

Once the filler has hardened, excess can be removed using a metal plane or file. From then on, progressively finer grades of abrasive paper should be used, starting with a 40 grade production paper and finishing with 400 grade wet-and-dry paper. Always wrap the abrasive paper around a flat rubber, cork, or wooden block – otherwise the surface of the filler will not be completely flat. During the smoothing of the filler surface the wet-and-dry paper should be periodically rinsed in water.

This will ensure that a very smooth finish is imparted to the filler at the final stage.

At this stage the 'dent' should be surrounded by a ring of bare metal, which in turn should be encircled by the finely 'feathered' edge of the good paintwork. Rinse the repair area with clean water, until all of the dust produced by the rubbing-down operation has gone.

Spray the whole repair area with a light coat of primer – this will show up any imperfections in the surface of the filler. Repair these imperfections with fresh filler paste or bodystopper, and once more smooth the surface with abrasive paper. If bodystopper is used, it can be mixed with cellulose thinners to form a really thin paste which is ideal for filling small holes. Repeat this spray and repair procedure until you are satisfied that the surface of the filler, and the feathered edge of the paintwork are perfect. Clean the repair area with clean water and allow to dry fully.

The repair area is now ready for final spraying. Paint spraying must be carried out in a warm, dry, windless and dust free atmosphere. This condition can be created artifically if you have access to a large indoor working area, but if you are forced to work in the open, you will have to pick your day very carefully. If you are working indoors, dousing the floor in the work area with water will help to settle the dust which would otherwise be in the atmosphere. If the repair area is confined to one body panel, mask off the surrounding panels; this will help to minimise the effects of a slight mix-match in paint colours. Bodywork fittings (eg chrome strips, door handles etc) will also need to be masked off. Use genuine masking tape and several thicknesses of newspaper for the masking operations.

Before commencing to spray, agitate the aerosol can thoroughly, then spray a test area (an old tin, or similar) until the technique is mastered. Cover the repair area with a thick coat of primer; the thickness should be built up using several thin layers of paint rather than one thick one. Using 400 grade wet-and-dry paper, rub down the surface of the primer until it is really smooth. While doing this, the work area should be thoroughly doused with water, and the wet-and-dry paper periodically rinsed in water. Allow to dry before spraying on more paint.

Spray on the top coat, again building up the thickness by using several thin layers of paint. Start spraying in the centre of the repair area and then, using a circular motion, work outwards until the whole repair area and about 2 inches of the surrounding original paintwork is covered. Remove all masking material 10 to 15 minutes after spraying on the final coat of paint.

Allow the new paint at least two weeks to harden, then, using a paintwork renovator or a very fine cutting paste, blend the edges of the paint into the existing paintwork. Finally, apply wax polish.

5 Major body damage – repair

Where serious damage has occurred or large areas need renewal due to neglect, it means certainly that completely new sections or panels will need welding in and this is best left to professionals. If the damage is due to impact, it will also be necessary to completely check the alignment of the bodyshell structure. Due to the principle of construction, the strength and shape of the whole car can be affected by damage to one part. In such instances the services of a VW agent with specialist checking jigs are essential. If a body is left misaligned, it is first of all dangerous as the car will not handle properly, and secondly uneven stresses will be imposed on the steering, engine and transmission, causing abnormal wear or complete failure. Tyre wear may also be excessive.

6 Maintenance – hinges and locks

1 Every 10 000 miles (15 000 km) lubricate the door, bonnet and tailgate/boot lid hinges with a little oil. Similarly lubricate the bonnet release mechanism and door, bonnet and tailgate/boot lid locks.
2 At the same time lubricate the door check straps with a little multi-purpose grease.
3 Do not attempt to lubricate the steering lock.

7 Door rattles – tracing and rectification

1 Check first that the door is not loose at the hinges, and that the latch is holding the door firmly in position. Check also that the door lines up with the aperture in the body. If the door is out of alignment, adjust it as described in Section 15.
2 If the latch is holding the door in the correct position but the latch still rattles, the lock mechanism is worn and should be renewed.
3 Other rattles from the door could be caused by wear in the window operating mechanism, interior lock mechanism, or loose glass channels.

8 Bonnet – removal, refitting and adjustment

1 Support the bonnet in its open position, and place some cardboard or rags beneath the corners by the hinges.
2 Mark the location of the hinges with a pencil then loosen the four retaining bolts (photo).
3 Disconnect the windscreen washer tubes from the jets on the bonnet (photo).
4 With the help of an assistant, release the stay, remove the bolts, and withdraw the bonnet from the car.
5 Refitting is a reversal of removal, but adjust the hinges to their original positions and check that the bonnet is level with the surrounding bodywork. If necessary adjust the height of the bonnet front edge by screwing the rubber buffers in or out (photo), and also adjust the bonnet lock if necessary with reference to Section 9.

9 Bonnet cable and lock – removal, refitting and adjustment

1 Inside the car, remove the trim on the left under the dash. The cable is accessible on the inside end. Before it can be removed it must be released from the lock which is bolted to the centre support of the grille.
2 Open the bonnet, remove the radiator grille and disconnect the cable.
3 Now back inside the car, remove the bonnet catch release handle bracket and lift the bracket away from the trim. In the centre of the upper end of the operating handle is a small clamping plate. Bend this outwards and the handle may be released from the bracket. The cable

8.2 Bonnet hinge

8.3 Disconnecting the windscreen washer tubes from the bonnet

8.5 Bonnet rubber buffer

This sequence of photographs deals with the repair of the dent and paintwork damage shown in this photo. The procedure will be similar for the repair of a hole. It should be noted that the procedures given here are simplified — more explicit instructions will be found in the text

In the case of a dent the first job — after removing surrounding trim — is to hammer out the dent where access is possible. This will minimise filling. Here, the large dent having been hammered out, the damaged area is being made slightly concave

Now all paint must be removed from the damaged area, by rubbing with coarse abrasive paper. Alternatively, a wire brush or abrasive pad can be used in a power drill. Where the repair area meets good paintwork, the edge of the paintwork should be 'feathered', using a finer grade of abrasive paper

In the case of a hole caused by rusting, all damaged sheet-metal should be cut away before proceeding to this stage. Here, the damaged area is being treated with rust remover and inhibitor before being filled

Mix the body filler according to its manufacturer's instructions. In the case of corrosion damage, it will be necessary to block off any large holes before filling — this can be done with aluminium or plastic mesh, or aluminium tape. Make sure the area is absolutely clean before ...

... applying the filler. Filler should be applied with a flexible applicator, as shown, for best results; the wooden spatula being used for confined areas. Apply thin layers of filler at 20-minute intervals, until the surface of the filler is slightly proud of the surrounding bodywork

Initial shaping can be done with a Surform plane or Dreadnought file. Then, using progressively finer grades of wet-and-dry paper, wrapped around a sanding block, and copious amounts of clean water, rub down the filler until really smooth and flat. Again, feather the edges of adjoining paintwork

The whole repair area can now be sprayed or brush-painted with primer. If spraying, ensure adjoining areas are protected from over-spray. Note that at least one inch of the surrounding sound paintwork should be coated with primer. Primer has a 'thick' consistency, so will find small imperfections

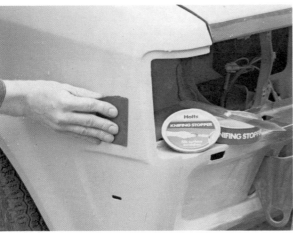

Again, using plenty of water, rub down the primer with a fine grade wet-and-dry paper (400 grade is probably best) until it is really smooth and well blended into the surrounding paintwork. Any remaining imperfections can now be filled by carefully applied knifing stopper paste

When the stopper has hardened, rub down the repair area again before applying the final coat of primer. Before rubbing down this last coat of primer, ensure the repair area is blemish-free – use more stopper if necessary. To ensure that the surface of the primer is really smooth use some finishing compound

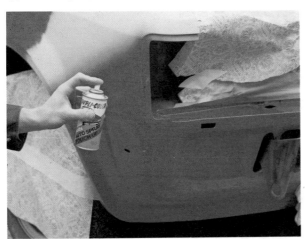

The top coat can now be applied. When working out of doors, pick a dry, warm and wind-free day. Ensure surrounding areas are protected from over-spray. Agitate the aerosol thoroughly, then spray the centre of the repair area, working outwards with a circular motion. Apply the paint as several thin coats

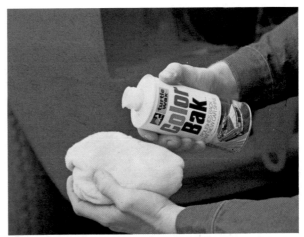

After a period of about two weeks, which the paint needs to harden fully, the surface of the repaired area can be 'cut' with a mild cutting compound prior to wax polishing. When carrying out bodywork repairs, remember that the quality of the finished job is proportional to the time and effort expended

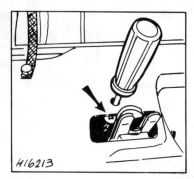

Fig. 11.1 Tightening the bonnet lock inner cable securing screw (Sec 9)

may now be pulled out of the handle and out of the car. Tie a piece of thin wire or cord to the inside end and pull that into the place the cable occupied to make fitting a new cable more simple.

4   Refitting is a reversal of removal, but make sure that the cable is positioned without any sharp bends. With the handle fully released bend the end of the inner cable to attach it to the lock, but make sure it is free of tension. With the outer cable free of tension tighten the cross-head screw on the lock.

5   To remove the lock remove the radiator grille and disconnect the cable.

6   Using an Allen key remove the retaining bolts and withdraw the lock (photo).

7   Refitting is a reversal of removal, but if necessary adjust the height of the bonnet front edge by loosening the retaining bolts and repositioning the lock within the elongated holes. The safety catch and anti-rattle spring should be checked for condition at the same time (photo).

10 Radiator grille – removal and refitting

1   Support the bonnet in its open position.
2   Release the clips from the top of the grille (photos).
3   Withdraw the grille upwards from the front valance.
4   Refitting is a reversal of removal.

11 Tailgate support strut – removal and refitting

1   Open and support the tailgate.
2   Unhook the spring clip from the end of the strut attached to the

9.6 Bonnet lock and retaining bolts

9.7 Bonnet safety catch and anti-rattle spring

10.2A Depress the plastic tab with a screwdriver ...

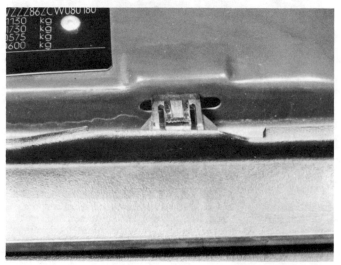

10.2B ... and pull out the radiator grille

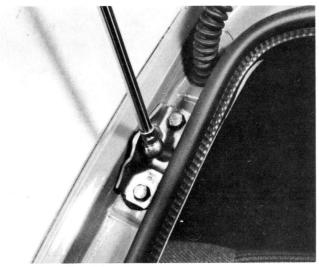

11.2 Body mounting of the tailgate strut

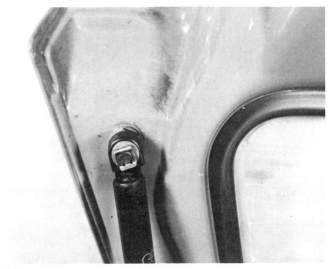

11.3 Strut mounting on the tailgate

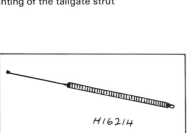

H16214

Fig. 11.2 Showing vice mounting area when depressurising the tailgate support strut (Sec 11)

body, pull up the ball head, and disconnect the strut from the ball-pin (photo).
3 Lever the spring clip from the other end of the strut, remove the washer, and withdraw the strut from the pivot pin (photo).
4 If the strut is to be renewed, the old unit can be depressurised by clamping it in a vice within the area shown in Fig. 11.2, then using a hacksaw to cut into the cylinder within the first third of the cylinder measured from the piston rod end. *Protective glasses and clothing must be worn and in addition rag should be wrapped around the area to be cut.*
5 Refitting is a reversal of removal.

12.3 Tailgate hinge

12 Tailgate – removal and refitting

1 Open and support the tailgate.
2 Remove the trim panel using a wide blade screwdriver, and disconnect the wiring from the heated rear window and wiper motor. Disconnect the washer tube and pull the wiring and tube from the tailgate.
3 Pull the weatherseal from the body aperture by the hinge positions (photo).
4 Carefully pull the headlining down to reveal the hinge bolts.
5 Lever the spring clips from the struts, remove the washers, and disconnect the struts from the tailgate.
6 Unscrew the hinge bolts and withdraw the tailgate from the car.
7 Refitting is a reversal of removal, but before tightening the hinge bolts make sure that the tailgate closes centrally within the body aperture. If necessary adjust the lock as described in Section 13.

13 Tailgate lock – removal, refitting and adjustment

1 Open the tailgate and using an Allen key unscrew the two lock retaining screws. Withdraw the lock (photo).

13.1 Tailgate lock

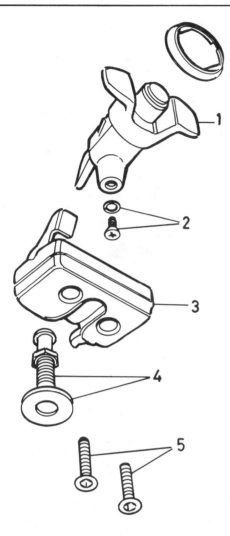

Fig. 11.3 Tailgate lock components (Sec 13)

1 *Lock cylinder with housing*
2 *Fillister head screw with washer*
3 *Tailgate latch*
4 *Locking pin with washer*
5 *Socket head screws*

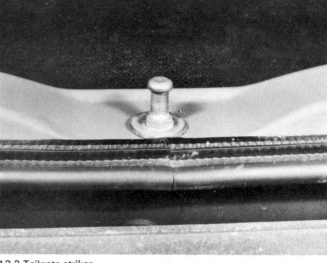

13.2 Tailgate striker

14.2 Removing the door inner handle surround

2 If necessary remove the cross-head screw and withdraw the lock cylinder and seal. Unscrew the striker from the body and remove the washer (photo).

3 Refitting is a reversal of removal, but before fully tightening the striker, close and open the tailgate two or three times to centralise it.

14 Door trim panel – removal and refitting

1 Unscrew and remove the locking knob.

2 Remove the inner handle surround by sliding it to the rear (photo).

3 Prise the covers from the door pull with a small screwdriver, remove the cross-head screws, and withdraw the door pull (photos).

4 Note the position of the window regulator handle with the window shut then prise off the cover, remove the cross-head screw and withdraw the handle and washer (photos).

5 Remove the self-tapping screws and withdraw the storage compartment panel (where applicable).

6 Prise out the stoppers and remove the cross-head screws from the trim panel (photos).

7 Using a wide blade screwdriver prise the trim panel clips from the door taking care not to damage the panel. Remove the panel (photos).

8 Remove the window regulator handle packing.

14.3A Prise off the covers ...

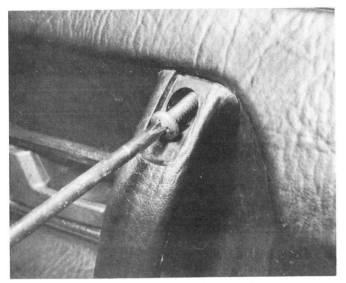

14.3B ... and remove the door pull screws

14.4A Remove the screw ...

14.4B ... and withdraw the window regulator handle

14.6A Prise out the plastic stoppers ...

14.6B ... and remove the door trim panel screws

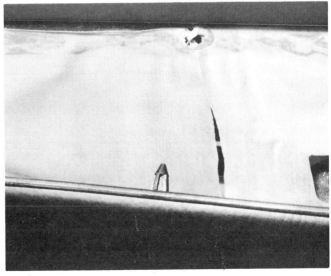

14.7A Door trim panel upper clips

14.7B Door trim panel lower clips

15.1 Door check strap

15.3 Door hinge and bolt

15.4 Door striker

9   If necessary peel the protective sheet from the door.
10 Refitting is a reversal of removal, however it is recommended that the window regulator handle retaining screw is locked by coating its threads with a liquid locking agent.

15 Door – removal and refitting

1   Open the door and use a punch to drive the pivot pin up from the check strap (photo).
2   Mark the position of the door on the hinges.
3   Support the door then unscrew and remove the lower hinge bolt followed by the upper hinge bolt, and withdraw the door from the car (photo).
4   Refitting is a reversal of removal, but if necessary adjust the position of the door on the hinges so that, when closed, it is level with the surrounding bodywork and central within the body aperture. Lubricate the hinges with a little oil and the check strap with grease. If necessary adjust the position of the door striker (photo).

16 Door handle (exterior) – removal and refitting

1   Remove the trim panel as described in Section 14.

16.4 View of exterior door handle from inside the door

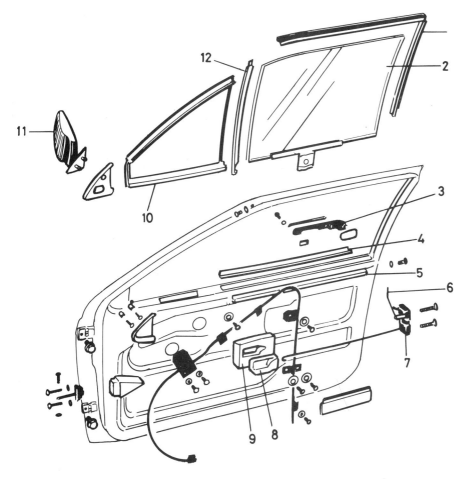

Fig. 11.4 Exploded view of door components (Secs 16 to 20)

1   Window channel
2   Glass
3   Door handle
4   Outer window slot seal
5   Inner window slot seal
6   Locking rod with sleeve
7   Door lock
8   Door lock remote control
9   Remote control seal
10 Fixed corner window with seal
11 Mirror
12 Front guide rail with window channel

2   Using a small screwdriver lever the plastic strip from the exterior door handle.

3   Remove the cross-head screws from the handle grip and the end of the door.

4   Withdraw the handle and release it from the lock (photo). Remove the gaskets.

5   Refitting is a reversal of removal, but fit new gaskets if necessary.

17 Door handle (interior) – removal and refitting

1   Remove the trim panel as described in Section 14.

2   Pull the foam seal away then prise the retainer from the bottom of the handle (photo).

3   Press the fingerplate forwards out of the door and unhook it from the rod (photo). Remove the foam seal.

4   Refitting is a reversal of removal.

18 Door lock – removal and refitting

1   It is not necessary to remove the trim panel. First open the door and set the lock in the locked position either by moving the interior knob or by turning the exterior key.

2   Using an Allen key, unscrew the retaining screws and withdraw the lock approximately 12 mm (0.5 in) to expose the operating lever (photo).

3   Retain the operating lever in the extended position by inserting a screwdriver through the hole in the bottom of the lock.

17.2 Interior door handle and foam seal

17.3 Removing the interior door handle and fingerplate

18.2 Door lock

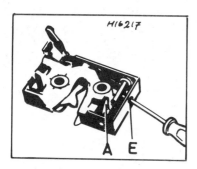

Fig. 11.5 Using a screwdriver through the door lock hole (E) to retain the operating lever (A) in the extended position (Sec 18)

4   Unhook the remote control rod from the operating lever and pull the upper lever from the sleeve. Withdraw the lock from the door.
5   Refitting is a reversal of removal, but remember to set the lock in the locked position first, and make sure that the lugs on the plastic sleeve are correctly seated.

19 Window regulator – removal and refitting

1   Remove the trim panel as described in Section 14.
2   Temporarily refit the window regulator handle and lower the window until the lifting plate is visible.
3   Remove the bolts securing the regulator to the door and the bolts securing the lifting plate to the window channel (photos).
4   Release the regulator from the door and remove it through the aperture.
5   Refitting is a reversal of removal, but ensure that the inner cable is adequately lubricated with grease and if necessary adjust the position of the regulator so that the window moves smoothly.

20 Windows – removal and refitting

Door windows
1   Remove the window regulator as described in Section 19.
2   With the window fully lowered unclip the inner and outer mouldings from the window aperture.
3   Remove the bolt and screw and pull out the front window channel abutting the corner window.
4   Withdraw the corner window and seal.
5   Lift the window glass from the door.
6   Refitting is a reversal of removal. If the glass is being renewed, make sure that the lift channel is located in the same position as in the old glass.

Windscreen and fixed glass
7   Removal and refitting of the windscreen and fixed glass windows is best left to a VW garage or windscreen specialist who will have the necessary equipment and expertise to complete the work properly.

21 Boot lid and lock (Classic models) – removal and refitting

1   Open the boot lid and mark the position of the hinges with a pencil.
2   With the help of an assistant unscrew the bolts and withdraw the boot lid.
3   The boot lock and striker are each secured by two cross-head screws, but when removing the lock it will be necessary to unhook the connecting rod.
4   Refitting is a reversal of removal, but make sure that the boot lid is central within the aperture and adjust its position on the hinge bolts if necessary. To adjust the boot lock striker, loosen the mounting screws then tighten them just sufficiently to hold the striker in position. Fully close the boot lid then open it again and fully tighten the screws. Adjust the stop rubbers if necessary.

19.3A Window regulator control mounting bolts

19.3B Window regulator tube mounting bolts

22 Front wing – removal and refitting

1   A damaged front wing may be renewed complete. First remove the front bumper as described in Section 23.
2   Remove the screws and withdraw the splash guard from inside the wing (in Coupé models also drill out the rivets).
3   Remove all the screws and lever the wing from the guides. If necessary warm the sealing joints with a blowlamp to melt the adhesive underseal, *but be sure to take the necessary fire precautions.*
4   Clean the mating faces and treat with rust inhibitor if necessary.
5   Apply sealer along the line of the screws before fitting the wing. Once in place, apply underseal as necessary. Paint the wing then fit the splash guard and front bumper.

23 Bumpers – removal and refitting

Front bumper
1   Working inside the engine compartment first disconnect the battery negative lead, then disconnect the wiring to the direction indicator lights.
2   Unscrew the bumper nuts on each side then pull the bumper

forwards out of the side guides and at the same time feed the direction indicator wiring through the body channels.

3 Refitting is a reversal of removal.

Rear bumper

4 Disconnect the battery negative lead.
5 Working in the luggage compartment remove the screw and detach the earth cable from the body.
6 Disconnect the number plate wiring at the connector then pull the wires out from the rear of the body together with the grommet.
7 Unscrew the bumper nuts on each side then pull the bumper rearwards out of the side guides.
8 Refitting is a reversal of removal.

24 Exterior mirror – removal and refitting

Non-remote control type

1 Prise the plastic cover from inside the door (photo).
2 Unscrew the cross-head screws and remove the clips.
3 Withdraw the outer cover and mirror.
4 Refitting is a reversal of removal.

Remote control type

5 Pull off the adjusting knob and bellows from the inside of the door.
6 Remove the door trim panel as described in Section 14.
7 Unscrew the locknut and remove the adjusting knob from the bracket.
8 Prise off the plastic cover then unscrew the cross-head screws and remove the clips.
9 Withdraw the mirror together with the adjusting knob and gasket.
10 Refitting is a reversal of removal, but fit a new gasket if necessary.

25 Sunroof – removal, refitting and adjustment

1 Half open the sunroof then prise off the trim clips.
2 Close the sunroof and push the trim to the rear.

24.1 Removing the inner plastic cover when removing the exterior mirror

3 Unscrew the guide screws from the front of the sunroof and remove the guides.
4 Disengage the leaf springs from the rear guides by pulling them inwards.
5 Remove the screws and withdraw the rear support plates.
6 Lift the sunroof from the car.
7 To refit the sunroof locate it in the aperture and fit the front guides.
8 With the sunroof closed and correctly aligned, fit the rear guides and leaf springs.
9 The correct adjustment of the sunroof is shown in Fig. 11.8 – the front edge must be level with or a maximum of 1.0 mm (0.040 in) below the roof panel, and the rear edge must be level with or a maximum of 1.0 mm (0.040 in) above the roof panel.

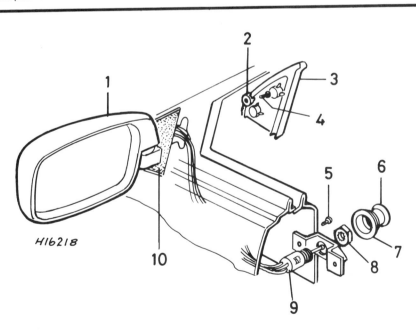

H16218

Fig. 11.6 Exploded diagram of remote control exterior mirror (Sec 24)

1 Outer mirror	4 Fillister head screw	7 Bellows	9 Retainer
2 Retainer	5 Phillips screws	8 Lock nut	10 Mirror mounting
3 Cover	6 Adjusting knob		

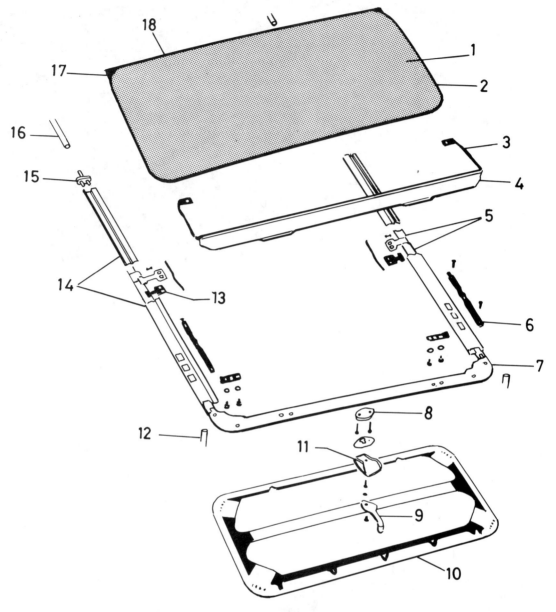

Fig. 11.7 Exploded view of the sunroof (Sec 25)

1	Sliding roof panel	6	Cover moulding	11	Finger plate	15	Guide rails end section
2	Moulded seal	7	Cable guide	12	Front water drain hose	16	Rear water drain hose
3	Deflector arm	8	Cable drive mechanism	13	Support plate	17	Water trap plate
4	Wind deflector	9	Crank	14	Guide rail	18	Panel seat
5	Rear guide with cable (one part)	10	Panel headlining				

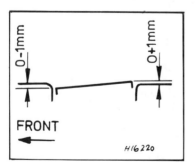

Fig. 11.8 Sunroof adjustment dimensions (Sec 25)

10 To adjust the front edge of the sunroof loosen the front guide screws and turn the adjustment screws as necessary, then tighten the guide screws.

11 To adjust the rear edge, detach the leaf springs, loosen the slotted screws and move the sunroof as necessary in the serrations. Tighten the screws and refit the leaf springs after making the adjustment.

12 Refit the trim with the clips.

26 Seats – removal and refitting

Front seats

1 Remove the screw and small clip at the front of the seat.

2 Slide the seat rearwards from the runners and remove from the car.

3 When refitting guide the seat onto the runners and refit the clip.

Rear seat

4 Remove the covers and mounting screws from the front of the cushion.

5 Lift the rear of the cushion to disengage the hooks then withdraw the cushion.

6 Working in the luggage compartment prise the backrest upper hooks from the panel, then withdraw the backrest from the car.

7 Refitting is a reversal of removal.

27 Heater unit and matrix – removal and refitting

1 Drain the cooling system with reference to Chapter 2.

2 Remove the sealing strip and cover from the plenum chamber at the rear of the engine compartment.

3 Pull the wiring block from the terminals on the heater (photo).

4 Note the locations of the hoses then loosen the clips and disconnect them (photo).

5 Release the clip and disconnect the temperature control cable (photo).

6 Prise out the clips, ease the heater from the fresh air box, and withdraw it from the bulkhead. Remove all traces of gasket and sealing compound (photos).

27.3 Removing the heater wiring block

27.4 Disconnecting the heater hoses

27.5 Showing heater temperature control cable

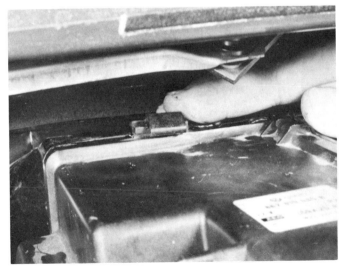

27.6A Prise off the clips ...

27.6B ... and withdraw the heater

27.6C Showing the heater air box on the bulkhead

27.7A Matrix retaining screw locations in the heater body

27.7B Removing the heater matrix

27.7C Heater matrix and temperature control valve

27.8 Heater motor connections

27.9 Showing flow direction arrow on the upper heater outlet – beneath the outlet with temperature valve fitted

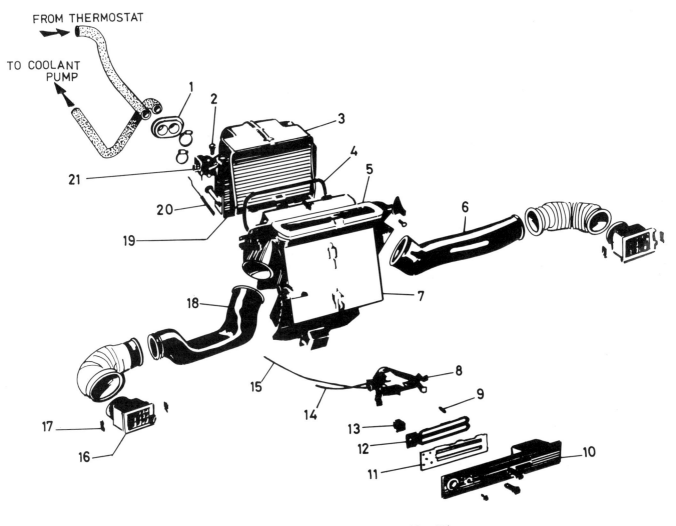

Fig. 11.9 Exploded view of the heater (Sec 27)

1	Double grommet	7	Fresh air box	12	Lighting strip	17	Spring clip
2	Bleeder screw with seal	8	Fresh air and heater	13	Fresh air blower switch	18	Air duct, left
3	Fresh air blower		controls	14	Cut-off flap valve	19	Non-hardening sealant
4	Seal	9	Fresh air controls light	15	Regulating valve cable	20	Regulating valve cable
5	Seal	10	Trim panel	16	Outlet vent	21	Regulating valve
6	Air duct, right	11	Light carrier				

7 Remove the cross-head screws and slide the matrix from the housing (photos).

8 Clean all the components. The motor can be removed by separating the housing halves but the motor is not obtainable as a separate item (photo).

9 Refitting is a reversal of removal, but fit a new gasket if necessary.

Make sure that the hoses are correctly fitted (photo). To fit the temperature control cable turn the lever fully clockwise to the closed position, pull the inner cable out of the outer cable, then locate the inner cable on the lever and secure the outer cable with the clip. Bleed the cooling system as described in Chapter 2.

Chapter 12 Supplement:
Revisions and information on later models

Contents

1 Introduction

This Supplement contains details of modifications and improvements made to the Polo range since 1983 when the main Chapters were written.

The Sections in this Supplement follow the same order as the main Chapters and, although the Specifications are grouped together, they too follow Chapter order.

It is recommended that before any work is undertaken, both the main Chapters and relevant Sections of this Supplement are studied, so that any changes to procedure are fully understood.

2 Specifications

These are revisions of, or supplementary to, the Specifications at the beginning of each of the preceding Chapters

Engine – 1986 on
General

	HZ	MH
Code letters		
Cubic capacity	1.05 litre	1.3 litre
Bore	75 mm (2.95 in)	75 mm (2.95 in)
Stroke	59 mm (2.33 in)	72 mm (2.84 in)
Compression ratio	9.5:1	9.5:1
Output	37 kW (50 bhp) at 5900 rpm	40 kW (54 bhp) at 5200 rpm
Torque (max)	74 Nm at 3600 rpm	96 Nm at 3400 rpm

Cylinder head
Minimum dimension after machining (skimming) .... 135.6 mm (5.34 in)

Camshaft
Run-out (max) .... 0.01 mm (0.0004 in)
Radial play (max) .... 0.1 mm (0.004 in)

Valves
Head diameter:
    Inlet .... 36 mm (1.42 in)
    Exhaust .... 29 mm (1.14 in)
Valve length:
    Inlet .... 98.9 mm (3.897 in)
    Exhaust .... 99.1 mm (3.905 in)
Seat width .... 2.2 mm (0.087 in)

Hydraulic tappets
Free travel (max) .... 0.1 mm (0.004 in)

Valve timing
(at 1.0 mm/0.04 in valve lift, zero valve clearance)

	HZ	MH
Inlet opens	12° ATDC	5° ATDC
Inlet closes	28° ABDC	29° ABDC
Exhaust opens	25° BBDC	33° BBDC
Exhaust closes	9° BTDC	9° BTDC

Lubrication system
Capacity:
    Without filter change .... 3.0 litres (5.3 pints)
    With filter change .... 3.5 litres (6.2 pints)
Dipstick MIN to MAX .... 1 litre (1.8 pints)
Oil pump:
    Gear teeth backlash:
        New .... 0.05 mm (0.002 in)
        Wear limit .... 0.20 mm (0.008 in)
    Gear teeth axial play (wear limit) .... 0.15 mm (0.006 in)
    Chain drive deflection .... 2.0 to 2.5 mm (0.08 to 0.10 in)

Torque wrench settings

	lbf ft	Nm
Camshaft sprocket bolt	59.0	80
Camshaft dust cover:		
Upper bolt	7.3	10
Lower bolt	14.7	20
Camshaft bearing cap nuts:		
Stage 1	4.4	6
Stage 2	Tighten by further 90°	
Number 5 cap screws	7.3	10
Cylinder head bolts:		
Stage 1	29.5	40
Stage 2	44.3	60
Stage 3	Tighten by further 180° (or 2 turns of 90°)	
Oil pump bolts	14.7	20
Stay bracket bolts	7.3	10
Strainer assembly to pump body	7.3	10
Socket-headed bolts in sump (new)	5.9	8

Fuel system – 1986 on
Pierburg 1B3 carburettor
Application .... 1.05 litre, HZ engine
Idling speed .... 800 ± 50 rpm
CO content .... 2.0 ± 0.5%
Accelerator pump capacity .... 1.0 ± 0.15 cm³/stroke
Choke valve gap .... 2.2 ± 0.2 mm
Fast idle speed .... 2000 ± 100 rpm

Pierburg 2E3 carburettor
Application .... 1.3 litre, MH engine
Idling speed .... 800 ± 50 rpm
CO content .... 3.0 ± 0.5%
Accelerator pump capacity .... 1.0 ± 0.15 cm³/stroke
Choke valve gap .... 2.0 ± 0.1 mm
Fast idle speed .... 2000 ± 100 rpm

Weber 32 TLA carburettor
Application	1.05 litre, HZ engine
Venturi	22 mm
Main jet	105
Air correction jet	80
Emulsion tube	F96
Idling fuel jet	47
Idling air jet	100
Accelerator pump capacity	1.05 ± 0.15 cm³/stroke
Float needle valve diameter	1.75 mm
Float needle washer thickness	0.75 mm
Float setting	28 ± 1.0
Fast idle speed	2000 ± 100 rpm
Choke valve gap (pull-down)	2.5 ± 0.2 mm
Choke valve gap (wide open kick)	2.0 ± 0.5 mm
Idling speed	800 ± 50 rpm
CO content	2.0 ± 0.5%

Fuel tank capacity
9.2 Imp gal (42 litres)

Ignition system – 1986 on
General
Type	TCI-H breakerless transistorized system

Spark plugs
Type	Bosch W7 DTC
	Beru 14-7 DTU
	Champion N7 BYC
Gap	0.6 to 0.8 mm (0.024 to 0.032 in)

Ignition timing (at idling speed)
All models (vacuum hose disconnected)	5° ± 1 BTDC

Clutch
Friction disc diameter
Later models	190 mm (7.48 in)

Manual gearbox and final drive
Four-speed
Ratios (teeth):	**GX**
1st	3.45:1 (38:11)
2nd	1.95:1 (41:21)
3rd	1.25:1 (60:48)
4th	0.89:1 (51:57)
Reverse	3.38:1 (44:13)
Final drive	4.06:1 (65:16)
Speedo drive	0.60:1 (12:20)

Five-speed
Code	085

At the time of writing no additional information was available – see Section 7

Suspension and steering – 1986 on
Tyre pressures – bar (lbf/in²)

	Front	Rear
135 SR 13:		
Half load	1.7 (25)	1.7 (25)
Full load	2.1 (30)	2.4 (34)
145 SR 13:		
Half load	1.6 (23)	1.6 (23)
Full load	1.9 (28)	2.3 (33)
155/70 SR 13:		
Half load	1.6 (23)	1.6 (23)
Full load	1.9 (28)	2.3 (33)
165/65 SR 13:		
Half load	1.6 (23)	1.6 (23)
Full load	1.9 (28)	2.3 (33)

3 Engine (1986 on)

General description
1 The 1.05 litre and 1.3 litre engines, code letters HZ and MH, produced since August 1985 have a redesigned cylinder head incorporating hydraulic 'bucket' type tappets in place of the previous rocker finger tappets, and a redesigned engine oil pump, driven by chain from the crankshaft.

2 Additionally, different ancillary components are fitted, such as carburettor and distributor. Where differences to the servicing procedure described in the relevant Chapters of this book occur, they will be found in this Supplement.

3.4 New type valve cover

3.5 Plastic oil shield

3.10 Using two lengths of metal as a pair of 'scissors' to prevent the camshaft turning

Cylinder head – removal

3 The procedure for removing the cylinder head on engines with hydraulic tappets is basically the same as described in Chapter 1, but the following points should be borne in mind.

4 The valve cover is different, being held in place by three bolts (photo).

5 There is a plastic oil shield located at the distributor end of the engine (photo).

6 The fuel and coolant pipes differ, depending on model.

7 Spring type re-usable hose clips may be fitted. These are removed by punching the ends together to expand the clip and then sliding it down the hose.

8 The clips on the fuel hoses are designed to be used only once, so obtain new ones or replace them with screw type clips.

Camshaft – removal and inspection

Removal

9 Refer to Chapter 1, Section 10, all paragraphs up to number 4 (inclusive).

10 Devise a method to prevent the camshaft turning, and remove the sprocket bolt (photo). Remove the camshaft sprocket and Woodruff key.

11 The camshaft bearing caps must be refitted in the same places from which they were removed, and the same way round. They are usually numbered, but centre-punch marks on them, if necessary, to ensure correct refitting.

12 Remove bearing caps 5, 1 and 3 in that order. Now undo the nuts holding 2 and 4 in a diagonal pattern and the camshaft will lift them up as the pressure of the valve springs is exerted. When they are free, lift the caps off.

13 If the caps are stuck, give them a sharp tap with a hide-faced mallet to loosen them. Do not try to lever them off with a screwdriver.

14 Lift out the camshaft; the oil seal will come with it.

Inspection

15 Clean the camshaft in petrol, then inspect the journals and cam peaks for pitting, scoring, cracking and wear.

16 The camshaft bearings are machined directly into the cylinder head and the bearing caps.

17 Radial play in the bearings can be measured using the Plastigage method. Compare the results with the dimension in the Specifications.

18 If wear is evident, consult your VAG dealer.

Camshaft oil seal – renewal

19 This is straightforward if the camshaft is removed, but it is possible to renew the oil seal without removing the camshaft.

20 A VAG special tool exists for this job, but if it is not available the old seal will have to be removed by securing suitable screws into it and pulling it out with pliers. Note which way round it is fitted.

21 Whichever method is used, the timing cover and camshaft sprocket will have to be removed. Slacken the water pump bolts to release the tension in the timing belt.

22 Lightly oil a new seal and slide it onto the camshaft – the same way round as the one which was removed. Use a suitable socket and a bolt in the end of the shaft to press the new seal home. Push it in as far as it will go.

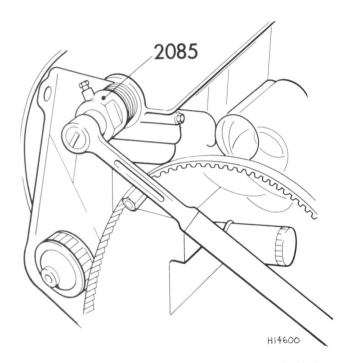

Fig. 12.1 Renewing the camshaft oil seal with the VAG special tool (Sec 3)

Camshaft endfloat

23 To check the camshaft endfloat, remove the camshaft and all the tappets.

24 Refit the camshaft using only number 3 bearing cap.

25 Set up a dial test indicator or use feeler gauges (photo) to measure the endfloat (see the Specifications in Chapter 1). If the endfloat is greater than specified, consult your VAG dealer.

Camshaft – refitting

26 Oil all the bucket tappets, the camshaft journals and the camshaft liberally with clean engine oil.

27 Place the camshaft in position on the cylinder head (photo).

28 Fit a new camshaft oil seal (photo).

29 Refit the bearing caps, ensuring they are the right way round and in their correct position (they are numbered 1 to 5 and these numbers should be readable from the exhaust manifold side of the head).

30 Thread on the cap retaining nuts loosely, then tighten the nuts on number 2 and 4 caps in a diagonal sequence to the Stage 1 torque figure given in the Specifications (photo).

31 Tighten the nuts on caps 1, 3 and 5 to the Stage 1 torque.

3.25 Measuring camshaft endfloat with feeler gauges

3.27 Refitting the camshaft

3.28 Camshaft oil seal

3.30 Tightening the camshaft bearing cap nuts

3.33 Fitting the camshaft sprocket bolt

3.41 Removing the bucket tappets

32 Once all nuts have been tightened to the Stage 1 torque, tighten all nuts a further 90° (Stage 2). Fit and tighten No 5 cap screws to the correct torque.
33 Refit the Woodruff key into its slot in the camshaft, fit the camshaft sprocket and tighten the bolt to the specified torque (photo).
34 If the cylinder head is in the car, follow the procedure given in Chapter 1, Section 38, paragraphs 9 to 18.
35 Ignore any reference to the oil spray tube, and be sure to refit the oil shield at the distributor end of the camshaft before the valve cover is refitted.
36 If the cylinder head is out of the car it will obviously have to be refitted before the timing belt can be reconnected. Refitting the cylinder head is described later in this Section.

Cylinder head – inspection
37 If, on examination, the valve seats are badly pitted or eroded they can be reworked, but this is a specialist job best left to your dealer or local engine overhaul specialists.
38 Similarly, the cylinder head surfaces can be skimmed, again by specialist engineers, if the head is warped.
39 On inspection, if it is found that there are cracks from the valve seats or valve seat inserts to the spark plug threads the cylinder head may still be serviceable. Consult your VAG dealer.

Hydraulic bucket tappets – removal, inspection and refitting
40 Remove the camshaft, as previously described.
41 Lift out the tappets one by one (photo), ensuring they are kept in their correct order and so are replaced in their original positions.
42 Place them, face down (cam contact surface), on a clean sheet of paper as they are removed.
43 Inspect the tappets for wear, indicated by ridging on the clean surface, pitting and cracks.
44 Tappets cannot be repaired, and if found worn must be renewed.
45 Before fitting the tappets, oil all parts liberally and slip the tappets back into their original bore.

Caution: if new tappets are fitted, the engine must not be started after fitting for approximately 30 minutes, or the valves will strike the pistons.

Hydraulic bucket tappets – checking free travel
46 Start the engine and run it until the radiator cooling fan has switched on once.
47 Increase engine speed to about 2500 rpm for about 2 minutes.
48 Irregular noises are normal when starting, but should become quiet after a few minutes running.
49 If the valves are still noisy carry out the following check to identify worn tappets.
50 Stop the engine and remove the valve cover from the cylinder head.
51 Turn the crankshaft clockwise, using a wrench on the crankshaft pulley securing bolt, until the cam of the tappet to be checked is facing upward, and is not exerting any pressure on the tappet.
52 Press the tappet down using a wooden or plastic wedge.
53 If free travel of the tappet exceeds that given in the Specifications the tappet must be renewed.

Inlet and exhaust valves – removal, inspection and refitting
54 Remove the cylinder head, camshaft and tappets, as described previously.
55 Using a valve spring compressor with a deep reach, compress the valve springs, remove the two cotters and release the compressor and springs.
56 Lift out the upper spring seat (photo).
57 Remove the outer and inner valve springs (photos).
58 Lift out the valve (photo).
59 The valves should be inspected as described in Chapter 1, Section 30. Refer to the Specifications for dimensions.
60 Valves cannot be reworked, but must be renewed if they are worn. They should be ground in the normal manner.
61 If possible, check the valve spring lengths against new ones. Renew the whole set if any are too short.
62 Refitting is a reversal of removal.

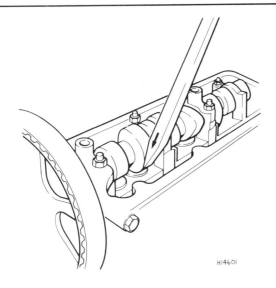

Fig. 12.2 Checking the hydraulic tappet free travel (Sec 3)

3.56 Lift out the valve spring upper seat

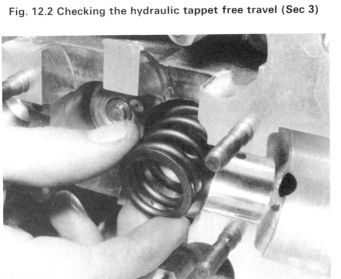

3.57A Remove the outer ...

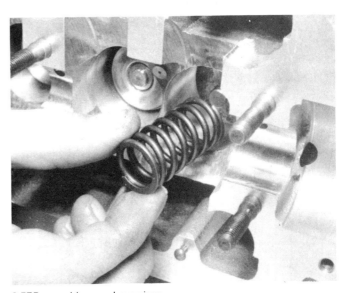

3.57B ... and inner valve springs

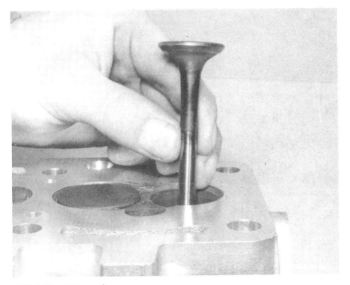

3.58 Lift out the valve

Valve stem oil seals – removal and refitting
63 The removal of the valve stem oil seals (photo) requires the use of special tools and compressed air, and is best left to your VAG dealer.

Cylinder head – refitting
64 Clean all traces of old gasket from the cylinder block and cylinder head faces.
65 Using a new gasket, fit the inlet manifold (photos).
66 If they have been removed, refit the oil pressure switches, using new copper sealing washers (photo).
67 Refit the thermostat housing using a new O-ring seal (photo).
68 Refit the coolant hoses, ensuring they are connected up in their positions (photo).
69 Lubricate the fuel pump driveshaft with clean engine oil and slip it into its housing in the cylinder head (photo).
70 Refit the fuel pump (photo) and fit and tighten the bolts, not forgetting the lifting eye (photo).
71 Slide the distributor into position and ensure that it goes fully home (photo).
72 Fit the distributor rotor arm (photo).
73 Fit the distributor cap and connect up the earth lead (photo).

3.63 Valve stem oil seal

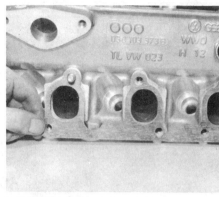
3.65A Fitting a new inlet manifold gasket

3.65B Fitting the inlet manifold, complete with carburettor

3.66 Use a new copper sealing washer when refitting an oil pressure switch

3.67 Use a new O-ring seal (arrowed) when refitting the thermostat housing

3.68 Coolant hoses in position

3.69 Fitting the fuel pump driveshaft (arrowed)

3.70A Fitting the fuel pump ...

3.70B ... not forgetting the lifting eye

3.71 Fit the distributor ...

3.72 ... rotor arm ...

3.73 ... cap and earth lead

74 Check the timing marks on the cylinder head and camshaft sprocket are lined up.

75 The pistons in the cylinder block **must not** be at TDC when refitting the cylinder head.

76 Position a new cylinder head gasket on the cylinder block (photo).

77 Lower the cylinder head gently into position. Special guides are used by Volkswagen both to line up the gasket and guide the cylinder head into position, but this can be done using suitable sized rods inserted in two cylinder head bolt holes.

78 Refer to Chapter 1 and refit the cylinder head bolts in the sequence given in Fig. 1.4, but use the torque figures and stages given in the Specifications section of this Supplement.

79 It is not necessary to retighten the bolts after a period of service, as is normally the case.

80 Refit the plastic oil shield (photo).

81 Using a new rubber sealing gasket, properly located over the dowels, refit the valve cover (photos).

82 Fit a new gasket to the exhaust manifold (photo).

83 Fit the exhaust manifold, do up the nuts (photo), and fit the hot air shroud (photo).

84 Connect up the exhaust downpipe and any other exhaust brackets loosened during removal.

85 Refit all remaining hoses of the cooling system, EGR and fuel system, referring to the relevant Chapter where necessary.

86 Refit all electrical connections disturbed during dismantling (distributor, carburettor, oil pressure transmitter, coolant temperarure, inlet manifold preheater etc). Do not forget the earth lead under the inlet manifold nut (photos).

87 Refit the distributor vacuum hose.

88 With reference to Chapter 1, Section 40, refit the timing belt and covers.

89 Refer to Chapter 3 and refit the throttle cable.

90 Refit the spark plugs, air cleaner and associated pipework and electrical leads.

91 Check oil and coolant levels, refilling as necessary.

3.76 Positioning a new cylinder head gasket

Oil pump
General description

92 The oil pump fitted to engines produced since August 1985 has been changed from the crescent type to a gear type pump, driven by chain from the engine crankshaft.

93 Only the oil pump has been changed, the rest of the lubrication system remains as before.

3.80 Refit the plastic oil shield

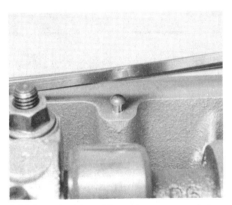

3.81 Locating dowel for valve cover gasket

3.82 Fitting a new exhaust manifold gasket

3.83A Exhaust manifold bolted into position

3.83B Fitting the hot air shroud

3.86A Distributor electrical connection

3.86B Coolant temperature sender electrical connection

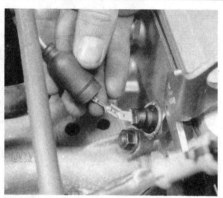

3.86C Oil pressure switch electrical connection

3.86D The earth lead under the inlet manifold nut

Removal and inspection
94 The oil pump can be removed with the engine still in the vehicle.
95 Drain the oil from the sump.
96 Refer to the relevant Chapters and disconnect the exhaust downpipe and inboard driveshaft to give room to remove the sump.
97 Remove the sump.
98 If it is only desired to check backlash in the gears this can be done by removing the oil pump cover and strainer assembly from the back of the pump.
99 Refer to Figs. 12.4 and 12.5 and check backlash and axial play against the tolerances in the Specifications.
100 If the tolerances are exceeded then the oil pump should be renewed, as follows.
101 Refer to the relevant Chapters and remove:

  (a) Camshaft drivebelt (timing belt)
  (b) Alternator drivebelt
  (c) Crankshaft pulley

  (d) Lower camshaft cover
  (e) Front cover and TDC setting bracket

102 If they are still in position remove the bolts holding the rear stay bracket.
103 Remove the two bolts holding the oil pump to the cylinder block.
104 This will release the tension on the chain and allow the pump to be removed.
105 If sufficient slack in the chain cannot be achieved by this method, then slide the pump, chain and crankshaft drive sprocket forward together.
106 Check the chain and teeth of the drive sprockets and renew any parts which are worn.
107 If a new pump is being fitted, it would be as well to renew all other parts at the same time.
Refitting
108 Refitting is a reversal of removal, but bear in mind the following points.

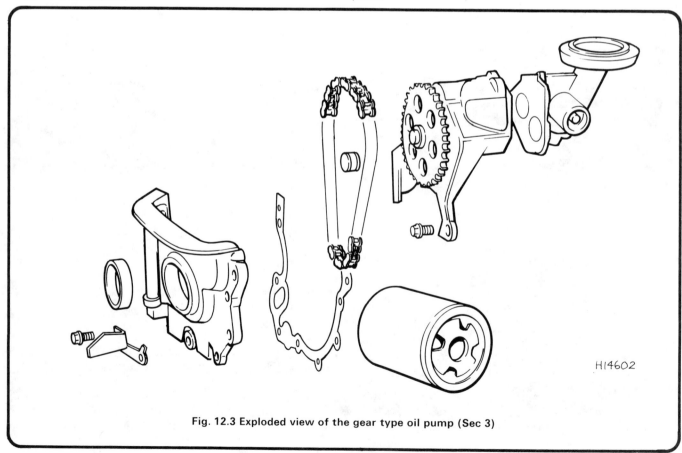

Fig. 12.3 Exploded view of the gear type oil pump (Sec 3)

H14602

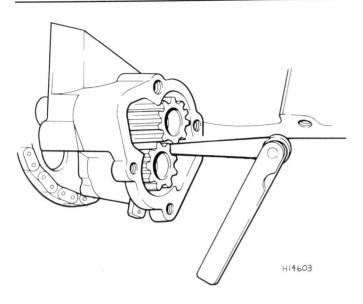

Fig. 12.4 Checking the oil pump gear backlash (Sec 3)

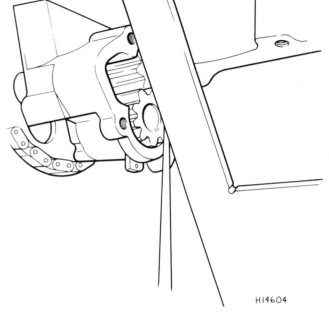

Fig. 12.5 Checking the oil pump gear axial play (Sec 3)

109 Use new gaskets on all components.
110 Oil all new parts liberally.
111 If the small plug in the front cover is at all damaged replace it.
112 Similarly, fit a new crankshaft oil seal to the cover. The old seal can be prised out and a new one pressed fully home.
113 The chain is tensioned by moving the pump housing against its mounting bolts.
114 With light thumb pressure exerted on the chain, deflection should be as given in the Specifications.
115 Whenever the sump is removed with the engine *in situ*, the two hexagon screws in the sealing flange at the flywheel end should be replaced by socket-headed screws and spring washers, and tightened to the figure given in the Specifications.

4 Cooling system

General

The cooling system continues unchanged apart from the modification to the thermostat housing on engines fitted with an automatic choke. These differences are covered in the Fuel system Section.

5 Fuel system

General description (1986 on)

1 In conjunction with the newly designed cylinder head, different carburettors are used, according to engine size.
2 They are either the Weber 32 TLA or Pierburg 1B3, fitted to engines code lettered HZ, or the Pierburg 2E3 fitted to engines code lettered MH.
3 The following sub-sections deal only with those operations not fully covered, or different from those described in Chapter 3; where these are the same, cross-reference to Chapter 3 will be made.
4 The Specifications Section of this Supplement should also be referred to before carrying out any servicing or adjustment, to ensure all relevant information is taken into account.

Carburettor (1986 on) – removal and refitting

5 Disconnect the battery negative lead.
6 Remove the air cleaner as described in Chapter 3.
7 Drain half of the coolant from the cooling system, with reference to Chapter 2.
8 Disconnect the coolant hoses from the automatic choke.

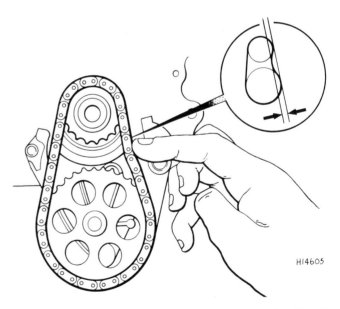

Fig. 12.6 Checking the oil pump drive chain tension (Sec 3)

9 As applicable, disconnect the wiring from the automatic choke and fuel cut-off solenoid.
10 Disconnect the accelerator cable.
11 Disconnect the fuel and vacuum hoses.
12 Unscrew the through-bolts or nuts, and lift the carburettor from the inlet manifold. Remove the insulating flange gasket.
13 Refitting is a reversal of removal, but clean the mating faces of the carburettor and inlet manifold and always fit a new gasket. Tighten the mounting bolts evenly.

Carburettor (1986 on) – dismantling, servicing and reassembly (general)

14 Wash the exterior of the carburettor with a suitable solvent and allow to dry.

15 Dismantle the carburettor with reference to the relevant Figs. and photos. Before dismantling, obtain a set of gaskets. Be sure to mark the relationship of the automatic choke to the carburettor body before separating them.

16 Clean the internal components with a suitable solvent. **Do not** probe any jets or orifices with wire or similar to remove dirt; blow them through with an air line.

17 **Do not** alter or remove the full throttle stop, or adjust the Stage II throttle valve screw settings (if applicable).

18 Reassembly is a reversal of dismantling, but renew all gaskets and rubber rings. Refer to the following sub-sections for checks and adjustments.

Pierburg 2E3 carburettor – servicing and adjustment

19 Before undertaking any carburettor adjustments, be sure all jets etc are clean. Dismantling and reassembly are described in the previous sub-sections (photos).

20 If the port throttle enrichment valve is removed it must be renewed.

Cut-off valve

21 To check the cut-off valve, apply battery voltage. The valve must be heard to click when voltage is applied.

Choke valve gap

22 To check the choke valve gap the choke cover must be removed. Move the throttle valve and the fast idle cam so that the adjustment screw is against the highest cam stop. Now push the choke valve operating rod fully towards the adjustment screw (and pull-down unit), then check the choke valve-to-barrel clearance using a twist drill as a gauge. If necessary turn the adjuster screw as required to provide the specified choke valve gap (Figs. 12.8 and 12.9).

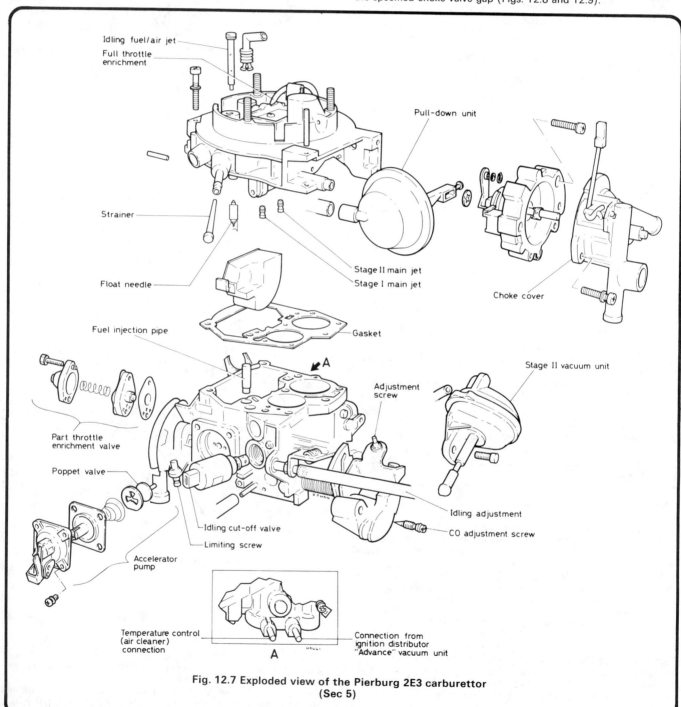

Fig. 12.7 Exploded view of the Pierburg 2E3 carburettor (Sec 5)

5.19A Top cover securing screws (arrowed) – 2E3 carburettor

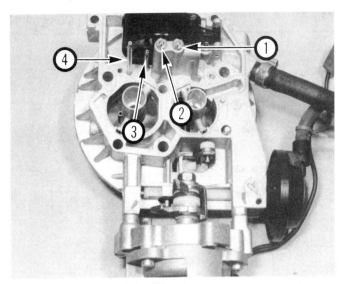

5.19B Underside view of the 2E3 carburettor
1 Stage I main jet
2 Stage II main jet
3 Full throttle enrichment lift pipe
4 Stage II progression lift pipe

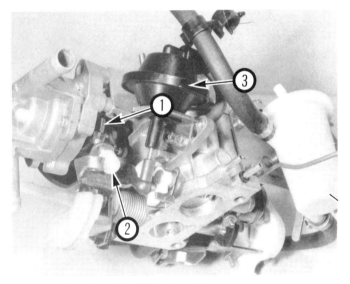

5.19C Outside view of the 2E3 carburettor
1 Fast idle cam
2 Fast idle adjustment screw
3 Stage II vacuum unit

5.19D Choke housing and cover must be correctly aligned – 2E3 carburettor

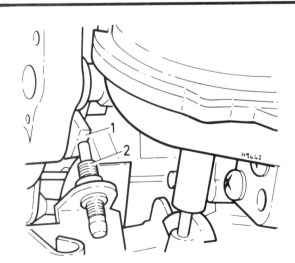

Fig. 12.8 Fast idle cam (1) and choke valve gap adjusting screw (2) – 2E3 carburettor (Sec 5)

Fig. 12.9 Checking the choke valve gap – 2E3 carburettor (Sec 5)

1 Choke valve operating rod
   (push in direction of arrow)
2 Twist drill

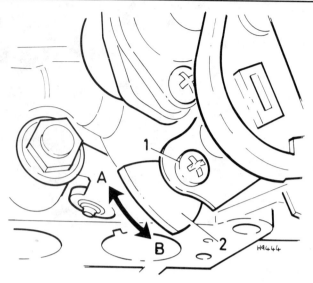

Fig. 12.10 Accelerator pump adjustment – 2E3 carburettor
(Sec 5)

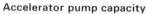

1 Fast idle cam locking screw   A Increases injection capacity
2 Fast idle cam   B Decreases injection capacity

Accelerator pump capacity

23 The accelerator pump injection capacity can be checked in the
same manner as that described in Chapter 3, Section 12. Allow 1
second per stroke, and 3 seconds between strokes. If necessary, refer
to Fig. 12.10 and make suitable adjustments. Ensure the injection pipe
is correctly positioned (photo).

Automatic choke and pull-down unit

24 Ensure that the automatic choke cover and the choke housing
alignment marks correspond. To check the choke, connect up a test
lamp between a battery positive terminal and the choke lead. The test
lamp should illuminate; if it doesn't then the choke unit is defective and
must be renewed.

25 The choke pull-down unit can be checked whilst it is removed but,
as this requires the use of a vacuum pump and gauge, it is a check best
entrusted to your VAG dealer. The pull-down unit can also be tested
when the carburettor is in position in the car. The air cleaner unit must
be removed. Run the engine at idle speed then close the choke valve by
hand and check that a resistance is felt over the final 3 mm (0.12 in) of
travel. If no resistance is felt, there may be a leak in the vacuum
connections, or the pull-down unit diaphragm broken, in which case
the unit must be renewed.

Stage II throttle valve

26 The basic Stage II throttle valve adjustment is made during
manufacture and cannot be further adjusted.

Idle speed and mixture

27 Refer to Chapter 3, Section 13, paragraphs 1 to 7 (photo).

Fast idle speed

28 To check and adjust the fast idle, first check that the engine is still
at normal operating temperature. The air cleaner must be removed and
the other provisional conditions must apply as for the idle adjustment.
Plug the air cleaner temperature control hose.

29 Restart the engine and open the throttle to give an engine speed of
2500 rpm (approximately). Press down the fast idle cam to its stop
then move the throttle valve back so that the adjuster screw is on the
second highest stop on the fast idle cam. In this position the fast idle
speed should be as specified. If the setting is incorrect, turn the
adjustment screw in the required direction until it is correct – Fig.
12.11. (Note that the screw may have a tamperproof cap fitted.)

30 On completion unplug the temperature control connector and refit
the air cleaner.

Pierburg 1B3 carburettor – servicing and adjustment

31 Before undertaking any carburettor adjustments, be sure all jets,
etc, are clean. Dismantling and reassembly are described previously in
this Section.

5.23 Injection pipe must align with recess (arrows) – 2E3
carburettor

Fig. 12.11 Fast idle adjustment screw (2) – 2E3 carburettor
(Sec 5)

5.27 Outside view of 2E3 carburettor
1 Idle speed screw and guide sleeve   2 Mixture screw

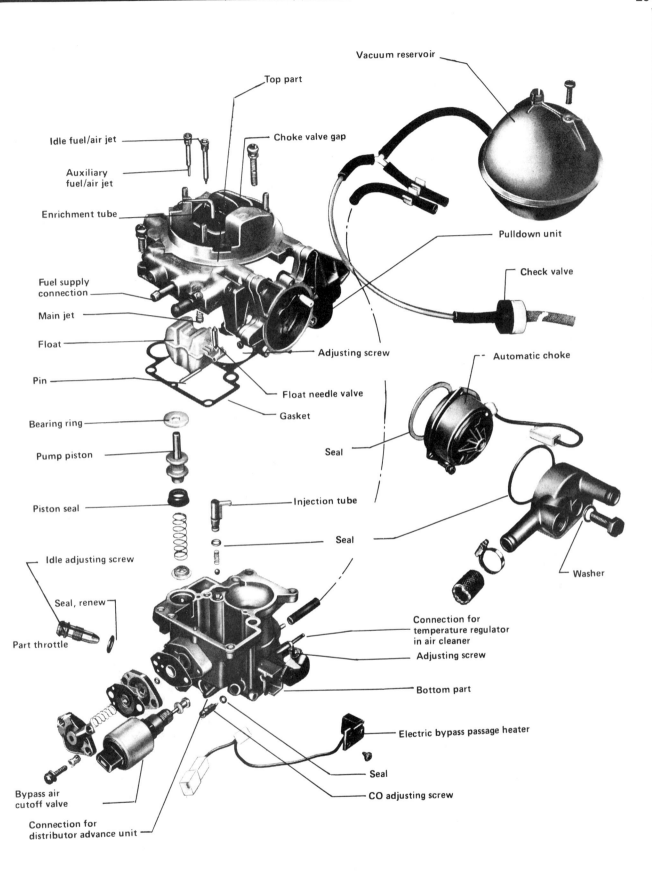

Vacuum reservoir

Top part

Idle fuel/air jet

Choke valve gap

Auxiliary fuel/air jet

Enrichment tube

Pulldown unit

Check valve

Fuel supply connection

Main jet

Float

Adjusting screw

Automatic choke

Pin

Float needle valve

Gasket

Seal

Bearing ring

Pump piston

Piston seal

Injection tube

Seal

Idle adjusting screw

Washer

Seal, renew

Connection for temperature regulator in air cleaner

Part throttle

Adjusting screw

Bottom part

Electric bypass passage heater

Seal

Bypass air cutoff valve

CO adjusting screw

Connection for distributor advance unit

Fig. 12.12 Exploded view of the Pierburg 1B3 carburettor (Sec 5)

32 When inserting the accelerator pump piston seal, press it towards the opposite side of the vent drilling. The piston retaining ring must be pressed flush into the carburettor body.

General

33 All checks and adjustments are as described for the Pierburg 2E3 carburettor, with the following additions.

Enrichment tube

34 With the choke valve closed, the bottom of the enrichment tube should be level with the upper surface of the valve, as shown in Fig. 12.13.

Idle speed and mixture

35 Before making any adjustment, make sure that the automatic choke is fully open, otherwise the throttle valve linkage may still be on the fast idle cam.

Fast idle speed

36 With the engine at normal operating temperature and switched off, connect a tachometer and remove the air cleaner.

37 Fully open the throttle valve, then turn the fast idle cam and release the throttle valve so that the adjustment screw is positioned on the highest part of the cam.

38 Without touching the accelerator pedal, start the engine and check that the fast idling speed is as given in the Specifications. If not, turn the adjustment screw on the linkage as necessary. If a tamperproof cap is fitted renew it after making the adjustment.

Choke valve gap

39 Fully open the throttle valve, then turn the fast idle cam and release the throttle valve so that the adjustment screw is positioned on the highest part of the cam.

40 Press the choke operating rod as far as possible towards the pull-down unit.

41 Using the shank of a twist drill, check that the distance from the choke valve to the carburettor wall is as given in the Specifications. If not, adjust the screw behind the automatic choke.

Electric bypass air heating element

42 Disconnect the wiring from the cut-off valve and thermo-switch, and connect a test lamp to the heating element wire and the battery positive terminal.

43 If the lamp lights up, the heater element is in good working order.

Accelerator pump capacity

44 Hold the carburettor over a funnel and measuring glass.

45 Turn the fast idle cam so that the adjusting screw is off the cam. Hold the cam in this position during the following procedure.

46 Fully open the throttle ten times, allowing at least three seconds per stroke. Divide the total quantity by ten and check that the resultant injection capacity is as given in the Specifications. If not, refer to Fig. 12.14 and loosen the cross-head screw, turn the cam plate as required, and tighten the screw.

47 If difficulty is experienced in making the adjustment, check the pump seal and make sure that the return check valve and injection tube are clear.

Weber 32 TLA carburettor – servicing and adjustment

48 Before undertaking any carburettor adjustments, be sure all jets, etc, are clean. Dismantling and reassembly are described previously in this Section.

49 **Note:** Before loosening the throttle lever, the accelerator pump cam must be held in place with an M4 screw (Fig. 12.17).

Float level

50 With the upper part of the carburettor inverted and held at an angle of approximately 45°, the measurement 'a' in Fig. 12.18 should be as shown in the Specifications.

51 The ball of the float needle should not be pressed in against the spring when making the measurement.

Idle speed and mixture

52 The procedure for checking and adjusting the idling speed and CO content are basically the same as given previously for the Pierburg carburettors.

53 However, refer to Figs 12.19 and 12.20 for the location of adjustment screws and to the Specifications in this Supplement for settings.

Choke valve gap (pull-down)

54 Remove the choke cover.

55 Place the cold idling speed adjusting screw on the highest step of the cam (Fig. 12.21). Press the pullrod in the direction of the arrow.

56 Measure the choke flap gap using a drill shank (Fig. 12.22). The gap should be as given in the Specifications. Adjustment is made on the screw at the end of the pulldown device. Ensure that the spring (2 in Fig. 12.22) is not compressed when making the check.

Idle cut-off valve

57 To check the cut-off valve, apply battery voltage. The valve must be heard to click when voltage is applied.

Fast idle speed

58 Before carrying out this check, ensure that ignition timing and manual idling adjustments are correct. The engine should be set at a minimum temperature of 60°C.

59 Remove the air cleaner.

60 Plug the temperature regulator connection.

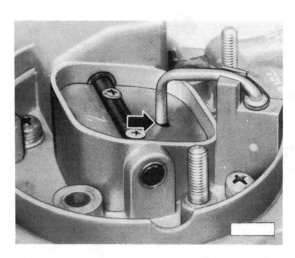

Fig. 12.13 Correct position of the enrichment tube – 1B3 carburettor (Sec 5)

Fig. 12.14 Accelerator pump adjustment – 1B3 carburettor (Sec 5)

a   Cam locking screw   b   Cam plate

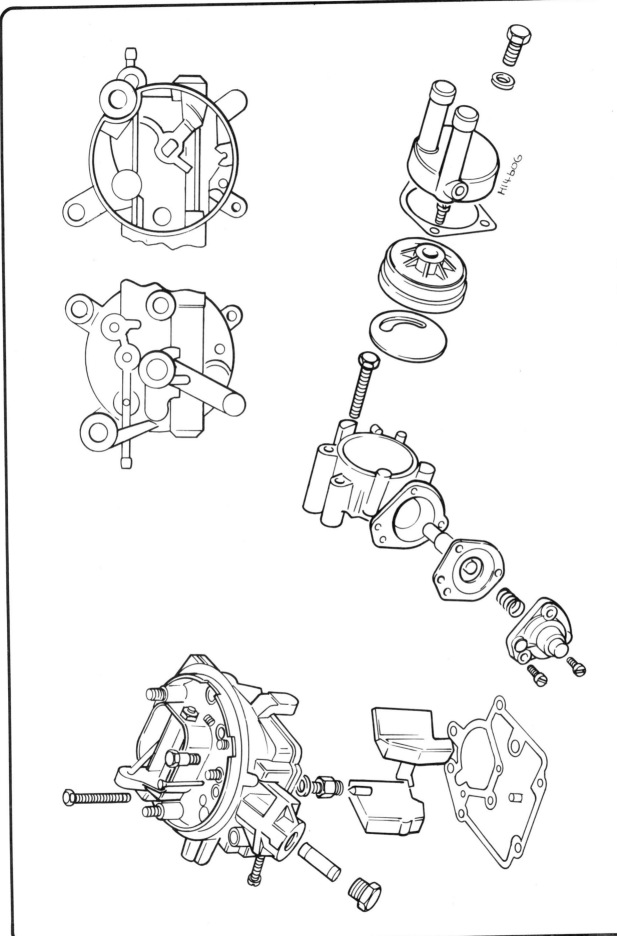

Fig. 12.15 Exploded view of upper part of Weber 32 TLA carburettor (Sec 5)

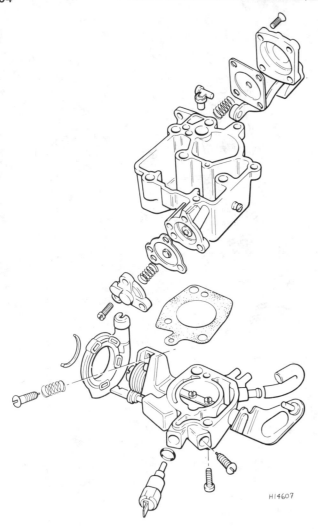

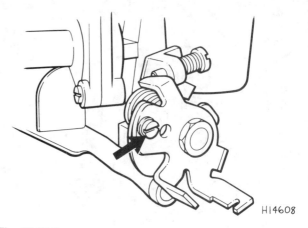

Fig. 12.17 Secure the accelerator pump cam with an M4 screw (arrowed) before loosening the throttle lever – 32 TLA carburettor (Sec 5)

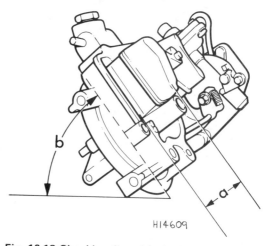

Fig. 12.16 Exploded view of lower part of Weber 32 TLA carburettor (Sec 5)

Fig. 12.18 Checking float level – 32 TLA carburettor (Sec 5)

$a = 28 \pm 1.0$ mm $b = 45°$

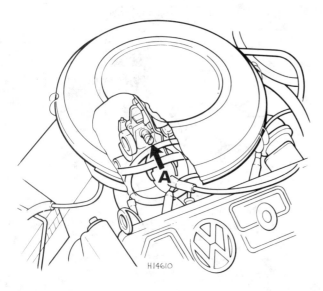

Fig. 12.19 Idle speed adjusting screw (A) – 32 TLA carburettor (Sec 5)

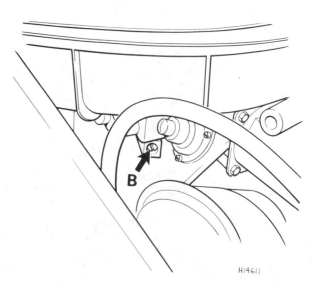

Fig. 12.20 Mixture (CO content) adjusting screw (B) – 32 TLA carburettor (Sec 5)

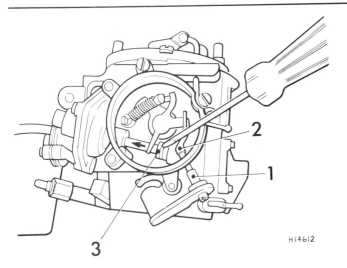

Fig. 12.21 Cam setting prior to checking choke valve gap
(pull-down) – 32 TLA carburettor (Sec 5)

1   Idle speed adjusting screw   3   Pullrod
2   Cam

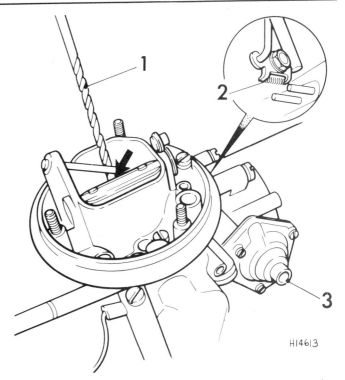

Fig. 12.22 Checking the choke valve gap (pull-down) –
32 TLA carburettor (Sec 5)

1   Twist drill   3   Adjusting screw
2   Spring

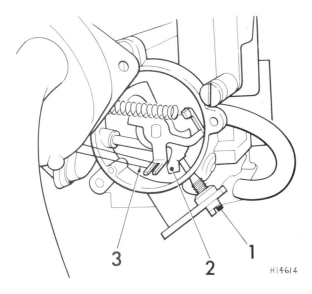

Fig. 12.23 Fast idle speed adjustment – 32 TLA carburettor
(Sec 5)

1   Fast idle adjusting screw   3   Rubber band
2   Cam

61   Connect up a rev counter.
62   Remove the choke cover and set the fast idle speed adjusting screw
on the second highest step on the cam (Fig. 12.23).
63   Tension the operating lever with a rubber band so that the choke
flap is fully open.
64   Without touching the accelerator pedal, start the engine, which
should run at the fast idle speed given in the Specifications.
65   Adjust on the screw as necessary.
Choke valve gap (wide open kick)
66   Remove the air cleaner.
67   Fully open the throttle and hold it in this position.
68   Refer to Fig. 12.24 and press the lever (1) upwards.
69   Check the gap with a twist drill, which should be as given in the
Specifications. Adjust by binding the lever (Fig. 12.25).

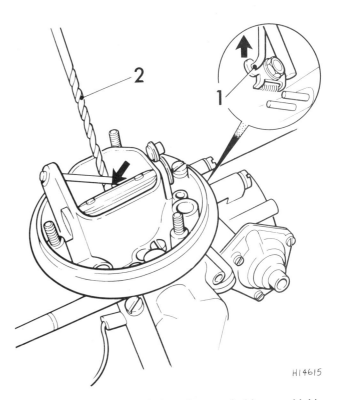

Fig. 12.24 Checking the choke valve gap (wide open kick) –
32 TLA carburettor (Sec 5)

1   Press upwards   2   Twist drill

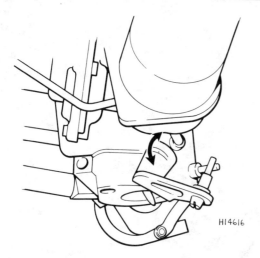

**Fig. 12.25 Adjusting the choke valve gap (wide open kick) –
32 TLA carburettor (Sec 5)**

Bend the lever to make adjustments

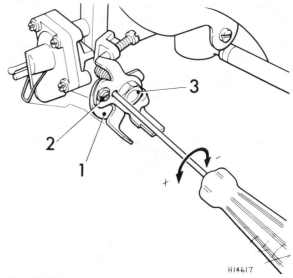

**Fig. 12.26 Accelerator pump adjustment – 32 TLA
carburettor (Sec 5)**

1 Cam	*3 Cam locking nut*
2 M4 screw securing cam	

Accelerator pump capacity

70 This can be checked by following the procedure in Chapter 3,
Section 12 with the following differences.

71 Open the throttle valve quickly when operating the pump (ie 1
second per stroke, with pauses of 3 seconds between strokes).

72 The amount of fuel injected can be altered, but only very slightly, as
follows:

73 Take the accelerator cable cam off the throttle valve lever.

74 Secure the cam for the accelerator pump with an M4 screw (Fig.
12.26).

75 Loosen the locknut on the cam securing screw. Loosen the screw
and turn the cam with a screwdriver – clockwise to decrease injected
fuel and anti-clockwise to increase injected fuel. Tighten the screw
and locknut and recheck the injection capacity.

Solex 31 PIC-7 carburettor – modification

76 From May 1983, the 31 PIC-7 carburettor on 1.05 litre models has
been fitted with a float needle valve which is hung on the float to give a

forced opening (Fig. 12.27). Carburettors with this modification have
the numbers 146-3 in their code number.

77 When refitting the float and needle, ensure the needle valve is
located correctly in the slot in the float suspension arm.

Air cleaner with vacuum-operated control

78 Since January 1984 some air cleaners have been modified by
having the thermostatic control of the air intake changed to purely
vacuum control (Fig. 12.28).

79 Both types of air cleaner are interchangeable.

6   Ignition system (1986 on)

General description

1   On later models the contact breaker type distributor is replaced by a
breakerless transistorized unit.

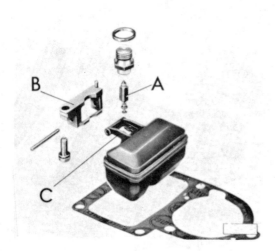

**Fig. 12.27 Float and needle valve assembly on 31 PIC-7
carburettor with forced opening (Sec 5)**

A Needle valve	*C Float arm*
B Bracket	

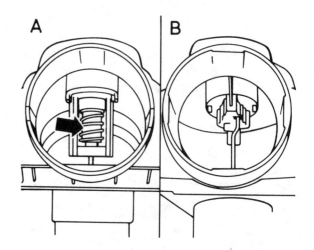

Fig. 12.28 Air cleaner intake control (Sec 5)

A Thermostatic control	*B Vacuum control*

2   This system (TCI-H) functions in a similar manner to that described for the conventional system (Chapter 4), but an electronic sender unit replaces the contact points and condenser in the distributor, and a remotely-mounted electronic switch unit controls the coil primary circuit.

Precautions

3   On models equipped with transistorized ignition certain precautions must be observed in order to prevent damage to the semi-conductor components and in order to prevent personal injury.

4   Before disconnecting wires from the system make sure that the ignition is switched off.

5   When turning the engine at starter speed without starting, the HT lead must be pulled from the centre of the distributor cap and kept earthed to a suitable part of the engine or bodywork.

6   Disconnect the battery leads before carrying out electric welding on any part of the car.

7   If the system develops a fault and it is necessary to tow the car with the ignition key switched on, the wiring must be disconnected from the TCI-H switch unit.

8   Do not under any circumstances connect a condenser to the coil terminals.

9   Take care to avoid receiving electric shocks from the HT system.

7   Manual gearbox (1986 on)

General

1   Some later models are fitted with a five-speed manual gearbox; code number 085. This transmission is essentially the same as the four-speed 084 unit, but with a fifth gear and associated components fitted in a housing adjacent to the other geartrains.

2   At the time of writing no specific information was available for this gearbox; but routine maintenance, and removal and refitting procedures remain as given in Chapter 6. The drain and filler plugs are in the same places.

8   Braking system

Modifications

1   Later Polo and Polo Coupe models are fitted with VW 'Mk 1' brake calipers on the front axle.

2   The instructions given in Chapter 8 are sufficient to cover the servicing of these brake calipers, but the following point should be noted.

3   The wheel bearing housing has also been modified, and if a new brake caliper and wheel bearing housing of VW design are being fitted to older vehicles, then a new brake hose should also be fitted to allow the rubber brake hose retainer to be located correctly (Fig. 12.29).

9   Electrical system

Automatic stop-start system

1   From March 1984, Formel E models are equipped with an automatic stop-start (SSA) system, in addition to the gearshift/consumption indicator (GCI).

2   The system required specialist test equipment to check its operation and diagnose faults, and if it fails to operate satisfactorily, it is recommended that the vehicle is taken to your local VAG dealer.

Description of operation

3   The SSA system is switched on or off, as required, by a switch on the facia panel.

4   For the system to become operative, the coolant temperature must be above 55°C (131°F) and the vehicle road-speed in excess of 5 km/hour (3 mph).

5   The engine is automatically switched off when road-speed drops below this point and 1st, 2nd or reverse gears are not engaged.

6   When the SSA system is in operation, the heated rear window and oil pressure warning light are switched off.

7   The engine will be started automatically when the gear lever is moved from neutral toward 1st, 2nd or reverse, and the clutch pedal depressed.

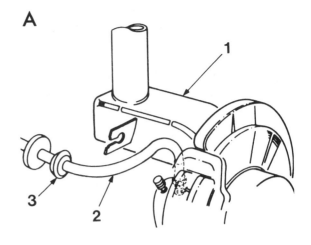

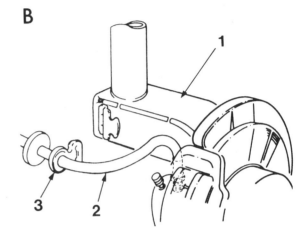

Fig. 12.29 Brake hose retainers on the wheel bearing housing (Sec 8)

A Old type	2 Brake hose
B New type	3 Retainer
1 Wheel bearing housing	

8   Should the engine stall when moving off, the engine may be restarted by moving the gear lever back to neutral and then into 1st, 2nd or reverse gear within 6 seconds of stalling.

9   Wiring diagrams for the SSA system appear in the wiring diagrams; the following paragraphs and figures show component location and removal/refitting procedures for individual components.

SSA components – removal and refitting

10   The stop-start automatic control unit is located under the facia panel.

11   Remove the two screws (Fig. 12.30) and pull the control unit off the relay plate.

12   The heated rear window and oil pressure warning cut-off relay is located on the double relay plate by the steering column, behind the shelf (Fig. 12.31).

13   To remove the relay, first remove the shelf and then pull the relay off the relay plate.

14   The gearshift indicator control unit is on the same relay plate.

15   The speed sensor is located in the instrument panel (Fig. 12.32).

16   Remove the instrument panel, undo the screws (arrowed) and remove the speed sensor unit.

17   The SSA master switch is located on the facia panel (Fig. 12.33).

18   To remove it, carefully lever the switch out and pull off the connector.

19   The SSA gearbox switch is located on the underside of the gearbox (Fig. 12.34).

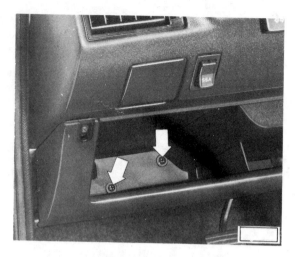

Fig. 12.30 Stop-start system automatic control unit
retaining screws – arrowed (Sec 9)

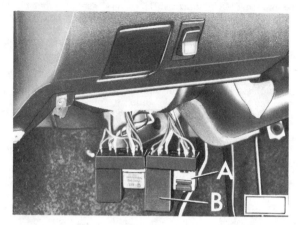

Fig. 12.31 The double relay plate (Sec 9)

A   Heated rear window and oil pressure warning cut-off relay
B   Gearshift indicator control unit

Fig. 12.32 Speed sensor retaining screws – arrowed (Sec 9)

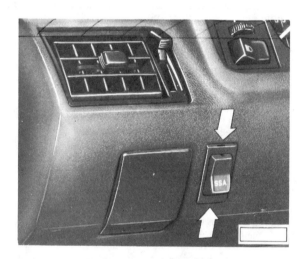

Fig. 12.33 The SSA master switch (Sec 9)

Lever out at arrows

20 To remove the switch, disconnect the wiring connector and
unscrew the switch. Retain the shim.
21 When refitting the switch, use a shim of the same thickness as that
removed.
22 The gearbox switch for gearshift/consumption indicator can also
be seen in Fig. 12.34.
23 Refitting for all items is a reversal of the removal procedure.
24 Check gearbox oil level and top up as necessary.

Oil pressure warning system (1983 on)
General description
25 All models from 1983 on are equipped with an optical and acoustic
oil pressure warning system.
26 The oil pressure switches for these warning systems are mounted
on the cylinder head.
27 The switches are 1.8 bar (white insulation) and 0.3 bar (brown
insulation).
28 On starting the engine, as soon as the oil pressure rises above 0.3
bar, the oil pressure warning light will go out.
29 At engine speeds above 2000 rpm the high pressure switch comes
into operation, and should the oil pressure drop below 1.8 bar, the oil
warning light will come on and the buzzer will sound.
30 On some earlier models, the buzzer will also sound in the low
pressure mode on start-up.
31 Apart from changing the oil pressure switches, little can be done by
way of maintenance, and your VAG dealer should be consulted if the
system malfunctions.

Fig. 12.34 The SSA gearbox switch (Sec 9)

A   SSA switch   B   Gearshift/consumption
                                          indicator switch

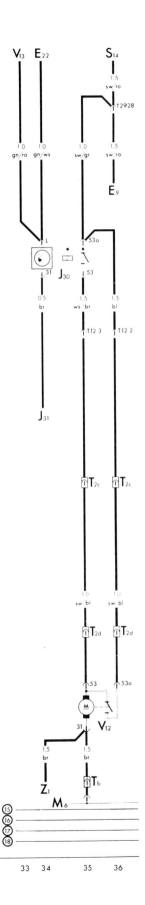

Fig. 12.35 Wiring diagram amendment for 1982 CL and GL models

Use with Fig. 9.18 in Chapter 9

Designation		in current track
E9	To fresh air blower switch	36
E22	To intermittent wiper switch	34
J30	Rear window wiper/washer relay	34,35
J31	To intermittent wash/wipe relay	34
M6	To rear left turn signal	
S14	Fuse in fuse box	
T1i	Connector, single in boot rear left	
T2d	Connector, 2 point, in tailgate near wiper motor	
T2c	Connector, 2 point, in tailgate near wiper motor	
T12/	Connector, 12 point behind dash	
T29	Connector, 29 point behind dash	
V12	Rear wiper motor	35,36
V13	To rear washer pump motor	33
Z1	To heated rear window	34

15. Earthing point in insulating sleeve of left engine compartment loom

16. Earthing point in insulating sleeve of right engine compartment loom

17. Earthing point, bound with insulating tape in dash loom

18. Earthing point, bound with insulating tape in instrument loom

Colour code

bl	Blue
br	Brown
gn	Green
gr	Grey
ro	Red
sw	Black
ws	White

Key to wiring diagram for Polo models from 1985

Designation		In current track
A	Battery	1
B	Starter	5 to 7
C	Alternator	3 to 4
C1	Voltage regulator	3 to 4
D	Ignition/starter switch	6 to 9
E1	Lighting switch	71 to 75
E2	Turn signal switch	60,61
E3	Emergency light switch	55 to 63
E4	Headlight dimmer/flasher switch	75 to 77
E9	Fresh air blower switch	37,38
E15	Heated rear window switch	82
E19	Parking light switch	69,70
E20	Instrument/instrument panel lighting control	67
E22	Intermittent wiper switch	25 to 31
F	Brake light switch	90
F1	Oil pressure switch	44
F2	Front left door contact switch	84
F3	Front right door contact switch	83
F4	Reversing light switch	17
F9	Handbrake warning system switch	40
F18	Radiator fan thermoswitch	91
F22	Oil pressure switch	45
F34	Brake fluid level warning contact	41
F35	Thermoswitch for automatic choke	14
G	Fuel gauge sender	47
G1	Fuel gauge	47
G2	Coolant temperature gauge sender	48
G3	Coolant temperature gauge	48
H	Horn plate	18
H1	Horn	18
J2	Emergency light relay	56 to 58
J6	Voltage stabilizer	50
J30	Rear window wiper/washer relay*	31 to 33
J31	Intermittent wash/wipe relay	26 to 30
J59	Relief relay for X contact	79 to 82
J81	Intake manifold preheating relay	13,14
J114	Oil pressure monitor control unit	43 to 45
K1	Main beam warning lamp	51
K2	Generator warning lamp	42
K3	Oil pressure warning lamp	46
K5	Turn signal warning lamp	53
K6	Emergency light system warning lamp	54
K10	Heated rear window warning lamp	81
K14	Handbrake warning lamp	40
K28	Coolant temp. warning lamp (overheating, red)	49
L1	Twin filament headlight bulb, left	74,78
L2	Twin filament headlight bulb, right	75,77
L9	Lighting switch light bulb	39
L10	Instrument panel insert light bulb	66,67
L16	Fresh air controls light bulb	63
L32	Rear cigarette lighter light bulb	88
L39	Heated rear window switch bulb	80
M1	Sidelight bulb, left	69
M2	Tail light bulb, right	71
M3	Sidelight bulb, right	70
M4	Tail light bulb, left	68
M5	Front left turn signal bulb	60
M6	Rear left turn signal bulb	59
M7	Front right turn signal bulb	61
M8	Rear right turn signal bulb	62
M9	Brake light bulb, left	90
M10	Brake light bulb, right	89
M17	Reversing light bulb right	17
N	Ignition coil	10
N1	Automatic choke	15
N3	By-pass air cut-off valve	16
N6	Series resistance	10
N23	Series resistance for fresh air blower	37

Designation		In current track
N51	Heater resistance for intake manifold preheating	13
O	Ignition distributor	10 to 12
P	Spark plug connector	11,12
Q	Spark plugs	11,12
R	Radio connection	
S1 to S16	Fuses in fusebox	
T1	Connector, single, in engine compartment, rear carburettor	
T1a	Connector, single, in boot, rear left	
T1b	Connector, single, behind dash panel, near fusebox	
T1c	Connector, single, in boot, left	
T1d	Connector, single, in boot, rear left	
T1e	Connector, single, in boot on lock carrier plate	
T1f	Connector, single, behind dash panel, near fusebox	
T1g	Connector, single, behind dash panel, near fusebox	
T1h	Connector, single, behind dash panel, near fusebox	
T1i	Connector, single, in engine compartment, near carburettor	
T2	Connector 2 pin, in engine compartment, near carburettor	
T2a	Connector 2 pin, in engine compartment, left	
T2c	Connector 2 pin, in boot, rear left	
T2d	Connector 2 pin, in tailgate, near wiper motor	
T2e	Connector, 2 pin, in engine compartment, front left	
T2f	Connector 2 pin, behind dash panel, near fusebox	
T2g	Connector 2 pin, behind dash panel, near fusebox	
T2h	Connector, 2 pin, in engine compartment, front right	
T2i	Connector, 2 pin, behind dash panel, near fusebox	
T3a	Connector, 3 pin, behind dash panel, near fusebox	
T4	Connector, 4 pin, behind dash panel, (radio bracket)	
T8/	Connector, 8 pin, on fusebox	
T12/	Connector, 12 pin, behind dash panel	
T14/	Connector, 14 pin, on dash panel insert	
T20/	Connector, 20 pin, on fusebox	
T20a/	Connector, 20 pin, on fusebox	
T29/	Connector, 29 pin, behind dash panel	
T32/	Connector, 32 pin, on fusebox	
U1	Cigarette lighter	87
V	Windscreen wiper motor	23 to 27
V2	Fresh air blower	38
V5	Windscreen washer pump	36
V7	Radiator fan	91
V12	Rear wiper motor*	33,34
V13	Rear washer pump motor*	35
W	Interior light, front	84,85
X	Number plate light	72,73
Y	Clock	86
Z1	Heated rear window	82

* Polo and Polo Coupe only

Earthing points

①	Earthing strap, from battery, via body to gearbox
②	Earthing strap, from engine to body
⑩	Earthing wire, on steering gear
⑪	Earthing point, under rear seat
⑭	Earthing point, on tailgate lock carrier plate
⑮	Earthing point, in insulating tube of wiring loom in engine compartment, left
⑯	Earthing point, in insulating tube of wiring loom in engine compartment, right
⑰	Earthing point, bound up with insulating tape in dash panel wiring loom
⑱	Earthing point, bound up with insulating tape in wiring loom for instruments

Positive (+) connections

㉒	58b in wiring loom for instruments

Colour code

bl	Blue	gn	Green	ro	Red	ws	White
br	Brown	gr	Grey	sw	Black		

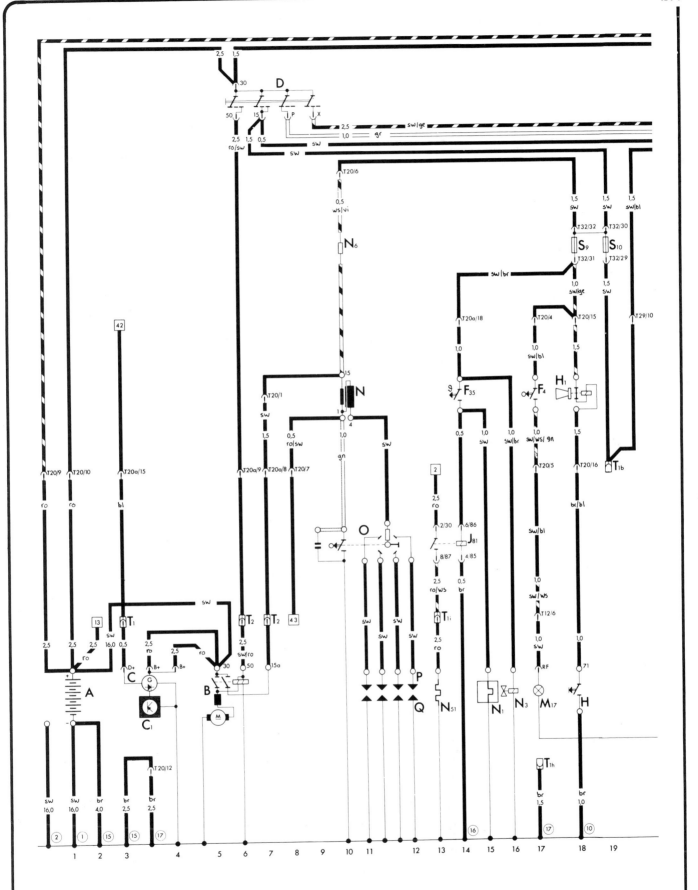

Fig. 12.36 Wiring diagram for Polo models from 1985

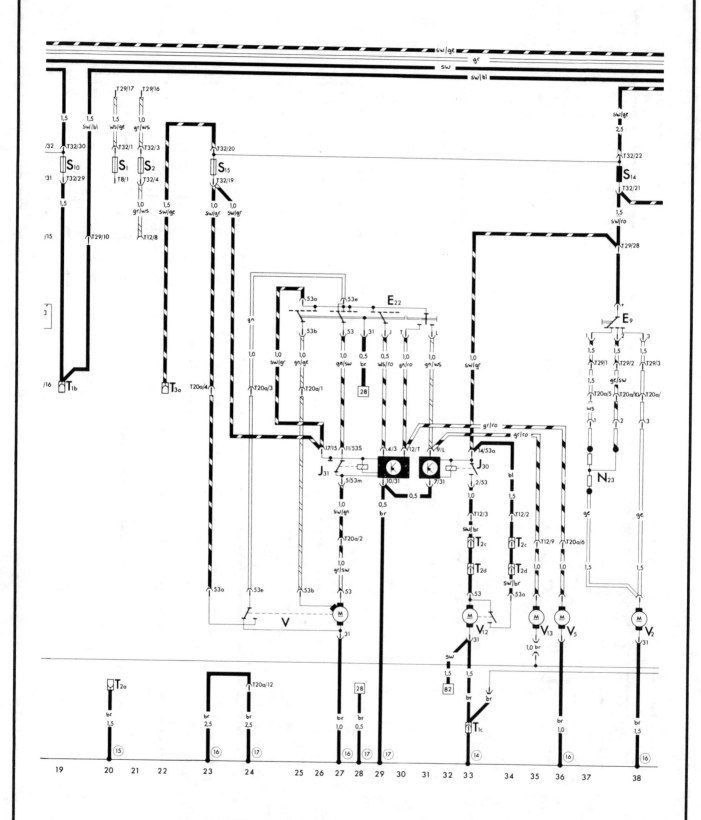

Fig. 12.36 Wiring diagram for Polo models from 1985 (continued)

213

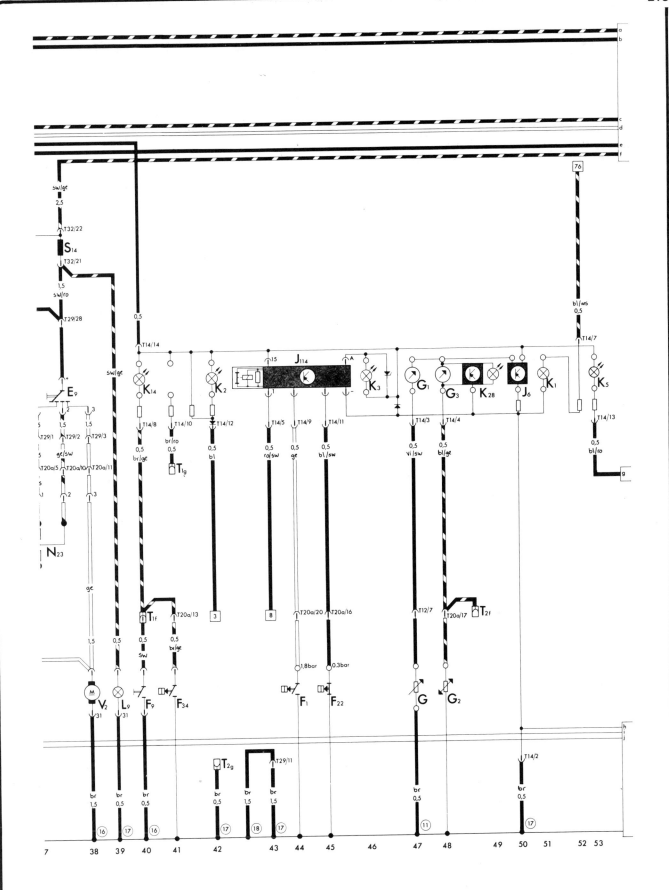

Fig. 12.36 Wiring diagram for Polo models from 1985 (continued)

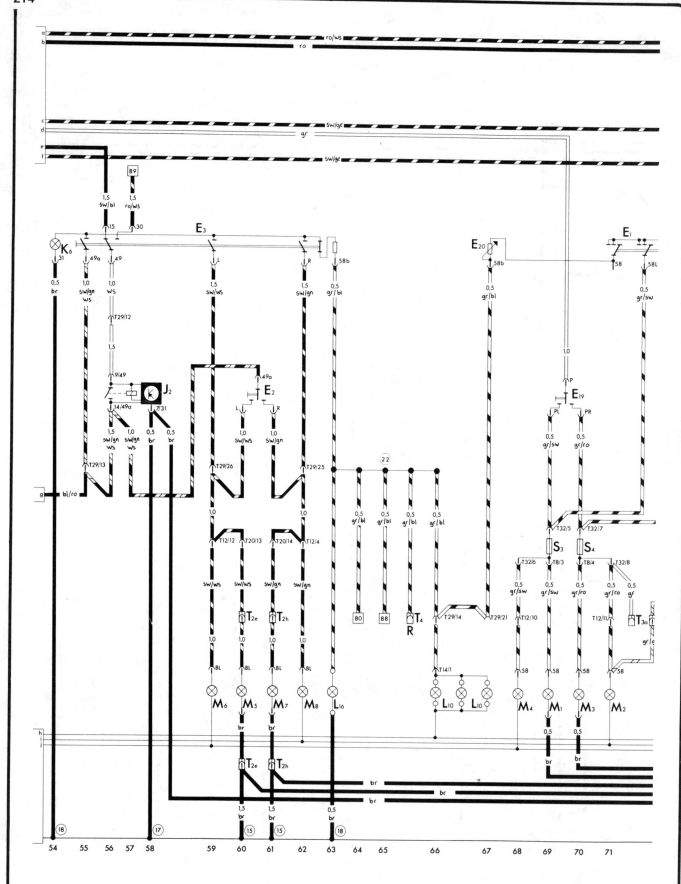

Fig. 12.36 Wiring diagram for Polo models from 1985 (continued)

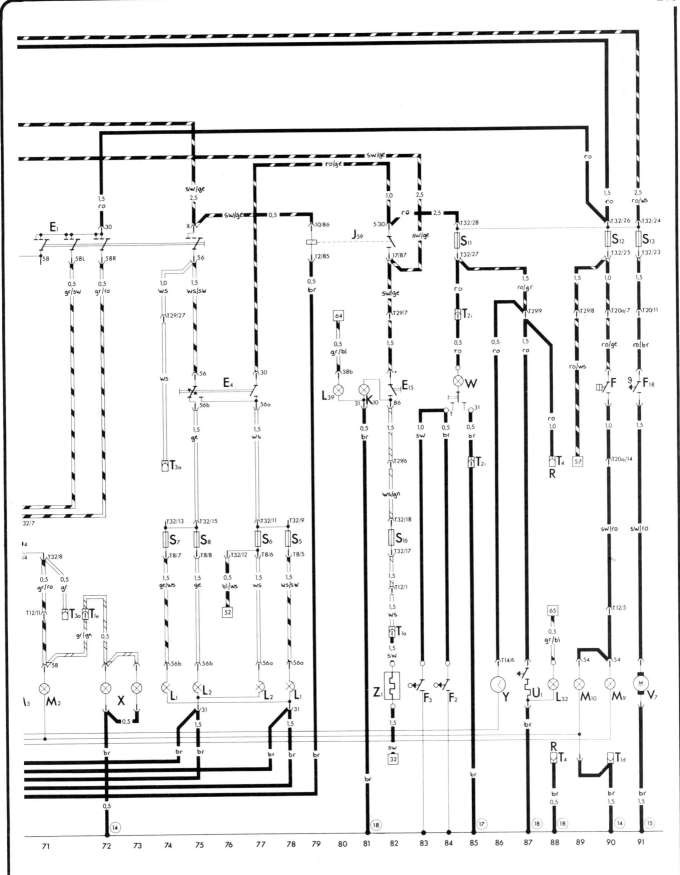

Fig. 12.36 Wiring diagram for Polo models from 1985 (continued)

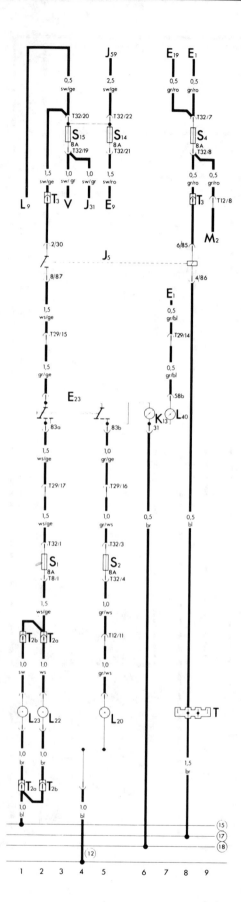

Fig. 12.37 Additional wiring diagram for front and rear foglights

August 1983 on

Designation		in current track
E1	Lighting switch (terminal 58R)	7.8
E9	Fresh air blower switch	5
E19	Parking light switch (terminal PR)	7
E23	Foglight and rear foglight switch	2 to 5
J5	Foglight relay	2 to 8
J31	Intermittent wash/wipe relay (terminal 15)	4
J59	Relief relay (for X contact) terminal 87	5
K13	Rear foglight warning lamp	6
L9	Lighting switch light bulb	1
L20	Rear foglight bulb	5
L22	Foglight bulb, left	2
L23	Foglight bulb, right	1
L40	Front and rear foglight switch bulb	7
M2	Tail light bulb, right	9
S1,S2,S4,S14,S15	Fuses in fusebox	
T	Junction box, behind dash	
T2a	Connector, two pin, in engine compartment front left	
T2b	Connector, two pin, in engine compartment front right	
T3	Connector, three pin behind dash	
T8/	Connector, eight pin on fusebox	
T12/	Connector, twelve pin behind dash	
T29/	Connector 29 pin behind dash	
T32/	Connector 32 pin on fusebox	
V	Windscreen wiper motor (terminal 53a)	3

Earthing points

- ⑫ Earth point, on rear cross panel left
- ⑮ Earth point, in insulating sleeve of engine compartment loom left
- ⑰ Earth point, bound with insulating tape in dash loom
- ⑱ Earth point, bound with insulating tape in instrument loom

Colour code

bl	Blue
br	Brown
ge	Yellow
gr	Grey
ro	Red
sw	Black
ws	White

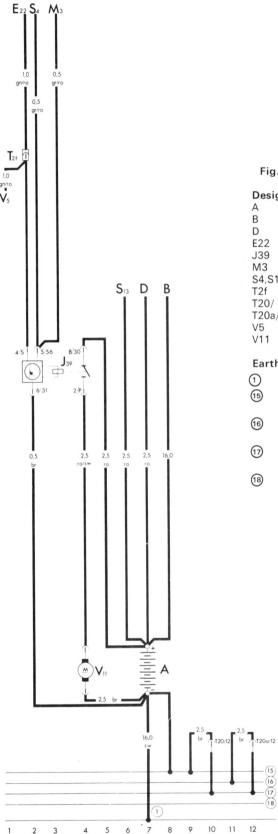

Fig. 12.38 Additional wiring diagram for headlight washer

Designation		in current track
A	Battery	7
B	Starter (terminal 30)	8
D	Ignition/starter switch (terminal 30)	7
E22	Intermittent wiper switch (terminal T)	2
J39	Headlight washer system relay	2 to 4
M3	Sidelight bulb, right	3
S4,S13	Fuses in fusebox	
T2f	Connector, two pin behind dash	
T20/	Connector 20 pin on fusebox	
T20a/	Connector 20 pin on fusebox	
V5	Windscreen washer pump	1
V11	Headlight washer pump	4

Earth points

① Earth strap, from battery via body to gearbox

⑮ Earth point, in insulating sleeve of engine compartment loom left

⑯ Earth point, in insulating sleeve of engine compartment loom right

⑰ Earth point, bound with insulating tape in dash loom

⑱ Earth point, bound with insulating tape in instrument loom

Colour code

br	Brown
gn	Green
gr	Grey
ro	Red
sw	Black
ws	White

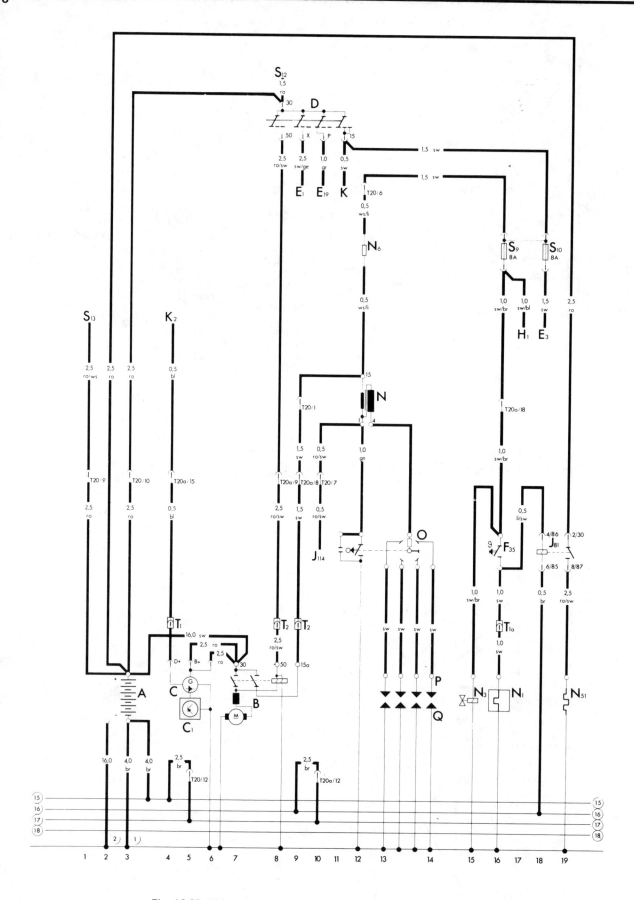

Fig. 12.39 Additional wiring diagram for 1.3 litre 40 kW engine

Key to additional wiring diagram for 1.3 litre 40 kW engine

Designation		In current track
A	Battery	3
B	Starter	7,8
C	Alternator	4 to 6
C1	Voltage regulator	4 to 6
D	Ignition/starter switch	8 to 11
E1	Lighting switch (terminal X)	9
E3	`Emergency light switch (terminal 15)	18
E19	Parking light switch (terminal P)	10
F35	Thermoswitch for intake manifold preheating	16
H1	Horn	17
J81	Intake manifold preheating relay	18,19
J114	Oil pressure monitor switch unit (terminal T 14/5)	10
K	Dash insert (terminal T 14/14)	11
K2	Generator warning lamp (terminal T 14/12)	4
N	Ignition coil	12
N1	Automatic choke, left	16
N3	Bypass air cut-off valve	15
N6	Resistance wire	12
N51	Heater element for intake manifold preheating	19
O	Ignition distributor	12 to 14
P	Spark plug connector	13,14

Designation		In current track
Q	Spark plugs	13,14
S9,S10,S12,S13	Fuses in fusebox	
T1	Connector, single in engine compartment centre	
T1a	Connector, single in engine compartment near carburettor	
T2	Connector, two pin in engine compartment near carburettor	
T20/	Connector, 20 pin, on fusebox	
T20a/	Connector 20 pin, on fusebox	

Earth points

① Earth strap from battery via body to gearbox

② Earth strap from engine to body

⑮ Earth point in insulating sleeve of left engine compartment loom

⑯ Earth point in insulating sleeve of right engine compartment loom

⑰ Earth point bound with insulating tape in dash loom

⑱ Earth point bound with insulating tape in instrument loom

Colour code

bl	Blue	gn	Green	ro	Red
br	Brown	gr	Grey	sw	Black
ge	Yellow	li	Lilac	ws	White

Key to additional wiring diagram for gearshift/consumption indicator and automatic stop-start system January 1984 on

Designation		In current track
A	Battery	11
B	Starter	13
D	Ignition/starter switch	11,12,15,23
E1	Lighting switch	6,14
E3	Emergency light switch	11,14
E9	Fresh air blower switch	30
E15	Heated rear window switch	1
E101	Main switch for stop-start system	8
F	Brake light switch	15
F1	Oil pressure switch	21
F18	Radiator fan thermoswitch	13
F22	Oil pressure switch	2
F35	Thermoswitch for cold start device	11
F62	Gearshift indicator vacuum switch	17
F68	Gear switch for gearshift/consumption indicator	30
F90	Gearbox switch for stop-start system	4,5
G5	Rev counter	20
G51	Consumption indicator	27
G54	Speed sensor for stop-start system	18,19
H1	Horn	5
J6	Voltage stabilizer	20
J59	Relief relay for x contact	16,30
J81	Intake manifold preheating relay	15
J98	Gearshift indicator control unit	23 to 28
J107	Control unit – stop-start system	8 to 19
J112	Switch off relay for heated rear window, driving lights and oil pressure control	1 to 3
J114	Oil pressure monitor control unit	21 to 23

Designation		In current track
K3	Oil pressure warning lamp	24
K48	Gearshift indicator warning lamp	25
K67	Warning lamp for main switch stop-start system	7
L9	Lighting switch light bulb	31
L51	Bulb for main switch stop-start system light	6
M17	Reversing light bulb right	9
N	Ignition coil	10,19
N60	Solenoid valve for cosumption indicator	26
S9 to S16	Fuses in fusebox	
T3	Connector 3 pin, in engine compartment, right	
T3a	Connector 3 pin, behind instrument panel	
T6/	Connector 6 pin, on instrument panel insert	
T12/	Connector 12 pin, behind instrument panel	
T14/	Connector 14 pin, on instrument panel insert	
T20/	Connector 20 pin, on fusebox	
T20a/	Connector 20 pin, on fusebox	
T32	Connector 32 pin, on fusebox	
U1	Cigarette lighter	17
V	Windscreen wiper motor	29
W	Interior light, front	16
Z1	Heated rear window	1

Earthing points

⑪ Earthing point thermostat housing

⑰ Earthing point, bound with insulating tape, in instrument panel wiring loom

Colour code

bl	Blue	gn	Green	ro	Red
br	Brown	gr	Grey	sw	Black
ge	Yellow	li	Lilac	ws	White

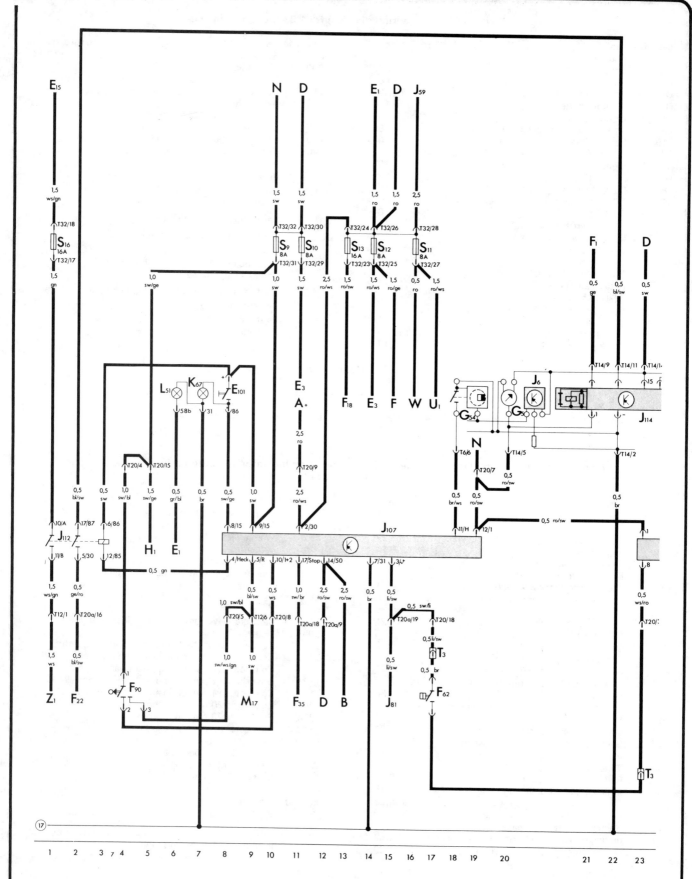

Fig. 12.40 Additional wiring diagram for gearshift/consumption indicator and automatic stop-start system
January 1984 on

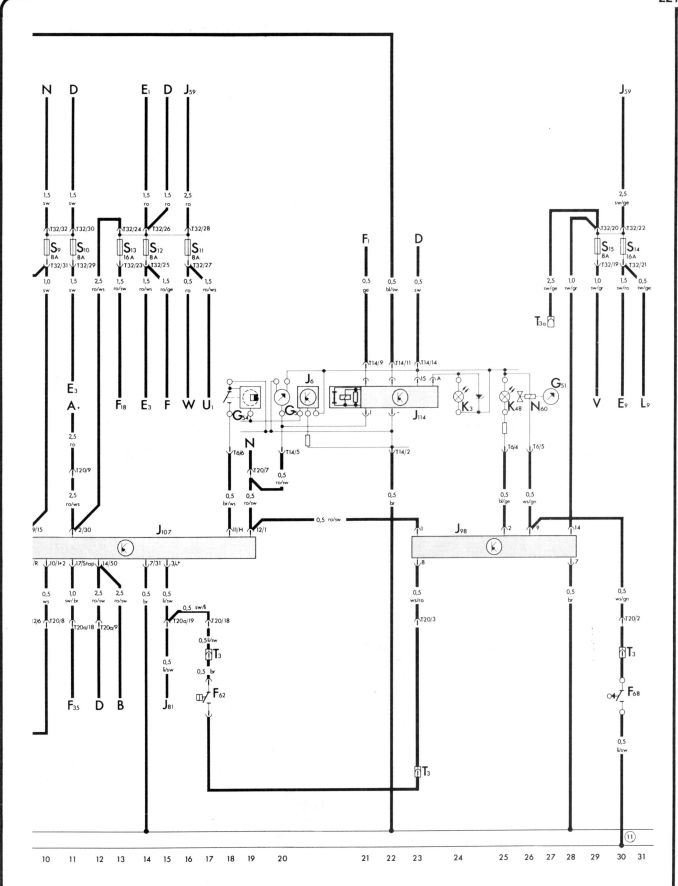

Fig. 12.40 Additional wiring diagram for gearshift/consumption indicator and automatic stop-start system (continued)
January 1984 on

10 Bodywork and fittings

Window regulator handles – later models
1   Access to the window regulator handle retaining screw is gained by prising off the plastic cover (photo).
2   Undo the screw, and the handle may be removed.
3   Reverse the operation to replace the handle.

Split rear seats – removal and refitting
4   To remove the seat squab, pull the seats upward using the plastic pull handles provided.
5   Tilt the seats right forward, which will allow access to the retaining screws (photo).
6   There are two screws for each seat squab.
7   Remove the screws and lift out the seat squabs.
8   The seat backrests may be removed by operating the seat back release mechanism and tilting the backrest forward.
9   Remove the spring clip from the centre pivot bracket, by pulling it vertically (photo).

10   Now undo the two screws securing each backrest to the luggage compartment floor (photo).
11   Remove the centre pivot pin, and the seat backs may be lifted out.
12   Refitting is a reversal of this procedure.

Seat back release mechanism – removal and refitting
13   With the seat backs released, the release mechanism can be removed by prising off the retaining clip, unhooking the return spring, and sliding the mechanism off the spigot (photo).
14   Refit in the reverse order to removal.

Front seat belts – removal and refitting
Lower outboard mounting
15   Push the front seat right forward.
16   Pull back the plastic cover from the lower seat belt mounting (photo).
17   Count the number of coils in the spring.
18   Unhook the spring and gently allow the tension to be released by allowing the spring to unwind.
19   Remove the spring from the retaining bolt head.
20   Undo the bolt.

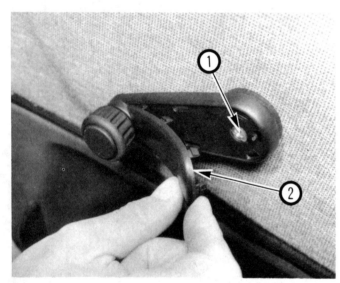

10.1 Later type window regulator handle
1   *Retaining screw*   2   *Plastic cover*

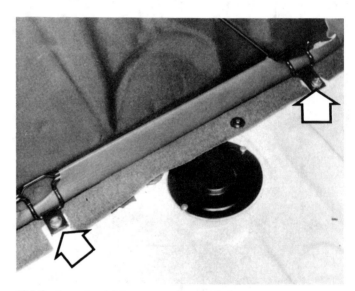

10.5 Seat squab retaining screws (arrowed)

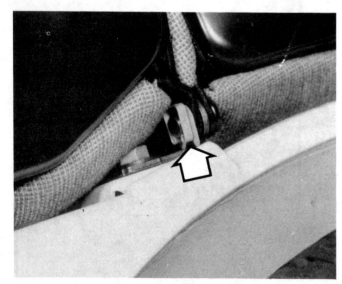

10.9 Centre pivot bracket spring clip (arrowed)

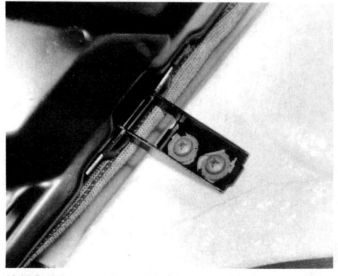

10.10 Backrest securing screws

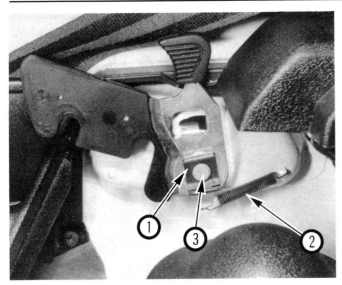

10.13 Seat back release mechanism
1   Spring clip   3   Spigot
2   Return spring

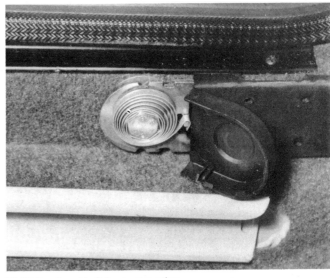

10.16 Front seat belt lower mounting

Top mounting
21 Prise off the plastic cover and undo the retaining bolt (photo).
Inertia reel mounting
22 Remove the trim panel from the side of the passenger rear seat.
23 Undo the retaining bolt holding the inertia reel in place (photo).
All mountings
24 Refitting of all three mountings is a reversal of removal.

Rear seat belts – removal and refitting
25 The rear seat belts are removed in much the same way as the front belts.
26 The outer mountings are held by one bolt (photo).
27 The inboard mounting is undone after lifting the seat squabs (photo).
28 The inertia reel mechanism is held in place in the double skin of the luggage compartment by two bolts (photo).
29 Refit in the reverse order of removal.

10.21 Front seat belt top mounting

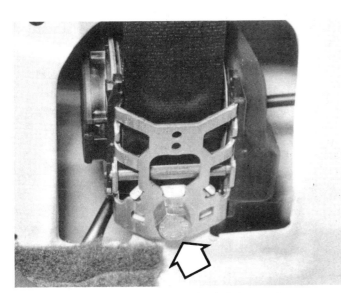

10.23 Front seat belt inertia reel mounting bolt (arrowed)

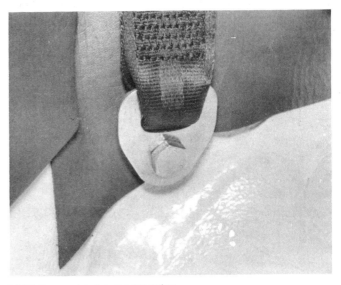

10.26 Rear seat belt outer mounting

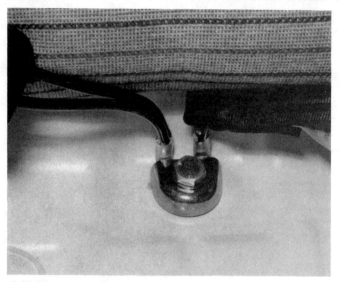

10.27 Rear seat belt inner mounting

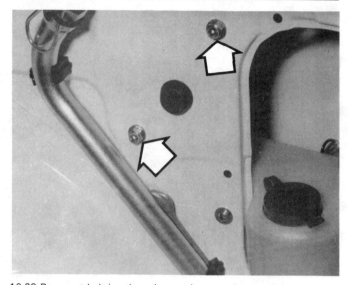

10.28 Rear seat belt inertia reel mounting nuts (arrowed)

Centre console – removal

30 A centre console may be fitted to models which do not have one as standard; the screw retainers on the gear lever housing and air ducting under the facia are provided.
31 Remove the gear lever knob.
32 Unclip and remove the rubber boot.
33 Remove the screws from the front end of console (Fig. 12.41).
34 Pull the console rearward, and lift it from the retainers.
35 Lift out the console in the direction of the arrows.

Front apron trim – removal and refitting

36 Drill the rivet heads (arrowed in Fig. 12.42).
37 Lift the trim forward and clear of the towing eye.
38 Knock out the rest of the rivets inwards with a punch.
39 When refitting a new trim, start riveting from the centre and work outwards.

Wheel arch mouldings – removal and refitting

40 The wheel arch mouldings are removed and refitted in the same way as the front apron trim.

Roof railing (roof rack) – description

41 A roof railing is available as an extra for 'square back' Polo models from 1986.
42 The railing can also be installed on 'square back' models from March 1985.
43 Fitting of the roof railing is best left to your VAG dealer.

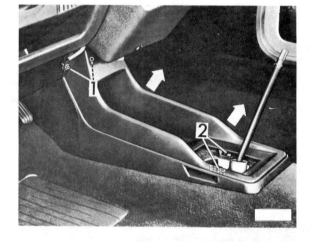

Fig. 12.41 Removing the centre console (Sec 10)

1 Retaining screws   *2 Retainers*

Lift out in direction of arrows

Fig. 12.42 Front apron trim rivets – arrowed (Sec 10)

Fig. 12.43 Wheel arch moulding rivets – arrowed (Sec 10)

General repair procedures

Whenever servicing, repair or overhaul work is carried out on the car or its components, it is necessary to observe the following procedures and instructions. This will assist in carrying out the operation efficiently and to a professional standard of workmanship.

Joint mating faces and gaskets

Where a gasket is used between the mating faces of two components, ensure that it is renewed on reassembly, and fit it dry unless otherwise stated in the repair procedure. Make sure that the mating faces are clean and dry with all traces of old gasket removed. When cleaning a joint face, use a tool which is not likely to score or damage the face, and remove any burrs or nicks with an oilstone or fine file.

Make sure that tapped holes are cleaned with a pipe cleaner, and keep them free of jointing compound if this is being used unless specifically instructed otherwise.

Ensure that all orifices, channels or pipes are clear and blow through them, preferably using compressed air.

Oil seals

Whenever an oil seal is removed from its working location, either individually or as part of an assembly, it should be renewed.

The very fine sealing lip of the seal is easily damaged and will not seal if the surface it contacts is not completely clean and free from scratches, nicks or grooves. If the original sealing surface of the component cannot be restored, the component should be renewed.

Protect the lips of the seal from any surface which may damage them in the course of fitting. Use tape or a conical sleeve where possible. Lubricate the seal lips with oil before fitting and, on dual lipped seals, fill the space between the lips with grease.

Unless otherwise stated, oil seals must be fitted with their sealing lips toward the lubricant to be sealed.

Use a tubular drift or block of wood of the appropriate size to install the seal and, if the seal housing is shouldered, drive the seal down to the shoulder. If the seal housing is unshouldered, the seal should be fitted with its face flush with the housing top face.

Screw threads and fastenings

Always ensure that a blind tapped hole is completely free from oil, grease, water or other fluid before installing the bolt or stud. Failure to do this could cause the housing to crack due to the hydraulic action of the bolt or stud as it is screwed in.

When tightening a castellated nut to accept a split pin, tighten the nut to the specified torque, where applicable, and then tighten further to the next split pin hole. Never slacken the nut to align a split pin hole unless stated in the repair procedure.

When checking or retightening a nut or bolt to a specified torque setting, slacken the nut or bolt by a quarter of a turn, and then retighten to the specified setting.

Locknuts, locktabs and washers

Any fastening which will rotate against a component or housing in the course of tightening should always have a washer between it and the relevant component or housing.

Spring or split washers should always be renewed when they are used to lock a critical component such as a big-end bearing retaining nut or bolt.

Locktabs which are folded over to retain a nut or bolt should always be renewed.

Self-locking nuts can be reused in non-critical areas, providing resistance can be felt when the locking portion passes over the bolt or stud thread.

Split pins must always be replaced with new ones of the correct size for the hole.

Special tools

Some repair procedures in this manual entail the use of special tools such as a press, two or three-legged pullers, spring compressors etc. Wherever possible, suitable readily available alternatives to the manufacturer's special tools are described, and are shown in use. In some instances, where no alternative is possible, it has been necessary to resort to the use of a manufacturer's tool and this has been done for reasons of safety as well as the efficient completion of the repair operation. Unless you are highly skilled and have a thorough understanding of the procedure described, never attempt to bypass the use of any special tool when the procedure described specifies its use. Not only is there a very great risk of personal injury, but expensive damage could be caused to the components involved.

Conversion factors

Length (distance)
Inches (in)	X	25.4	= Millimetres (mm)	X 0.0394	= Inches (in)
Feet (ft)	X	0.305	= Metres (m)	X 3.281	= Feet (ft)
Miles	X	1.609	= Kilometres (km)	X 0.621	= Miles

Volume (capacity)
Cubic inches (cu in; in^3)	X	16.387	= Cubic centimetres (cc; cm^3)	X 0.061	= Cubic inches (cu in; in^3)
Imperial pints (Imp pt)	X	0.568	= Litres (l)	X 1.76	= Imperial pints (Imp pt)
Imperial quarts (Imp qt)	X	1.137	= Litres (l)	X 0.88	= Imperial quarts (Imp qt)
Imperial quarts (Imp qt)	X	1.201	= US quarts (US qt)	X 0.833	= Imperial quarts (Imp qt)
US quarts (US qt)	X	0.946	= Litres (l)	X 1.057	= US quarts (US qt)
Imperial gallons (Imp gal)	X	4.546	= Litres (l)	X 0.22	= Imperial gallons (Imp gal)
Imperial gallons (Imp gal)	X	1.201	= US gallons (US gal)	X 0.833	= Imperial gallons (Imp gal)
US gallons (US gal)	X	3.785	= Litres (l)	X 0.264	= US gallons (US gal)

Mass (weight)
Ounces (oz)	X	28.35	= Grams (g)	X 0.035	= Ounces (oz)
Pounds (lb)	X	0.454	= Kilograms (kg)	X 2.205	= Pounds (lb)

Force
Ounces-force (ozf; oz)	X	0.278	= Newtons (N)	X 3.6	= Ounces-force (ozf; oz)
Pounds-force (lbf; lb)	X	4.448	= Newtons (N)	X 0.225	= Pounds-force (lbf; lb)
Newtons (N)	X	0.1	= Kilograms-force (kgf; kg)	X 9.81	= Newtons (N)

Pressure
Pounds-force per square inch (psi; lbf/in^2; lb/in^2)	X	0.070	= Kilograms-force per square centimetre (kgf/cm^2; kg/cm^2)	X 14.223	= Pounds-force per square inch (psi; lbf/in^2; lb/in^2)
Pounds-force per square inch (psi; lbf/in^2; lb/in^2)	X	0.068	= Atmospheres (atm)	X 14.696	= Pounds-force per square inch (psi; lbf/in^2; lb/in^2)
Pounds-force per square inch (psi; lbf/in^2; lb/in^2)	X	0.069	= Bars	X 14.5	= Pounds-force per square inch (psi; lbf/in^2; lb/in^2)
Pounds-force per square inch (psi; lbf/in^2; lb/in^2)	X	6.895	= Kilopascals (kPa)	X 0.145	= Pounds-force per square inch (psi; lbf/in^2; lb/in^2)
Kilopascals (kPa)	X	0.01	= Kilograms-force per square centimetre (kgf/cm^2; kg/cm^2)	X 98.1	= Kilopascals (kPa)

Torque (moment of force)
Pounds-force inches (lbf in; lb in)	X	1.152	= Kilograms-force centimetre (kgf cm; kg cm)	X 0.868	= Pounds-force inches (lbf in; lb in)
Pounds-force inches (lbf in; lb in)	X	0.113	= Newton metres (Nm)	X 8.85	= Pounds-force inches (lbf in; lb in)
Pounds-force inches (lbf in; lb in)	X	0.083	= Pounds-force feet (lbf ft; lb ft)	X 12	= Pounds-force inches (lbf in; lb in)
Pounds-force feet (lbf ft; lb ft)	X	0.138	= Kilograms-force metres (kgf m; kg m)	X 7.233	= Pounds-force feet (lbf ft; lb ft)
Pounds-force feet (lbf ft; lb ft)	X	1.356	= Newton metres (Nm)	X 0.738	= Pounds-force feet (lbf in; lb in)
Newton metres (Nm)	X	0.102	= Kilograms-force metres (kgf m; kg m)	X 9.804	= Newton metres (Nm)

Power
Horsepower (hp)	X	745.7	= Watts (W)	X 0.0013	= Horsepower (hp)

Velocity (speed)
Miles per hour (miles/hr; mph)	X	1.609	= Kilometres per hour (km/hr; kph)	X 0.621	= Miles per hour (miles/hr; mph)

Fuel consumption*
Miles per gallon, Imperial (mpg)	X	0.354	= Kilometres per litre (km/l)	X 2.825	= Miles per gallon, Imperial (mpg)
Miles per gallon, US (mpg)	X	0.425	= Kilometres per litre (km/l)	X 2.352	= Miles per gallon, US (mpg)

Temperature

Degrees Fahrenheit = (°C × 1.8) + 32

Degrees Celsius (Degrees Centigrade; °C) = (°F − 32) × 0.56

*It is common practice to convert from miles per gallon (mpg) to litres/100 kilometres (l/100 km),
where mpg (Imperial) × l/100 km = 282 and mpg (US) = l/100 km = 235

Index

Printed by
J H Haynes & Co Ltd
Sparkford Nr Yeovil
Somerset BA22 7JJ England